# TRAGIC HOLLYWOOD
## Beautiful, Glamorous, Dead

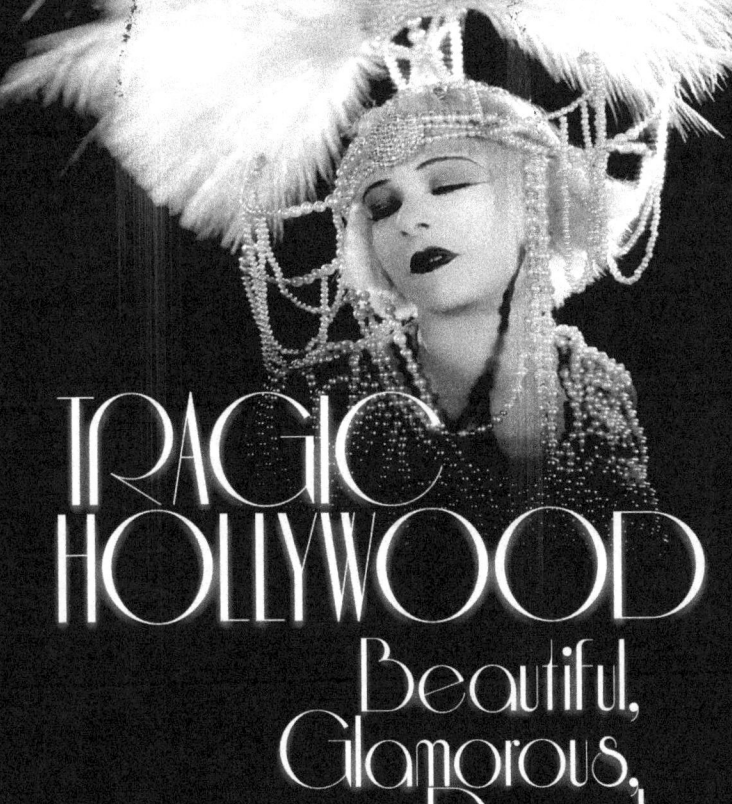

# TRAGIC HOLLYWOOD
## Beautiful, Glamorous, Dead

### Jackie Ganiy

Dedicated to the Facebook fans

of

Tragic Hollywood: Beautiful, Glamorous and Dead,

and to all lovers of Old Hollywood

everywhere.

TRAGIC HOLLYWOOD: BEAUTIFUL, GLAMOROUS, DEAD
Copyright © 2013, 2014, 2015, 2016 by Jackie Ganiy.
Fourth Edition

All photographs from public domain or author's private collection except where otherwise noted in the appendix.

All rights reserved. This book, whole or in part, may not be reproduced in any medium or used in any manner without the written permission of the publisher, except for the use of brief quotations in a book review, or article, except in the case of photographs already in the public domain, or used under license as described in the appendix, for which the copyright and/or license for reuse remains intact.

Published in the United States of America 2016.

Contact Jackie Ganiy at kashmere2u@aol.com

TRAGIC HOLLYWOOD: BEAUTIFUL, GLAMOROUS, **DEAD**

"This is my life! It always will be! There's nothing else. Just us, and the cameras, and those wonderful people out there in the dark..."

Norma Desmond
*Sunset Boulevard*

| | |
|---|---|
| Acknowledgments | 1 |
| Foreword | 2 |
| Introduction | 7 |
| Silenced Forever | 8 |
|     Rudolph Valentino | 10 |
|     Florence Lawrence: The First Movie Star | 16 |
|     Martha Mansfield | 20 |
|     Wallace Reid | 24 |
|     Marie Prevost | 28 |
|     Olive Thomas | 32 |
|     Thomas Ince | 38 |
|     Alma Rubens | 44 |
| The Beautiful and the Doomed | 48 |
|     Natalie Wood | 50 |
|     Judy Tyler | 58 |
|     Heath Ledger | 64 |
|     Suzan Ball | 70 |
|     Vivien Leigh | 74 |
|     Clara Bow | 80 |
| The Forgotten & The Forsaken | 86 |
|     Yvette Vickers | 88 |
|     Linda Darnell | 92 |
|     D.W. Griffith | 98 |
|     Charlie Chaplin | 106 |
|     Dorothy Dandridge | 118 |
|     Tom Neal | 124 |
|     Montgomery Clift | 130 |
| Live Fast Die Young | 140 |
|     James Dean | 142 |
|     River Phoenix | 152 |
|     Errol Flynn | 160 |
|     Chris Farley | 168 |
|     Barbara La Marr | 174 |

## By Their Own Hand — 184

Freddie Prinze — 186
Peg Entwistle — 192
Marie McDonald — 196
Margaux Hemingway — 202
Lupe Velez — 208
Jean Seberg — 214
Dana Plato — 222

## Tragic Blondes — 230

Jayne Mansfield — 232
Sharon Tate — 246
Jean Harlow — 256
Dorothy Stratten — 274
Barbara Payton — 286
Marilyn Monroe — 294

## Hauntingly Tragic: Spectral Tales of The Famous & The Infamous — 318

The Paul Bern/Jay Sebring/Sharon Tate House — 320
Superman Just Won't Die - George Reeves' Ghost — 324
The Ghost of Marilyn Monroe — 328
Heath Ledger's Visit From Beyond — 330
Pickfair: The Haunting That Led to a Demolition — 332
Ozzie Nelson's Still at Home — 334
Lucille Ball & Roxbury Drive — 335
Errol Flynn Still Sailing — 336
Phantoms of The Opera Set — 338
Jayne Mansfield & the Haunting of the Pink Palace — 340
Peg Entwistle and the Hollywood Sign — 342
Haunted Hollywood Forever — 344
The Tate Murder House's Neighborhood — 348

## Conclusion — 350

## Bibliography & Credits — 354

## Index — 360

*Grauman's Egyptian Theater of Hollywood, in the 1920s.*

# Acknowledgements

Without the unwavering support, help, and enthusiastic encouragement of my family—my wonderful children and their long-suffering father—for my labor of love, it would have never been completed, and the world would be left wanting!

Without the incessant prodding and nagging of the fans on Facebook, I would never have even begun this project. It was them daring me to do it that finally got me to do it. Thanks to all of you!

# Foreword

I have always been fascinated with the movies. As a skinny little kid, living in a dead-end town in central California with limited entertainment options, I would sit in front of our fifteen-inch RCA television screen and watch old movies on the "cable" channel out of sheer boredom. At least that's how it started out. Gradually, I began to get into these films. I noticed that the women seemed more beautiful than anyone I'd ever seen in real life, and more beautiful than the current movie stars that filled the screens of my local theater. I noticed that the men were classier than the ones I encountered in my little town, or even in the big city to the south. The women and men were beautifully dressed, perfectly coiffed and, well, just so darn classy! They inhabited beautiful worlds where homes were perfect, and there was no ugliness on the public streets. Dinner was often mixed with a full swing orchestra and a marble dance floor. Women ran the simplest of errands dripping in fur and jewelry, always wearing some poof of a hat, perched ever so delicately atop their immaculate hairdos. In my world, women walked around in polyester pants and cotton blouses, not swing dresses and pumps. Men wore slacks and golf shirts, not elegant, tailored suits and Derbies.

Soon, I was hooked on old Hollywood glamour. I began looking for information about some of those people with whom I had grown familiar while watching all those old movies. I have no words to adequately describe my abject shock and disappointment when I looked into many of the old stars biographies only to discover how miserable their real lives were, and how tragically so many of them ended up. I realized that it was all just an illusion—a really good illusion—but still just an illusion...sort of like Disneyland. That world, the world of beauty and glamour, had never really existed, except on celluloid. This was worse than finding out there was no Easter Bunny for me. I still remember weeping over Vivien Leigh's biography, and never being able to watch her in *Gone with the Wind* with the same simple, innocent joy afterwards. This is still true for me today.

Far from dampening my interest in old Hollywood, however, I was more ensorcelled than ever. I had always been a weird kid, drawn to the darker side of life more than most. I preferred *Twilight Zone* to *Bugs Bunny*, and I loved a good ghost story. I obsessed over tragic stars and their sad stories. I would regularly entertain my friends and family with gruesome details of a particular star's life, while they tried to watch a movie with that star in it. This didn't win me any favors. I didn't care. Somehow, I felt empowered that I knew almost as much about these people as my parents, who had been the peers of many of these icons, and whose lives had paralleled theirs.

What my mother had dismissed as a passing fancy turned into a lifelong passion, which brings us to the present, and this book. I began this journey over a year ago, when I decided to create a page on Facebook dedicated to all things tragic of Hollywood. I had seen a few similar pages, but none of them contained the depth of knowledge and the level of commitment I felt I could give to such a page. So I just did it. After I put the page up, I noticed that I was getting attention rapidly. Within days, I had several hundred "fans". Within weeks, I had almost a thousand. I was having a wonderful time adding stories to my page, organizing each story into a photo album category, and honoring a star on their "deathiversary" nearly every day. A few people mentioned that I should write a book. I laughed the suggestion off, until I realized they were serious. "Why not?" I thought. "I could write this book with one hand tied behind my back!"

I knew from experience that most of the books on this subject that were already out there were dry, lifeless text books that never really went into any depth as to why a star crashed and burned. They were boring to read—an unpardonable sin for a book based on entertainment. Of course, the single exception to this rule was the infamous *Hollywood Babylon*, by Kenneth Anger. Oh yes, this book was juicy, fun, salacious and wicked. I lapped every bit of it up, licked the pages and begged for more! But I was young. The older I got, the more nastiness came out about *Hollywood Babylon*. Much of what Anger had written turned out to be either very exaggerated, or just plain wrong. Some of the information stained a star's reputation for decades, such as the decapitation story about Jayne Mansfield, and the horrible story of the dog making a meal out of poor Marie Prevost's corpse. None of this was true. Why make stuff up anyway? The real stories are tragic and bizarre enough! There really is no need to fabricate or exaggerate the tragedy of the lives of these piteous souls, who lived and died under the hot lights and unforgiving glare of public scrutiny.

This book is meant for pleasure and historical research. I have done my best to assure that what is published is factual and accurate. It disputes many previous assumptions, and attempts to shed new light on old controversies. Many of the stars that are featured herein are well-known. The memory of some of them has been swept away by time. All of them lived fascinating lives, and all of them died tragic, untimely deaths. May they rest in peace, and may the essence of their beauty be what lingers in our memories and our hearts.

Jackie Ganiy

*The Hollywood Theater in Portland, Oregon, during the 1920s.*

# Introduction

Everyone loves a good story. This love crosses cultural barriers, religious differences and ethnic boundaries. Once upon a time there was a magical place located in the Southern California desert of Los Angeles. The people who inhabited this place understood this fundamental truth, and sought to yoke its power for profit. The place was Hollywood, and the people who lived there created great fictional stories, both on and off the silver screen. Yet the stories of what really happened have a power to shock and fascinate beyond simple hype and mindless publicity. These real stories haunt us, swelling the ranks of the dark side of our collective cultural consciousness.

We are those in the dark: the fans, the curious, the silent observers of the glamorous and/or beautiful and/or doomed. These stories serve to remind us that all is not as it seems in these shimmering make-believe worlds of illusion. Scratch the surface, and an ugliness is revealed that, rather than causing us to turn away, draws us in deeper into the spell that is fame, stardom and beauty. These are the stories of those stars that shone brightly and briefly, then left a legacy of macabre mystery behind when their lights were extinguished. Read on...if you have the stomach and heart for a hardcore, glamor-free look at tragic Hollywood, and its piteous occupants.

# Silenced Forever
## Tragedies from the silver screen

Long before there was such a thing as CGI, before there existed a thing called Hollywood, and before most of the studios we take for granted today were founded, there was another place. This place existed on delicate, nitrite reels of flickering, silent images. On these images were faces: Garbo, Gilbert, Swanson...the pioneers of the modern film industry. They are all gone, as are most of their films, but their incredible lives and work are still remembered by those who are true lovers of the craft and magic of film.

These sirens of the silver screen were no shrinking violets either. The term "heroin baby" was coined in the '20s to describe some of the most prominent leading ladies of the day. In spite of prohibition, or because of it, the booze flowed freely and profusely, and many were miserable alcoholics. Promiscuity was a way of life, especially among the "Hollywood crowd", and life was one wild party after another.

Until it wasn't.

# Rudolph Valentino

Has there ever been a sex god of the silver screen that titillated and stimulated the female imagination more than the "Latin lover"? Much has been written to suggest that he was not what his work on the screen implied. They wrote that he was bisexual, effeminate, and dominated by lesbian women, some who sought only to emasculate him, both personally and professionally. Whispers teased that the reigning god of sex never actually had sex.

He was born in Castellaneta, Italy in 1895, to a domineering mother who spoiled and coddled him. His first experience in entertainment came after he arrived in New York in 1913, where he was on the street until he took a job as a 'taxi dancer' in a chic nightclub called Maxim's. He got involved with Blanca de Saulles—a Chilean socialite who was not very happily married to socially prominent businessman, John de Saulles. Instead of minding his own business, Valentino testified against Mr. de Saulles at the couple's divorce hearing, which landed him in jail for a few days. Seems John de Saulles didn't take kindly to this "gigolo's" interference in his marriage, and used his political connections to have Valentino arrested on trumped-up vice charges. This scandal was well-publicized, and as a result, Valentino could not get work. To make matters worse, Mr. de Saulles also soon found himself at the wrong end of his ex-wife's gun, when she shot him dead over a custody dispute. Valentino fled New York to avoid becoming even further ensnared in scandal.

In Hollywood he played bit parts, but caught the eye of screenwriter, June Mathis. She insisted he play the Latin Lover in the epic film, *The Four Horsemen of the Apocalypse.* He did, and it made him a star, and no wonder! His tango dancing scene with Beatrice Dominguez is—even by modern standards—one of the most openly erotic scenes _ever_ filmed. Around this time, he got into a bizarre relationship with actress, Jean Acker, who was a known lesbian to everyone but Valentino. She thought they were getting married as a cover for their homosexual lifestyles, and he thought she really loved him. The night they were wed, she locked him out of her hotel room. Valentino continued to send love letters to Acker for quite some time, until someone clued him in on her preferences, at which point he moved on.

*Valentino in A Sainted Devil (1924)*

Whether he *actually was* bisexual is still debatable, but the rumors of his bisexuality were both commonplace and widespread. In 1926, the *Chicago Tribune* famously painted him a "Pink Powder Puff" and "Painted Pansy", and the rumormill pegged he and screen icon, Ramon Novarro, as lovers. In his infamous book, *Hollywood Babylon*, Kenneth Anger claimed Rudy gave Novarro an "art deco dildo", whatever that is. Novarro publicly stated he barely knew Rudy, and had enough romances with women to allay suspicions that he was gay (though still possibly bi), while his flamboyant gestures and dress may have been more down to his Italian heritage than sexual preference. 1920s America had strict rules on what proper masculine behavior was. Valentino, the hottest male sex symbol of the time, often colored outside those lines, to the delight of women everywhere.

His meteoric rise in films continued with *Camille, The Sheik,* and *Blood and Sand*. He ran off with actress Natacha Rambova, marrying her in Mexico, seeming to forget that he was already married to Jean Acker. Returning to the states, he was immediately arrested for bigamy, and spent several hours in jail, until Mathis with others bailed him out. The charges were dropped.

Much was said of his marriage to Rambova: how she gave him a slave bracelet to show him who was boss. She had many public lesbian *and* heterosexual affairs, and some saw theirs as purely a "lavender" marriage; never to be consummated at all. It's amusing to ponder what went on behind that bedroom door. Extremely possessive, she controlled nearly all aspects of his life and career, and alienated him from the studio and his friends. Her unfortunate picks for his film projects resulted in the worst films of his career, including *A Sainted Devil, Cobra* and *Monsieur Beaucaire*—all flops that further drove masculinity from the public's perception of Rudy.

Eventually, the marriage fell apart. She had a fling with a cameraman on the set of one of her films, and fled to New York, eventually obtaining a divorce in France. Despondent, Rudy bought the now famous Bel Air mansion, Falcon's Lair, to win her back, unsuccessfully. Depressed and near-suicidal, he saught solace in screen femme fatale, Pola Negri, who was also known to take both male and female lovers. He signed with the just-formed United Artists, and starred in two very successful films, *The Eagle* and *The Son of the Sheik*. It was 1926, and things were looking up for Rudy. Sadly, these good times were not to last.

Valentino had been suffering from severe stomach pains for several days, but had refused to go to a doctor. On Monday, August 16, while conducting a publicity tour for *The Son of the Sheik*, he collapsed in his New York hotel room, and was admitted to the hospital with a bleeding ulcer. They determined that his appendix had ruptured as well, spilling its toxins into his bloodstream, and causing an acute infection. In these days before antibiotics, little could be done to stem infections other than to hope the body was strong enough to survive the attack. He was operated on for the perforated ulcer, and given a good prognosis. Then he developed peritonitis, followed by pleuritis of the lungs, and his body began to fail. His doctors did not tell him he was dying, so Valentino chatted happily with them about the future, and where he planned to recuperate once released. He fell into a coma, from which he never woke. He passed away on August 23, 1926, at the age of thirty-one.

Normally, the story would end there, but this is Valentino. He was so popular, his death so sudden and unexpected, that the world went a bit nuts for a few days during his two (yes, two!) elaborate funerals. An estimated one hundred thousand people lined the streets of New York on August 24, to get a glimpse of his coffin. Fans broke windows, and vandalized property, in order to "pay their last respects." An all-day riot ensued, and one hundred mounted Police were called in to restore order. To top it off was the sublime performance of Pola Negri, swathed head to toe in black crape, swooning over his coffin multiple times, always in front of cameras. After this show of shows, his body was sent west on a train to Hollywood, where another, more dignified and controlled, final goodbye was arranged. Who could have guessed the ceremony in Tinseltown would be the more subdued of them? Rudy died without having made any burial arrangements, so June Mathis offered a spot in her family crypt in the ornate Cathedral Mausoleum at Hollywood Memorial Park Cemetery (now known as Hollywood Forever Cemetery). This arrangement was intended to be temporary, but June died the following year, and was buried next to Rudy, where the two remain in sweet repose to this day.

We're not done yet.

Shortly after the burial, a woman dressed entirely in black, a black veil covering her face, was spotted visiting Rudy's grave. She quietly left one red rose and departed without having said a word to anyone. Soon, this became a yearly ritual, the woman turned up on the anniversary of the great screen idol's death, her face completely shrouded in a black veil, leaving a single red rose at the tomb, then casually walking away. The press got wind of this, and cameras were dutifully set up to film the mysterious "lady in black" every year. She was filmed many times (nobody is really sure that it was always the same person), and questions were hurled at the figure by curious reporters and onlookers alike, while she maintained her stoic silence, simply leaving her rose, and walking away. Her identity (or identities) remains a mystery to this day.

Now we're done.

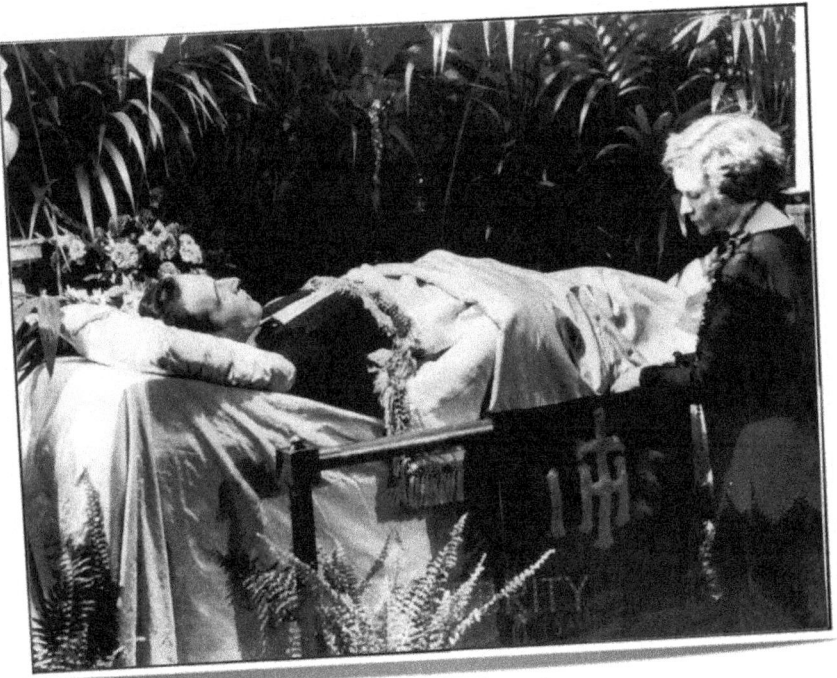

*Valentino at his funeral*

# Florence Lawrence

## The First Movie Star

*The grave of Florence Lawrence*

Florence Lawrence's epitaph, as written on her grave at the Hollywood Forever cemetery, reads "Florence Lawrence, 'The Biograph Girl', The First Movie Star." Who was she, and how did she earn that prestigious title?

Florence had been toiling away in subpar, one-reel affairs for a studio known as the Vitagraph Company, when she was noticed by a young actor named Henry Solter in 1908. He introduced her to D.W. Griffith of Biograph Pictures. She signed with Biograph, and married Solter that same year.

She went on to make sixty films for the studio, most of them directed by Griffith, the most prestigious director at the time. This was early twentieth century filmmaking however, and studios had made the unconscionable decision not to credit actors on screen, as they felt this would create "celebrities" out of mere performers, leading them to demand higher salaries.

Oh, the studios. Gotta admire them for trying.

Florence was extremely popular, but was known simply as "The Biograph Girl." She was well-compensated and seemed content, until a little German studio boss approached her with a wild scheme, and an offer she simply couldn't refuse.

Mr. Carl Laemmle was the head of Independent Motion Picture Company of America, or IMP for short. IMP would later form part of what is today known as Universal Pictures. To lure Lawrence away from Biograph, he offered her and Solter the leads in his next film, *The Broken Oath*, as well as their own names up on the marquee. This was unprecedented, and the couple jumped at the chance. Laemmle had one condition, though: he was going to stage the first "publicity stunt" on record, and he wanted his two new stars to participate. While the film was still in production, Laemmle sent out a fake notice which reported that Lawrence had been killed in a streetcar accident. The press lapped it up. "Biograph girl dead!" screamed the headlines, affording the film gobs of free publicity, and raising Lawrence's profile. A few days later, Laemmle sent out another press release stating "We Nail A Lie," which refuted the "scandalous" claim, and quoted Lawrence as saying she was very much alive, and would soon be making a public appearance to promote her new film, *The Broken Oath*. Genius. When Lawrence and Solter appeared together in St. Louis, Missouri, a near-riot ensued, assuring the film's success, and guaranteeing that she would go down in history as the first film actress to achieve name recognition with the public. In other words, she really was the first star.

Lawrence was unbelievably popular during this time. The press chased her everywhere she went, and she was quickly mobbed by adoring fans wherever she appeared in public. She supposedly received so much mail that her postman suffered a nervous collapse lugging the letters to her door every day. She also raced cars competitively, and was rumored to be the inventor of the first turning signal for cars.

Lawrence and her husband founded a production company of their own, Victor Film Company, and made several successful films under that name. In 1912, Lawrence declared her intention to retire, but was persuaded to make *Pawn's Destiny* for Universal, who acquired Victor Film Company in 1914. She was severely injured during filming, when a fire got out of control, burning her, and causing her to fall and injure her back. She was incapacitated for months. When she did return, she soon suffered a mental collapse. Several months later, the press awaited her when she pulled into the Universal lot in a massive, luxury automobile to make her comeback. She looked frail and depleted, yet she smiled and charmed her way through the interview, leaving them all with the impression that the movie business was a wonderful thing so long as stars like Florence Lawrence were around.

Sadly, her glory days were behind her, and a slow and painful decline was ahead. She divorced Solter after her accident, blaming him for making her do her own stunts. After two nervous breakdowns, she was unable to regain the leading lady stature she had once enjoyed. By the mid-1920s, she was hardly working at all, and when the stock market collapsed in 1929, she was wiped out financially. That same year, her beloved mother passed away, and she sank deeper into despair. Despite her finances, she paid for an elaborate burial for her mother which included a sculpted bust for the tomb. In 1933, she married Henry Bolton, a drunk who beat her the entire five-month span of the marriage. She also suffered from painful bone marrow disorder, myelofibrosis.

On the evening of December 27, 1938, Lawrence, in great pain, carefully set mementos of her former stardom around her, laid down, and swallowed ant paste. She was discovered the following day, alive, but in agony. She was rushed to the hospital, but died that afternoon. She was fifty-two.

Florence's real death garnered far less publicity than her faked death had, and she was buried at Hollywood Forever in an unmarked grave, a thousand yards from the elaborate tomb of her mother. Decades later, Roddy McDowall, then serving on The National Film Preservation Board, paid for the current marker and engraving, which finally restored some measure of recognition to this long-forgotten woman: Florence Lawrence, the screen's first movie star.

*Florence Lawrence*

Few stories of sudden, horrific, senseless death can rival that of lovely actress, Martha Mansfield. Mansfield was a stunning, seasoned performer in musical comedies, who had worked as a *Ziegfeld Follies* girl before migrating to Hollywood, and into the new medium of motion pictures. After years of playing secondary roles, she was finally cast in a movie that offered her a chance to work opposite the most famous actor of the day, John Barrymore. The movie was *Doctor Jekyll and Mr. Hyde*, and even though she did not garner the second lead, she did score a juicier role with more screen time. Martha thought this was her big break, but it proved to be an anomaly, and she went right back to secondary parts in B pictures.

In 1923, she won a costarring role in big-budget western, *The Warrens of Virginia*, and felt optimism about her future. Sadly, instead of being the start of big things for her, this was her final appearance before the cameras.

On the morning of November 30, filming was underway on location in San Antonio, Texas. The crew was on a break between scenes, when one of them lit his cigarette with a match, carelessly tossing it away. The match fell into the heavy, pure-cotton folds of Martha's hoopskirt costume, and smoldered there. Oblivious, she left the set, and got into her car. As she sat down and closed the door, her dress burst into flames, trapping her in an inferno of fiery fabric. Her costar, Wilfred Lytell, rushed in to put the flames out with his own coat, as did her chauffeur, but when the smoke cleared, Martha had severe burns over most of her body, save for her beautiful face. She was rushed to the hospital, but died the next day, at twenty-four years of age. It is hard to imagine a more gruesome way to die on a movie set, and the tragedy of such a young and promising actress, whose life was so carelessly cut short, haunted the industry for many years.

*Martha and John Barrymore, in Dr. Jekyll and Mr. Hyde*

*Martha Mansfield*

WALLACE REID
as Dusty Rhodes in
"Too Much Speed"

A Paramount Picture
Directed by Frank Urson

If ever there was a face that epitomized the tragedy wrought by the heartlessness of Hollywood studios, and their reckless worship of the bottom line, it would be that of good-natured megastar, Wallace Reid. Reid was the quintessential movie star; tall, dark, handsome, with laughing eyes, and an accommodating disposition. Born into the theater with a stage actress mother, and a father who both an acted in and wrote for films, he was also a skilled musician and outdoorsman. Reid preferred life behind the camera, and he wanted to be a cameraman and director when he arrived in Hollywood, but his good looks proved irresistible to casting directors, and he soon found himself working as an actor in several feature films, including *Birth of a Nation*.

Working as an actor he met Dorothy Davenport, a young actress, and soon married her. Not long after, he signed with Famous Players-Lasky (later Paramount Pictures), and began a frantic work schedule that would be his downfall. He had already made more than a hundred films—and given up on his dreams of working behind the camera—when he began working on several daredevil racing films for his new studio. He became a superstar in such films as *Excuse My Dust*, *The Roaring Road* and *Double Speed*—the *Fast and Furious* films of the day. He rarely took a day off.

It was suggested that he was having trouble keeping up with his relentless work schedule, and was offered a "pick me up" in the form of morphine. Other versions of the story say he became addicted to the drug after a back injury he suffered when a train he rode derailed while filming *The Valley of the Giants* in Oregon. An onsite physician prescribed daily doses of morphine to keep Reid working. By the time he returned to Hollywood, he was a dope fiend, and it wasn't long before the press began spreading it around. His clean-cut image was tarnished, and he began to drink.

Still, the studio kept pushing him to make racing films at that same inhuman pace, and the ever-obliging star complied. By the start of production for his last film, *Thirty Days*, he could barely function, and was committed to a sanatorium in a desperate attempt to regain control over both addictions. He was often confined to a padded cell, and restrained with a straight jacket. His weight dropped to a mere one-hundred-twenty pounds, down from one-hundred-seventy, and in that weakened state, he was defenseless against the influenza that followed. He died there, wrapped in Dorothy's arms, on January 18, 1923. He was thirty-two.

Dorothy went after Reid's friends, blaming them for leading him down the primrose path into substance abuse. She gave the studio a list with names, and referred to those listed as "The Bohemians". She worked to ruin their careers, yet she never laid blame where she should have: at the doorstep of Famous Players-Lasky. She also produced and starred in nice little anti-drug propaganda film, *Human Wreckage*, ironically herself in the process exploiting the young and overworked actress, Lucille Ricksen, who would later die from tuberculosis at only fourteen, a mere two years after Reid.

It is unfathomable how much control studios had over their stars during the era of silent film, willing and able to work them nearly to death in pursuit of the almighty dollar. Wallace Reid was a tragic casualty of this heartless system. He was just too nice for Hollywood.

**WALLACE REID**

*Wallace Reid's Ashes*

# Marie Prevost

> "She was a winner
> That became the doggie's dinner
> She never meant that much to me
> Poor Marie."

The chorus to this Nick Lowe song is sadly how the beautiful Marie Prevost is remembered by most people today. She is a profound example of the terrible fall from grace so many suffered when sound replaced the silence in film. Marie was barely seventeen when she signed with Mack Sennett's Keystone Studios as one of his original Bathing Beauties in 1915. She had worked as a secretary in the law firm representing the studio, and was discovered while running an errand to the set. That sounds like something right out of a fairytale—and for a while, it was.

Marie quickly rose to stardom, starting with eight comedies for Keystone, then in feature films for Warner Brothers, such as *The Beautiful and the Damned* and *The Marriage Circle*. She fell in love with a co-star on the set of *The Beautiful and the Damned*—Kenneth Harlan—and the studio arranged for them to be married on the set as a publicity stunt, to the delight of their fans. Problem was, Marie had neglected to get a divorce from her first husband, Sonny Gerke; a marriage she kept secret for years. When *The Daily Mirror* got wind of this wee hiccup, they ran a headline stating that Prevost would be a bigamist if she went through with the marriage. Needless to say, Jack Warner was not happy. In the end, she got the divorce, married Harlan, and went on to receive high praise for her performance in *The Beautiful and the Damned*. She and Harlan were Hollywood's golden couple for a brief, few years.

In 1926, a sequence of events mortally wounded her career. Her beloved mother, Hughlina Bickford, died in an car accident, devastating Marie, then Warner Brothers elected not renew Marie and her husband's contracts. Unable to cope with the loss of her last surviving parent, and hurt by the studio's unexpected rejection, she turned to alcohol for solace. Her marriage died the next year as she sank deeper into depression. A brief dalliance with Howard Hughes only made things worse, and her part in his film, *The Racket (1928)*, was her final starring role.

The final nail in her coffin was talking pictures. Marie's nasal voice wasn't a good fit for them, and as they got bigger, her roles got smaller, when she got work at all. She binged on food, gained a huge amount of weight, and her drinking got worse. By 1934–her career over–she hung on by a thread, in her small apartment off Vine Street in Hollywood.

She starved herself in an effort to reclaim some of her golden glamorous leading lady rep, but her drinking negated it. The combination of booze and a starvation diet is a dangerous one, as Marie found out. On January 23, after having listened for two days to the incessant barking of her dachshund, Maxie, neighbors called the apartment manager, who sent someone to check on Marie. Her body was found inside, face down in her bed, and somewhat decomposed. Several empty liquor bottles were found in the apartment, as well as an IOU made out to Joan

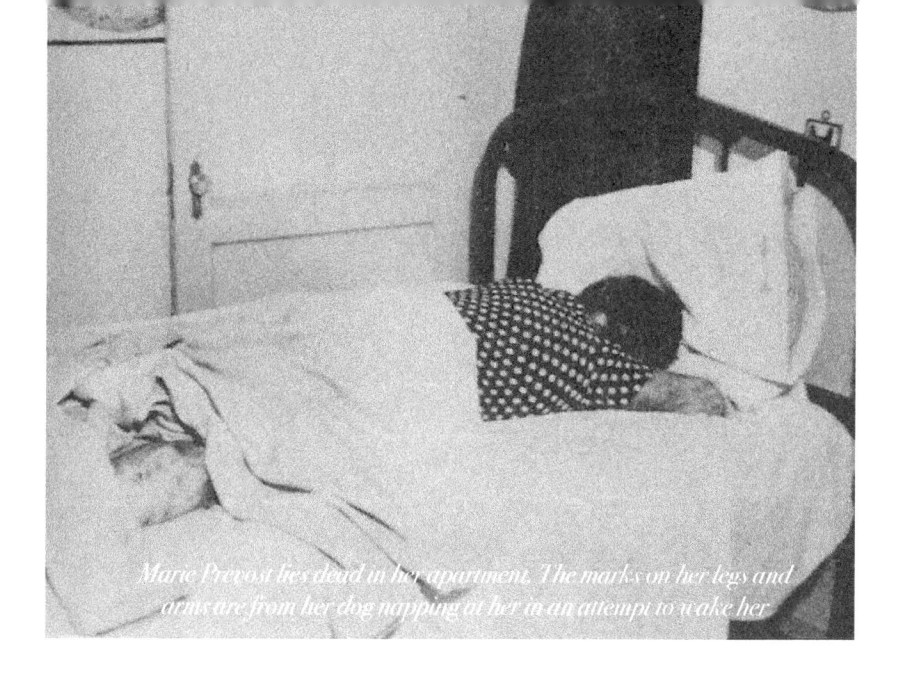

*Marie Prevost lies dead in her apartment. The marks on her legs and arms are from her dog nipping at her in an attempt to wake her*

Crawford. Kenneth Anger, in his book, *Hollywood Babylon*, famously claimed her dog had partially eaten her remains out of hunger, but the truth is that he was merely nipping at his mistress in a futile attempt to rouse her, which left marks on her fragile, decomposed skin. Her death certificate states she died of heart failure brought on by acute alcoholism, likely compounded by poor nutrition. She was thirty-eight.

Marie's funeral was held at Hollywood Memorial Park Cemetery (later known as Hollywood Forever), and attended by some of the period's biggest stars. Joan Crawford footed the bill, as it was revealed that Marie died with less than $300 in the bank. It would have been nice if Warner Brothers had sprung for it, considering how much money she made them in her prime, but hey, business is business.

One good thing did come out of this sad story. The industry, shocked by Marie's lack of resources after having been such a big star, founded a home for aging actors. On Mulholland Drive in Woodland Hills, and called The Motion Picture and Television Country House and Hospital, this facility still stands today, providing an invaluable service to the aging actors of the entertainment industry, the vast majority of which are not mega-millionaires, but independent contractors with no health coverage or retirement benefits. In the end, Marie would have been proud to be the inspiration for such an amazing organization. It has often been said that there is no crueler business than show business, and the sad, short life of Marie Prevost reaffirms this truth.

Olive Thomas

*Olive and her beloved Pekingese*

Long before Elizabeth Taylor, another violet-eyed, raven-haired beauty flitted across the silver screen, if only briefly, enchanting everyone who saw her. Her name was Olive Thomas, believed by many to be the most beautiful creature ever to grace films. Mary Pickford described her thus: "The girl had the loveliest violet blue eyes I have ever seen. They were fringed with long, dark lashes that seemed darker because of the translucent pallor of her skin."

Olive—or Ollie as her friends affectionately called her—began life in depressing, industrialized Pittsburg. Her father died when she was just a child, and she was forced to go to work at age fourteen to help support her family. She married Bernard Thomas when she was sixteen (probably to escape her miserable life), but the marriage was unhappy, and she separated from him two years later, moving to New York. While working in a department store in Harlem, she entered a contest for "The Most Beautiful Girl In New York" and won. This beauty title led to several prestigious modeling jobs for such well-known magazines as *Vogue* and *The Saturday Evening Post*. She also began posing nude for several illustrators and artists of the day, apparently little troubled by the strict moral code of contemporary society. She caught the attention of Florenz Ziegfeld, who immediately put her in his notorious *Midnight Frolics* show; a dubious affair, staged after-hours on the rooftop garden of the New Amsterdam Theater. The Frolics were nothing like Ziegfeld's famous *Follies*. The audience for the Frolics were usually wealthy men who paid a lot of money to see very young girls prance around in almost nothing. Ah, the scandalous turn-of-the-century!

33

*Olive and Jack Pickford*

Ollie became the toast of this wealthy, twisted men's underworld. She was showered with expensive gifts and lurid proposals. They were the lords of Wall Street, important businessmen, and politicians. A well-heeled foreign ambassador was said to have gifted her a ten thousand dollar pearl necklace, roughly a two hundred thousand dollar value today. She was introduced to the wild, dangerous world of the nonstop party, a world she embraced fully. In turn-of-the-century, pre-depression America, cocaine and heroin were still legal, even though booze was soon to be outlawed.

Ollie became Mr. Ziegfeld's mistress, as well as his most popular ingénue. Ziegfeld became quite angry when Jack Pickford (Mary Pickford's spoiled, reckless younger brother) entered Ollie's life, sweeping her away to Hollywood. There, Ollie signed with Triangle Pictures, and starred in a series of light comedies for them, which put her in direct competition with her new sister-in-law, Mary Pickford. Pickford's dislike of Thomas was well-known at the time. Mary did not think Olive—with her working class upbringing and dubious Frolics career—a suitable wife for her baby brother, nor cut from a cloth of the quality required to be admitted into her prestigious family. She completely ignored the fact that her brother was a notorious drug addict and philanderer on his own, who was already dealing with syphilis as a result of his flagrantly promiscuous behavior. She wrote in her autobiography: "I regret to say that none of us approved of the marriage at the time. Mother thought that Jack was too young, and Lottie and I thought that Olive, being in musical comedy, belonged to an alien world." Obviously, "musical comedy" was a euphemism for burlesque.

Screenwriter Frances Marion wrote of Jack and Olive: "Two innocent looking children, they were the gayest, wildest brats ever to stir the stardust on Broadway. Both were talented but they were much more interested in playing the roulette of life than concentrating on their careers."

Despite the pressure of the fuming disdain from her inlaws, Olive thrived in Hollywood. She performed in one successful film after another, and even came to be known as America's sweetheart...to the supreme irritation of Mary Pickford, no doubt.

Behind the scenes, Ollie was infamous for her high-energy, relentless curiosity about the process of filmmaking, as well as her shockingly unladylike language. One account tells of an elderly woman in a hotel lobby who dropped her knitting. Olive noticed, picked it the knitting, and handed it to the woman, her humungous diamond ring flashing in the woman's face. "My! How wonderful to have a ring as beautiful as that!" the old woman gushed. Olive replied, "It's easy, honey. I got this for two humps with a Jew, in Palm Beach." She reportedly crashed her car several times, always walking away with minor cuts and bruises. She and Jack were regulars at all the wildest, wickedest, and most decadent Hollywood parties.

Of course, it couldn't last. Though the press portrayed them as the happiest couple in town, the inner circle knew that the marriage was stormy and turbulent, with Jack juggling multiple affairs. Large quantities of alcohol and drugs were ingested nightly, and when the couple flew to Paris for a vacation in 1920, the consensus held that it was a last-ditch effort to save the marriage, and so yet another round of nonstop partying ensued in the bistros and nightclubs of the Montparnasse neighborhood of Paris. At one point, Jack left Olive in Paris, and went to London for a few days. The true reason he left is still a mystery, though his stated one was to "do some shopping." He couldn't do that in Paris? Some say that he and Olive had an argument, and afterwards Jack ran off to sulk in the arms of another woman. When he returned, he and Olive took up where they left off, hitting the party circuit with renewed and unmitigated vigor.

On September 5, at around 3 AM, Olive and Jack returned to their hotel suite in Montparnasse, after still another night of merrymaking. Jack immediately fell asleep, but Olive was restless, supposedly due to a headache. Pickford claimed that he woke to screams coming from the bathroom. He rushed in, only to find his wife in a panic. "Is the mercury bichloride in the medicine cabinet?" she stammered. Jack checked, and

**Olive Thomas, Film Star, Dies in Hospital in Paris; Took Mercury by Mistake**

Found Prostrated by Jack Pickford, Her Husband, Who Gave First Aid.

reported, "No. Only the aspirin is there." She became hysterical, and sobbed, "Then I've taken poison!" This was Jack's official version of the story. He also claimed—falsely—that the stuff that would kill his young, beautiful wife five agonizing days later was toilet cleaner. It was not. The pills were a prescription for Jack's syphilis sores.

The press went wild with suicide rumors and lurid tales of debauchery, even as Olive lay dying, grieving husband at her side. Many reports suggested Olive took the poison on purpose, thinking her life with Jack—whom she desperately loved—was unsustainable due to his inability to remain faithful, and his serious substance abuse issues. The fact that she did not take a small dose, but an ENTIRE BOTTLE, bears this out. How does someone swallow an entire bottle of poison by mistake, even if they are tired and/or drunk? A reporter from the *Los Angeles Examiner*, F. C. Bertelli, claimed he interviewed the doctor in charge of the case toward the end, Dr. Warden. Bertelli quoted Warden in his article as saying, "A police investigation would show whether she took the poison on purpose, as the medical evidence suggests, or by accident, as is claimed." Either way, Olive Thomas, one of film's brightest stars and most beautiful faces, was dead at twenty-six.

Her funeral in New York City drew thousands of grief-struck fans, with many fainting from stress. It was elaborate, expensive, and reportedly paid for in full—not by her husband—but her former lover: Mr. Ziegfeld. Seems he never got over Ollie, even keeping the nude oil painting of her by the famous artist, Vargas, behind his desk for decades, which must have annoyed the shit out of his loyal wife, actress Billie Burke.

The whole truth about Olive's death will never be known, as everyone involved is now long dead, and no official written record of the details of her death remain. Her beloved Jack died in 1933, from complications of syphilis and substance abuse, at the age of thirty-seven; adding one last, tragic footnote to the story of the 'Beauty and the Golden Boy', perched on the precipice of life–ever so delicately balanced–until their fatal fall.

*"Memories Of Olive", a painting of Ollie by Alberto Vargas*

# Thomas Ince

Whenever fame, money and scandal come together, there are the makings of a great story. Even today, the facts of the 'Thomas Ince Affair', as it has come to be known, are still passionately debated by historians and film buffs alike. Yet the man at the center of the scandal, Thomas Ince, was far more than some distant headline, or some unpleasant walk-on in someone else's biography. He was an actor, director, producer, writer, innovator and studio head, and rarely was or is recognized for his true accomplishments.

Ince was one of the most well-liked and innovative men in Hollywood, when he died at the age of forty-two. Starting with a history as a failed actor in vaudeville acts, he made his way to directing Westerns for the IMP film company in New York, owned by Carl Laemmle. Ince had bigger dreams, so he borrowed an expensive suit and a diamond ring, and arranged to meet with Charles O. Baumann, whose studio had just been contracted to open a new studio in Hollywood for the sole purpose of making westerns. Thomas laid it on thick, passing himself off as a more established filmmaker than he really was. Baumann ate it up. Ince was shocked when the ploy worked, and he was soon making movies in Hollywood, for the princely sum of one hundred fifty dollars a week.

Ince went on to change the entire film industry by building the first prototype of a modern Hollywood movie studio. He developed writing and filming techniques that are standard procedure today, such as the use of shooting scripts, and second unit directors to shoot separate scenes simultaneously. He realized that he needed a place where he could have more control over every aspect of filming, so he built a compound in the Santa Ynez Canyon near Santa Monica, that would later be known as Inceville—the first movie studio.

By all accounts, Inceville was amazing. Several thousand acres were filled with stages along with whole neighborhoods of multicolored houses; from the humblest shack to the most gigantic mansion. Architectural styles of many countries and periods were on hand, from Japanese villages to French chalets. He even hired performers from a wild west show to live onsite, including an entire Sioux tribe who happily pitched their teepees there. William S. Hart, famed western star, was first coaxed into film by Ince on a tour of Inceville. The story goes that Hart had a fear of horses, and so couldn't work in westerns, but Ince coaxed him to mount a pony so short his feet nearly touched the ground. This worked for Hart, who started doing westerns, and the rest was history. Inceville

*The town of Inceville, California circa 1918.*

was his Ince's kingdom, over it he reigned, and from the elaborate mansion he had built for himself, he could turn fear into a career.

Ince sold Inceville to Hart—who fell in love with it during that first tour—building a new studio in Culver City, Culver Studios. Inceville became Hartville, then fell into disrepair after several fires. Today, it is only a memory. Ince kept making movies at his Culver Studios, which still stands today on Culver Boulevard. The administration building is instantly familiar, not only for its likeness to Mount Vernon, but because the façade was the inspiration for Tara's exterior in *Gone with the Wind*. Culver Studios had forty colonial revival-style buildings, a fire department, a hospital, and a swimming pool. Royalty and presidents toured it and came away impressed. Ince had the world in his pocket for a little while. And then, well, there are many conflicting and contradictory versions of what happened the night of November 16, 1924, and most are pure speculation. What is known is: Ince's streak came abruptly to an end.

William Randolph Hearst, wealthy newspaper magnate, and his mistress, actress Marion Davies, hosted a party aboard Hearst's yacht, Oneida. Guests included Charlie Chaplin, and gossip columnist Louella Parsons, though both Davies and Parsons later insisted Parsons was not there, and Chaplin insisted for years that he wasn't either. Also onboard was physician Dr. Goodman. Some said this was a belated birthday party for Ince, but Davies denied this, saying it was just a party that Ince was invited to only at the request of his wife, Nell, who thought he could use the rest. However, there is a photo of Davies on a dock, dozens of giant balloons clutched in her arms, possibly welcoming Ince onto the Oneida, which lends credence to the birthday claim.

A lavish dinner and much merrymaking followed, but no drinking, claimed Davies. Others said the booze flowed freely. Later, Ince reportedly told doctors that he had consumed alcohol there. Hearst was a known teetotaler, who did not tolerate booze in his presence, but that would not stop guests from sneaking their own aboard, so the truth likely lies somewhere in-between.

During the night, Ince fell violently ill. He was dropped off in San Diego, and put on a train to Los Angeles. However, Dr. Goodman held that he was up early with Ince on Monday morning to leave the yacht with him, and return home before the others woke up. Ince suffered a heart attack while en route, and was taken from the train to a hotel, where another physician, Dr. T.A. Parker, was consulted. If Dr. Goodman believed Ince was having a heart attack, why didn't he see Ince to a hospital? Ince's wife was called, and she rushed to her husband's side. Again, rather than be taken to a hospital, Ince insisted he be taken home, and so was brought home to Los Angeles, where he died in his wife's arms the very next day.

The front page of the Wednesday morning edition of the *Los Angeles Times* blared "Movie Producer Shot On Hearst Yacht!" Hearst didn't own the *LA Times*. By the evening edition, the salacious headline was gone, and the Thursday morning edition read only that Ince had died of a heart ailment brought on by acute indigestion. If not for that single, errant headline, would Ince's death still pique the interests of people today? Doubtful.

Rumors said Hearst found Ince with Davies in a compromising position, then pulled out his diamond-encrusted pistol, shooting Ince. In another version, Hearst found them in a dark area of the yacht, and shot Ince, mistaking him for Charlie Chaplin. In another version, Hearst caught Chaplin and Davies together in bed, got his gun, and shot at Chaplin, who tried to escape by running down the gangplank. Hearst missed Chaplin, but hit Ince instead, who was in the wrong place at the wrong time. Chaplin made no secret of his infatuation with Davies, and credible evidence of an affair is extant. In her autobiography, however, Davies denied ever returning his affections, and expressed mild disdain for the director. "I don't think there was anything wrong with him," she said, "except that he was a little cracked." Allegedly, Parsons, who was elevated from lowly columnist to the top syndicated entertainment writer for Hearst publications soon afterwards, witnessed the entire incident.

The press went wild, at least those not controlled by Hearst Corporation, and the rumors spread like a grass fire. At least one eyewitness, Chaplin's secretary Toraichi Kono, reported seeing Ince carried off the boat with a bullet wound in his head. The San Diego District Attorney's office was finally forced to look into it. At least thirteen people were aboard the Oneida that night, not counting crew and paid performers. Yet, the investigation consisted of a single interview: Dr. Daniel Carson Goodman, who stated that Ince was not shot, but suffered from indigestion, or a heart ailment, or both. Why shouldn't the good doctor be taken at his word? That he was no longer a practicing physician, but was the head of production for Hearst's film company was irrelevant to the DA. The case was closed, the death ruled a result of "natural causes." Nell Ince immediately had her husband's body cremated, and left for Europe. She didn't leave empty-handed, however. For decades, rumors of a substantial Hearst-funded trust for her and the kids persisted, and say that he even paid off Ince's mortgage on an apartment building, the Chateau Elysee, still standing today at 5930 Franklin Avenue. The scientologists currently inhabiting it will be happy to give you a tour if you ask.

In a bizarre twist, Abigail Kinsolving—Davies' secretary—told police that Ince raped her that night. This sounds preposterous at first, but Kinsolving was not married, and did indeed give birth to a child nine months after the party, and then died in a mysterious automobile accident just a few months after that, an accident that occurred very near to Hearst's San Simeon Castle. Hearst security guards found her body. A strange suicide note was also discovered, and some said it appeared to be written by two different people. Her child was placed in an orphanage, and was supposedly financially supported by Davies for years.

Did Hearst kill Thomas Ince, deliberately or otherwise? Did he shoot Ince for raping Kinsolving? Ince was a well-liked man by all accounts. Marion said of him, "There was nothing wolfy about him, not a bit. He wanted to be friendly with everybody, and he was jovial and good-natured." Doesn't sound like a rapist. But then, there was the rumor that Ince had a secret room built in his new Benedict Canyon home, for which only he had a key. It connected to a passageway, and a secret viewing space from where he could observe his famous houseguests engaged in intimate activity undetected. Allegedly, this chamber was discovered after Nell Ince sold the home following his death. There are so many unanswered questions about this case that just won't go away. Why would all the physicians who attended Ince, including those that were never aboard the yacht, and therefore not subject to Hearst's influence, insist that he was suffering from a heart ailment? His own family physician listed the cause of death as a heart attack on the death certificate. A bullet wound is hard to miss, and he had nothing to gain by lying. It's not surprising that Hearst would try to help widowed Nell Ince, as he was known to be extremely generous, and probably felt partially responsible for her husband having fallen ill while being his guest. There is actually no real proof that he did provide for her, however, only speculation. If he did, it wasn't enough to ensure her financial security past the stock market crash of '29, and forestall her subsequent life as a taxi cab driver.

What is often lost when discussing the 'Thomas Ince Affair' is Thomas Ince himself. His contributions to the film industry, and his pioneering development of the first modern studio cannot be overstated. Yet he is little remembered today, save as a brief footnote in countless other publications. He will always be remembered as the man who was possibly murdered by William Randolph Hearst. What a sad legacy for such a remarkable and talented man.

*The Chateau Elysee, Hollywood*

# Alma Rubens

There once was a beautiful, delicate girl who enchanted everyone who knew her. She lit up the screen and quickly became a star. Her name was Alma Rubens, and her story is beyond sad.

Alma got her start in the world of show business at a very young age, first as a chorus girl in musical comedies. Soon, she was acting in the new medium of motion pictures. Quickly achieving success and recognition in such films as *Birth of a Nation* and *Intolerance*, she then made three high profile films with the extremely popular Douglas Fairbanks, and launched into real stardom.

With her captivating beauty, the doors of the Hollywood elite swung wide open. The parties glittering and decadent, the company intoxicating (in more ways than one), and the lifestyle exhausting. She was required to work nonstop during the day, and then to attend one social event after another in the evening. Soon, the endless schedule took its toll, and Alma showed signs of serious drug addiction. The offers slowed, and her lucid periods shrank, until it all came to a head one bizarre morning. People reported a crazy woman running down Hollywood Boulevard, tearing her clothes off, and screaming she'd been kidnapped. Two men in white lab coats chased her, and when they finally caught her, she stabbed one of them viciously in the shoulder with a concealed knife. Thus, Alma's secret was out. She had escaped while being transferred to a mental facility for treatment of her heroin addiction. With her worrisome fall from grace, the motion picture studio doors slammed shut to her, and her career was over.

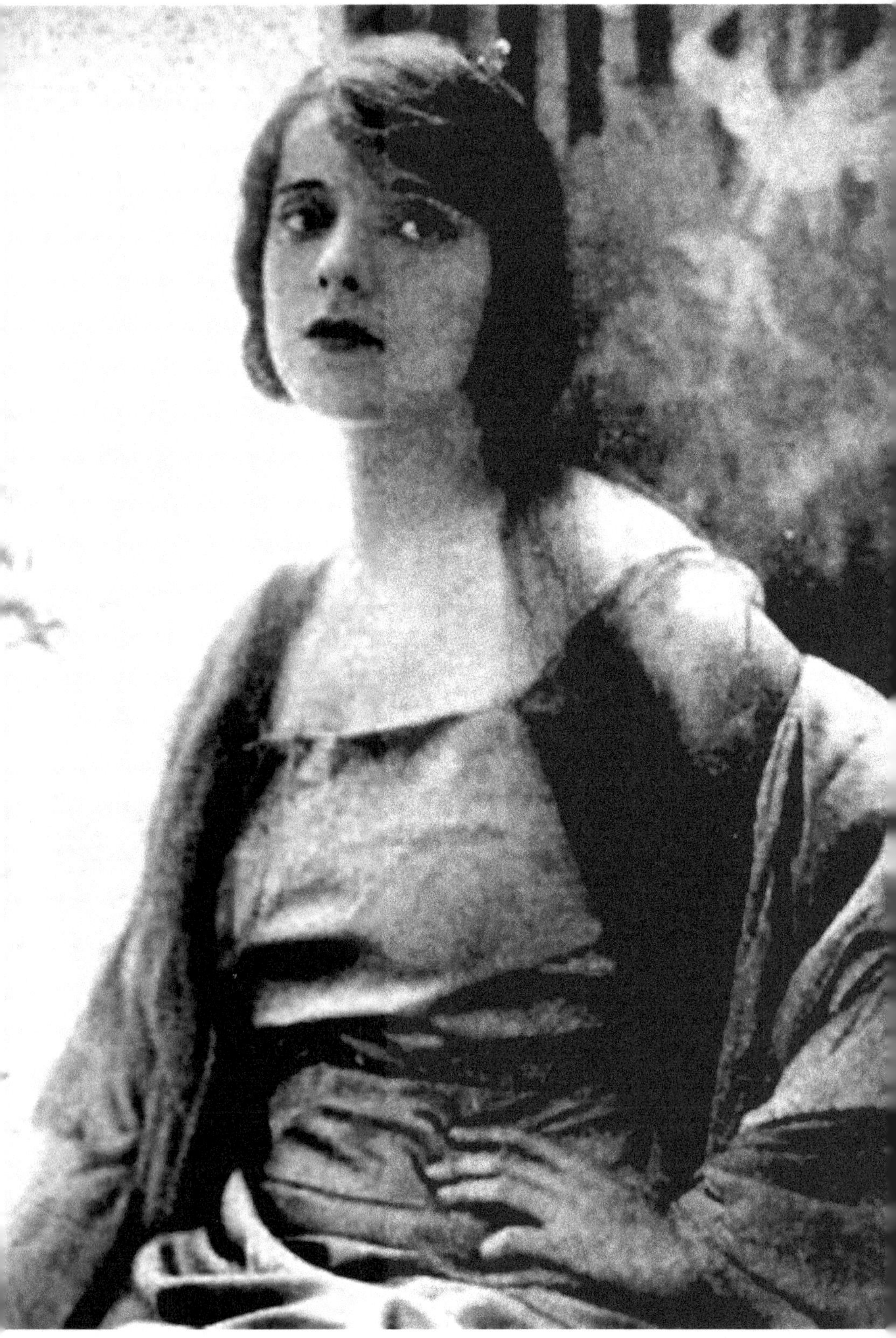

Alma had one friend left among the chosen, however: Marion Davies. Davies had befriended Alma years earlier, when Hearst produced some of her earlier films. Davies stood by Alma as the rest of Hollywood turned their backs. Broke, unable to work, and in dire straits, Davies convinced Hearst to support her, and pay her medical bills. If it weren't for this benevolence, Alma would probably have died on the streets. She died in a warm bed, from pneumonia, at the age of thirty-three.

In her last interview with the *Los Angeles Examiner*, Alma finally came clean. "I've been miserable for so long. As long as my money held out I could get drugs. I was afraid to tell my mother, my best friend. My only desire was to get drugs and take them in secrecy. If only I could go on my knees before the police or before a judge and beg them to make stiffer laws so that men will refuse to take dirty dollars from murderers who sell this poison and who escape punishment when caught by buying their way out."

Charlie Chaplin once said, "Nothing is permanent in this world, not even our troubles." Alma Rubens learned this truth the hard way.

# The Beautiful and the Doomed
## (Those who seemed doomed by misfortune)

There is an old saying that warns: "the good die young." Many old tales have been disproven, but more often than not, the good really do seem to have shorter lives. Perhaps it is merely that the impact of a lovely, vibrant life—cut tragically short—is more keenly felt, especially if that life brought joy and blissful distraction to thousands of fans. Hollywood seems to have seen more than its share of such sadness. Indeed, the real heartbreaking stories behind the screen far outnumber those projected onto it.

Natalie Wood

L ovely Natalie Wood. A precocious child star who morphed into a stunning beauty, while still retaining her sweet, approachable innocence. She truly was the girl next door. Everyone loved her, which may be why no one can let her rest in peace. The holes left in the hearts of fans everywhere when she died so tragically have only grown wider and deeper with each passing year, even as the memory of her living presence fades into the past. People seem to forget that she had been mostly written off by both her fans and the studios as a "once-was" on the pleasant November night she was taken from us.

It all began back in 1938, with a beautiful little girl born to Russian immigrants in San Francisco. They named her Natasha Nikolaevna Zacharenko. She was four, and living in small town in Northern California called Santa Rosa(made famous a few years later in Hitchcock's *Shadow of a Doubt*), when her mother took her downtown to watch the filming of the movie, *Happy Land*. Biographies often describe her mother, Maria, as the ultimate stage mom; determined to get her daughter into pictures. Maria arranged for Natasha to meet the director of *Happy Land*, Irving Pichel, with clear instructions to "Make Mr. Pichel love you." He did, and Natasha got a small role in his film, and a new, easier-to-pronounce name: Natalie Wood.

Two years later, when another role opened, Pichel remembered Natalie. It was an Orson Wells film, *Tomorrow Is Forever*. He called Maria, and asked her to bring Natalie out for a screen test. This was all Maria needed to hear to drop everything, immediately pack her bags, and drag her entire family off to Hollywood. For the test, Natalie was required to cry on cue. Not willing to risk failure, Maria showed Natalie a butterfly, and pulled off its wings right in front of her. This had the desired effect. Natalie wept openly and profusely, got the part, was wonderful in it, and a child star was born. The Christmas classic, *Miracle On 34th Street* followed, and Natalie became one of the most loved—and best paid—child actors of the time.

The filming of a scene for *The Green Promise* in 1949 led to Natalie's terror of drowning in black water. She was supposed to cross a bridge which spanned a raging river during a violent storm. The bridge was to collapse and pitch her into the water, where the waiting crew would quickly fish her out. Of course, things didn't turn out that way, and she spent several terrifying minutes struggling to keep her head above water before she was finally rescued. She nearly drowned. It was said that she wouldn't go in water any deeper than a bathtub after that.

She finished her childhood career with more than twenty pictures under her belt, and then entered the much-feared, awkward years of adolescence—usually a death sentence for the careers of child actors. Natalie avoided this fate by blossoming into a stunning beauty, as Elizabeth Taylor had, a few years earlier. She made a series of high-profile films during this time that would catapult her into fame, and cement her legacy as one of Hollywood's biggest stars, including *Rebel Without A Cause*, *Splendor in the Grass* and *West Side Story*.

Around this time, Natalie allegedly had an encounter with a well-known, established star. Rumor had it that this star lured Natalie to his hotel room, under the pretext of considering her for a big role in his next film. What happened to Natalie at the hands of this star has been the stuff of legend ever since. Supposedly, she was brutally raped, beaten, left to stagger out of the hotel and find her way home, dazed and injured. This star is still alive, so he will not be named, but if true, a dance around his grave when the time comes would not be inappropriate.

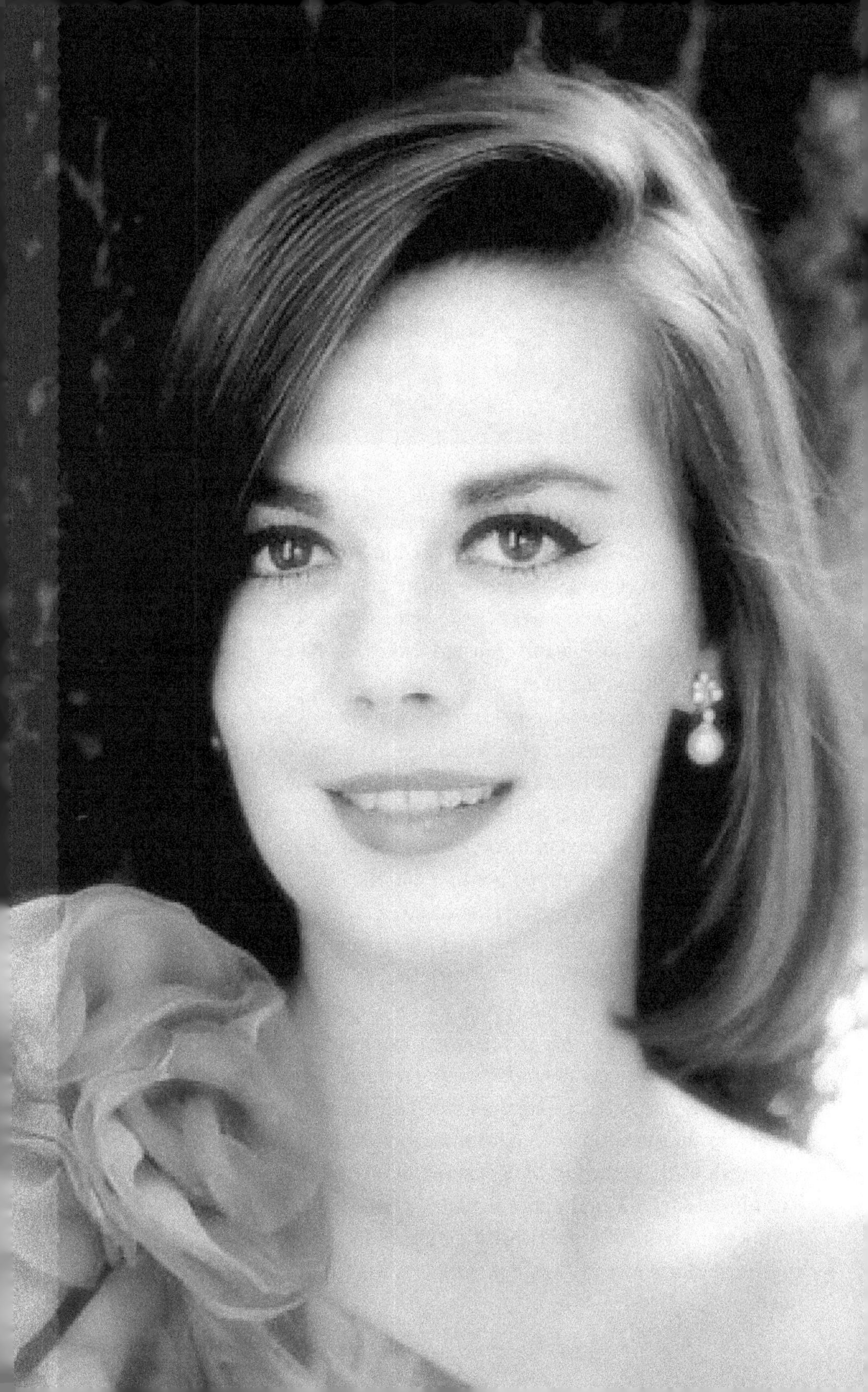

Seen with several eligible bachelors, including Elvis Presley and James Dean, Wood ended up marrying relatively unknown actor Robert Wagner in 1957. The marriage lasted a scant five years, and the cause of the divorce varies from storyteller to storyteller. Wagner said they couldn't merge their careers and personal lives, but in her biography on Natalie, author Suzanne Finstad wrote that she caught him in an intimate act with another man.

Natalie's onscreen transition from adolescent to adult proved more difficult than her seemingly effortless one from child star to teenage phenomenon. She made some very bad choices, in both her personal and professional lives, and by the early '70s, her career was at a standstill. She was on her second divorce, with one suicide attempt behind her. Robert Wagner reentered her life, and they decided to give their relationship another go, remarrying in 1972. During this period, she took several years off from movie making to raise her two daughters. Hollywood forgot about Natalie.

She had been off the big screen for so long that by the mid-'70s, she was relegated to acting in television movies. She received critical acclaim in such projects as *From Here To Eternity*, *Cat on a Hot Tin Roof* and *The Cracker Factory*, but she longed for the days when she was a major star on the silver screen. She was poised for a comeback when she began work on the big-budget sci-fi picture, *Brainstorm*, in 1983. The film costarred Christopher Walken—a hot commodity at the time—having won the best supporting actor award four years earlier for his riveting performance in *The Deer Hunter*. Alas, Natalie's comeback was not to be.

On November 27, 1983, the Friday after Thanksgiving, Walken joined both Wagners for a weekend pleasure cruise around Catalina Island, on the Wagners' yacht: Splendour (named for Natalie's favorite movie, *Splendor in the Grass*). Ominously, Natalie's eleven-year-old daughter, Natasha, begged her mother not to go, afraid she would never see her again. The Wagners argued as the boat left dock–a common pastime of theirs–and Natalie spent the first night in a hotel room on the island, allegedly with Dennis Davern: skipper of the Splendour. The next day began well, but got progressively worse. They began drinking early, and kept it up all day. Natalie left the yacht with Walken, arriving at Harbor Reef bar in the afternoon; long before RJ and Davern arrived. They were buzzed when they met back up for dinner. They were drunk when they left the restaurant, several witnesses reporting that the boisterous trio guzzled one bottle after another of champagne. Suzanne Finstad wrote in her book, *Natasha*, that waitresses saw Natalie and Walken holding hands under the table–openly flirting through dinner–as RJ's agitation grew each minute. A wine glass became airborne, shattered, and shards of glass flew everywhere.

Exactly what happened next still remains a mystery. Four people were aboard the Splendour that late Saturday night: Natalie, Wagner, Walken and Davern. Only three walked off in the morning. Natalie's body would be discovered seven hours later floating in the ocean, a mile from the yacht. She was floating upright, eyes wide open, wearing a down jacket, nightgown and socks. The untethered dinghy floated nearby. She was forty-three. What happened?

Exactly what happened next remains a mystery even today. Four people were aboard the Splendour that late Saturday night: Natalie, Wagner, Walken and Davern. Only three walked off in the morning. Natalie's body would be discovered seven hours later floating in the ocean, a mile from the yacht. She was floating upright, eyes wide open, wearing a down jacket, nightgown and socks. The untethered dinghy floated nearby. She was forty-three. What happened?

Wagner said he argued about Natalie's career with Walken after returning from the restaurant. Wagner told him to mind his own business, a bottle broke over a table, and Natalie left the room so the two "gentlemen" could "work it out" amongst themselves. Wagner and Walken called a truce, and Wagner headed off to his cabin. Later, he realized Natalie and the dinghy were missing. When her body was found, he said she must have slipped while trying to hitch up the dinghy, to keep it from banging against the side of the yacht, and keeping her awake. Wagner denied, for decades, that he and Natalie fought in the cabin after leaving Walken, but finally admitted that a fight had indeed occurred in his 2008 autobiography.

Dennis Davern backed up everything Wagner said back in 1981, and for thirty years afterwards. But in 2011, an attack of conscience led to his blabbing to CBS News[1] about all sorts of things that went down that fateful night. He said that the argument between Wagner and Walken was about Natalie herself, not her career, and remembers RJ yelling "You want to fuck my wife?!?" before bashing a wine bottle on a table. Davern reported that after everyone went to their separate corners, there was a serious—verging on violent—argument between Natalie and RJ that could be heard all over the boat, which ended with Natalie storming out of the room, RJ on her heels. Moments later, he claimed, he heard the couple shouting again, this time on the side of the boat where the dinghy was. In secret tapes handed over to the police by biographer Suzanne Finstad, Natalie's sister, Lana, is heard telling Finstad that Davern called her ten years after Natalie's death, and told her he saw RJ do the deed: "He shoved her away. She fell overboard."[1] RJ then decided to "teach her a lesson" by leaving

---

1 The tape can be accessed online here: http://losangeles.cbslocal.com/2012/09/13/audio-tapes-reveal-new-information-on-natalie-woods-death/

her there, while he and Davern went inside to have a few more drinks. They allegedly kept hearing her cries for help, and when the sounds stopped, RJ became panicked. On the tape, Lana claims that Davern told her he wanted to notify the Coast Guard immediately when they noticed she was missing, but Wagner wanted to wait and see if she would return in the dinghy. The authorities would not be notified for another two hours. Why didn't Davern say any of this closer to the time of the alleged crime? He claims he was pressured by RJ and his lawyer to lie to the cops to protect RJ.

This was enough for the police, who stated "substantial new evidence" as their reason for reopening the case, and it remains open as of this writing. Even the coroner decided to take a second look, and in doing so, amended Natalie's cause of death from accidental drowning to "Drowning and other causes undetermined," citing significant, unexplained bruising on her arms and legs as the reason for the change.

The timing of all of this is interesting. Davern coauthored a book about the case in 2008, *Goodbye Natalie, Goodbye Splendour*, which garnered no attention whatsoever when it was first published. But on the thirtieth anniversary of Natalie's death, and following a ten-minute interview on *48 Hours Mystery*, everyone was suddenly paying attention to this man and his story.

This is a mystery that should be solved. There are at least two people who know exactly what happened that night, but they have very different stories...so who is telling the truth? One has a financial motivation to lie, and the other has a legal motivation, so the chances that the truth will ever be told are not good. In the end, it doesn't really matter. Natalie is gone forever, and no amount of speculation or investigation will ever bring her back.

There is a touching scene in the film *Tomorrow Is Forever*, where she—as a tiny, frightened orphan—is walking away from the camera, her hand tightly clasped in the great bulk of a man: Orson Wells. The camera slowly fades out. Tomorrow *is* forever, unless your tomorrows are stolen in a cruel and senseless twist of fate, and swallowed by the dark November waters of your nightmares.

Rest in peace, Natasha.

# Judy Tyler

*The scene of the car accident that killed Judy Tyler*

When *Jailhouse Rock* was released in November of 1957, it was a huge hit, and elevated its young singing star—Elvis Presley—to even greater heights of fame. Many eyes were drawn, however, to his lovely costar: Judy Tyler. The chemistry between the two was palpable in the intimate publicity stills, and it oozed from them on the screen. Suddenly, everyone wanted to know who this sexy girl with the catlike eyes and tiny waist was. Elvis seemed genuinely smitten onscreen. Practically before the world had a chance to learn her name, it was reported that poor Judy had been tragically killed in an automobile accident six months prior to the release of the movie, just weeks after the shoot had wrapped. Judy, who seemed on the cusp of a promising career, was dead at twenty-three, before she ever really got started. So who was Judy Tyler?

Judy was born in Milwaukee, in 1932. Her father, Julian Hess, played trumpet for Benny Goodman's orchestra. Her mother, Loreleo, had been a *Ziegfeld Follies* girl. Judy grew into a stunning beauty herself, quitting school to model for Harry Conover, creator of the "Cover Girl" concept. She later moved to Manhattan, and danced in the Copacabana chorus line, all while still under eighteen years old. In 1952, she auditioned for the role of Princess Summerfallwinterspring on the wildly popular children's television show, *The Howdy Doody Show*, and won. The show gave Tyler national exposure, but she soon developed a reputation for wild behavior that did not fit at all with her squeaky-clean character. In his book about *The Howdy Doody Show*, *What Time Is It Kids?*, Stephan Davis, the show's writer/director, recounted numerous incidents that featured Tyler's insatiable appetite for sex and partying, as well as her very unladylike language. Her coworker, Bob Nicholson, said of her "I'd go out on weekend appearances with her, and while we'd get along fine, she would just as soon tell a store manager to go fuck himself as she would look at him." She also enjoyed stripping and dancing on tabletops on her days off, reportedly.

Tired of the limited scope of her character, Judy left *The Howdy Doody Show* two years later, and returned to the stage. In 1956, she again drew national attention when she won a Tony nomination for her role in the play, *Pipe Dream*. This landed her on the cover of *Life magazine*, an honor she shared with another tragic beauty, Jayne Mansfield.

*Judy as Princess Summerfallwinterspring*

This led to a guest appearance on *The Perry Mason Show,* and a role in the B movie, *Bop Girl Goes Calypso.* She was then approached by the producers of *Jailhouse Rock,* who cast her as Peggy Van Alden, opposite Elvis Presley.

By the time Judy was cast in *Jailhouse Rock,* she was already on her second marriage, this time to actor Greg Lafayette. The maid of honor at her Baltimore wedding had been Pattie Paige. The couple settled in New York, but Hollywood beckoned, and Judy and Greg flew to the west coast so she could begin filming.

Much was written about the sparks the flew right away between Elvis and Judy, and this was not lost on Greg, who became so disruptive that he was banned from the set. Elvis and Judy smolder in one double entendre-laden scene after the next, and witnesses said their ardor carried over into long lunch breaks and after hours rendezvous. One of Judy's best lines in the film is when Elvis asks why she's interested in him. She fixes him with those catlike eyes, and says, "I like the way you swing a guitar." Racy stuff in 1957.

*Judy as Peggy Van Alden with Elvis in Jailhouse Rock*

The film wrapped in June. Judy and her husband chose to drive, rather than fly, home. They were driving on Highway 30, through the wilderness of Wyoming, in late afternoon, when they neared a popular tourist trap: Wild Bills Curios and Petting Zoo. It was one of those weird little places that provided a distraction from the endless monotony of Wyoming's vast, open plains. As they drew near to the intersection by the store, another vehicle pulled out from the parking lot, and swung in front of them, causing Greg to wildly swerve their car at high speed. This led to an uncontrolled skid into oncoming traffic, and their vehicle was broadsided on the passenger's side by a northbound car. The impact was so violent, Judy was reportedly torn in half. She died instantly, of course, with Greg dying several hours later. The circumstances were similar to those in James Dean's accident, two years earlier. The time of day might have been a factor, as the sun was beginning to set, and the approaching car could have been blinded.

When Elvis found out, he was inconsolable, at least for a while. According to witnesses, he openly wept, and talked of never being able to watch *Jailhouse Rock* again. George Klein, one of Elvis's oldest friends, said he and Elvis drove around Memphis for hours that day, just talking about Judy. Elvis supposedly told a reporter "Nothing has hurt me as bad in my life. I just don't believe I can stand to see the movie we made together now. Just don't believe I can." Some say Elvis kept that vow, but others say he had already moved on, and was seeing Anita Wood within weeks of Judy's death.

When the reviews for *Jailhouse Rock* rolled in, they were polite to—when they were not raving for—Judy. *The Los Angeles Herald Express* wrote "Judy Tyler, as the pretty record promoter who helps the crude singer to success only to receive shameful treatment in return, gives a performance that makes her untimely death seem all the sadder." Margaret Harford, in the *Los Angeles Mirror*, lamented "Youthful Miss Tyler's death is a real loss, for she was a talented, fresh-looking beauty who probably would have done very well in the movies." Judy Tyler is just a footnote now, but once she was vibrant, gorgeous woman with a bright future, who turned Elvis Presley's head, both on and offscreen.

Heath Ledger

### "I wish I could quit you."

Heath Ledger delivered this iconic line to Jake Gyllenhaal, in the critically acclaimed 2005 film about bisexual cowboys, *Brokeback Mountain*. Just three years later, as he stood on the precipice of super-stardom, he would be found in his New York apartment, in the middle of the afternoon, dead. What could have gone so terribly wrong for this young man who seemed to have it all: youth, looks, charisma and serious talent?

Heath was a shy, sometimes withdrawn individual who turned to acting as a way of allowing his hidden personality to shine. He was born in Australia in 1979, and reportedly named after the character Heathcliff in the Emily Bronte novel, *Wuthering Heights*. He developed an early aptitude for playing chess, winning Australia's junior chess championship at the age of ten. His first foray into acting was in a grammar school production of *Peter Pan*, that same year.

When he was just sixteen, he struck out on his own, and moved to Sydney with his best friend, Trevor DiCarlo. After struggling in small roles, he was cast in the hit series, *Roar*, an adventure drama set in 400AD Ireland. The series was backed by the Fox network in the US. Fox executives quickly understood Heath's potential, and urged him to move across the pond to Hollywood.

His first major role was opposite Mel Gibson in the big-budget period piece, *The Patriot*. Next, a juicy role as the son of Billy Bob Thornton in critic's darling, *Monsters Ball*. He went from supporting to lead actor in a series of moderately successful films, such as *A Knights Tale*, *The Brothers Grimm* and *Casanova*. In 2001, he was named one of *People Magazine's* fifty most beautiful people. But Heath, by all accounts, was more embarrassed by his good looks than proud.

From 2001 to 2005, Heath stayed out of the limelight, concentrating on films that were independent, rather than mainstream. It's an odd choice, given that he appeared to be on the verge of serious commercial success. Perhaps he did not like the direction his career was taking, the type of press he was receiving, or the roles he was being offered by the studios. From the start, he was determined to be taken seriously as an actor, and not be known for only that last commercial success, or the pretty face.

In 2005, one of these independent films would thrust Heath back into the spotlight, and boost his image from edgy supporting actor to full-fledged star. The film was *Brokeback Mountain*, and in it, Heath played against type, as the doomed bisexual cowboy, Ennis Del Mar, who falls in love with fellow cowboy Jack Twist, played by Jake Gyllenhaal. This was a daring role for Heath to tackle, as his image as a heterosexual romantic lead could be tarnished. Heath cared more about acting than he did his image, however, putting his all into the role. It showed. Critics and audiences alike were stunned at the realism and subtle nature of his performance. *Rolling Stone* magazine's film critic, Peter Travers wrote: "Ledger's magnificent performance is an acting miracle. He seems to tear it from his insides. Ledger doesn't just know how Ennis moves, speaks, listens, he knows how he breathes. To see him inhale the scent of a shirt hanging in Jack's closet is to take measure of the pain of love lost." For this performance, Heath won the New York Critics Choice Award, as well as the San Francisco Film Critics Circle Award. He received a nomination for best actor from The Golden

Globes, and The Academy Of Motion Picture Arts and Sciences, but was passed over for both. Heath didn't care. He knew winning awards was not what it was about.

He followed *Brokeback Mountain* with another amazing, non-mainstream performance as young Bob Dylan—in the quirky, semi-autobiographical independent film, *I'm Not There*. Heath did not rest on his laurels, declaring in a 2007 interview "The day I say it's good is the day I should start doing something else."

A relationship blossomed between Heath and young *Brokeback Mountain* costar: Michelle Williams. Becoming parents in October of 2005, they set up a nest in Brooklyn, but Health still went home to Australia often. After several run-ins with the Australian paparazzi, whom he felt did not respect his privacy, Heath moved full-time into the Brooklyn nest with Michelle and baby.

When Heath was cast in Christopher Nolan's elaborate Batman film, *The Dark Knight*, he began suffering severe insomnia. His role as the maniacal Joker proved to be emotionally and physically draining, leaving him teetering on the edge of nervous collapse. He told reporters that he barely averaged two hours sleep a night while playing the "psychopathic, mass murdering, schizophrenic clown with zero empathy." Heath said, "I couldn't stop thinking. My body was exhausted, but my mind was still going." His relationship with Michelle suffered, and they broke up shortly after filming wrapped.

Early peeks at Ledger's Joker inspired serious prerelease buzz as the date for the film's premiere drew closer. The word was that this was the film that was going to make Heath a major star, and an artist who could stand proud in the ranks of Brando and Penn, as one of the greatest actors of modern cinema. Sadly, this prophecy would only be fulfilled within the confines of this single performance, as six months before *The Dark Knight* was released, Heath Ledger was dead.

On January 22, 2008, at approximately 2:45 PM, his housekeeper and his masseuse found Heath unconscious in his bed. Scattered on a nearby nightstand were several sleep medications, both prescription and over-the-counter. Oddly, instead of notifying authorities immediately, the masseuse, Diana Wolozin, used Heath's cell phone to call Mary-Kate Olsen, a good friend of Heath's, for advice. It was unclear what Olsen told her, but Wolozin ended up calling Olsen a second time, several minutes later, this time expressing her fears that Heath was dead. It is highly likely that she placed a third call to Olsen as well. Forty-five minutes passed between Heath being discovered, and the paramedics being finally called. Really? Though it probably wouldn't have made a difference if they had called immediately, we will never know.

Despite the swarming suicide rumors, the coroner's report—released two weeks later—lists the cause of death as an accidental overdose of oxycodone, hydrocodone(Vicodin), diazepam, temazepam, alprazolam and doxylamine. Vicodin and oxycodone alone would have done it. Heath's death was another sad example of the problem of prescription drug abuse that has plagued the celebrity community since the days of silent movies.

People were shocked and saddened. When the world finally got a look at Heath's final performance as the Joker in *The Dark Knight*—a role that likely contributed to the conditions that led to his death—his loss was all the more keenly felt. The snarling, grinning, evil monster who took pleasure in death and destruction will go down in history as one of the best villain performances ever filmed. Film critic Tim Teeman wrote, "With his face a peeling façade of clown paint and his mouth a blurred slash, the joker is the embodiment of anarchy and anti-order. Ledger is so terrifying and unpredictable that his very presence on screen makes you horribly nervous." Peter Travers of *Rolling Stone* agreed: "I can only speak superlatives of Ledger, who is mad crazy blazing brilliant as the Joker." *Total Film* wrote: "Dig out the thesaurus and run through the superlatives: chilling, gleeful, genius. It's a masterpiece of a performance...This is the definitive joker."

The posthumous awards flowed in: two People's Choice Awards, The Golden Globe Award, and finally, the Academy Award for Best Supporting Actor. Audiences flocked to see the film, and Heath's hypnotic performance, making *The Dark Knight* the fourteenth highest grossing film of all time. It is still considered the best film in its genre ever made.

Heath saw none of this, of course. His daughter will grow up without ever having known her father, and his potential as a brilliant actor will never fully be realized. His legacy is undeniable though, and rests with two performances that are not easily forgotten, even by the fickle standards of Hollywood. Goodnight, sweet prince. May flights of angels sing thee to thy rest.

*The Heath Ledger memorial in Melville, Australia.*

Suzan Ball

E veryone loved Lucy, but few remember her younger and more striking cousin, Suzan Ball—perhaps because Suzan did not live to see her twenty-second birthday.

She was born in Jamestown, New York—just like her famous cousin—in 1934. She began her career singing with Mel Baker's Orchestra, after moving with her family to North Hollywood in 1947. Inspired by cousin Lucille, and by having Universal Studios just around the corner from her house, she decided to strike out on her own and try to break into the movie business. She moved into a flophouse for struggling actresses, known as The House Of The Seven Garbos, high up in the Hollywood Hills. There she met fellow actress, Mary Castle, who arranged a meeting for Suzan with the big wigs at Universal-International. They set her up with a standard contract, and began casting her straightaway as the exotic love interest in a number of films.

Suzan had jet-black hair and olive complexion, so she was ideal for ethnically themed parts such as the Persian harem girl in *Aladdin and His Lamp*, and the Native American maiden in *War Arrow*. Captivated by her beauty, and her exotic (seeming) persona, the press dubbed her "Cinderella Girl of 1952". Hedda Hopper picked her as one of the stars to watch in 1953. Suzan's life was like something out of dream, and she had barely turned eighteen. In just three short years, however, her charmed ascent would slow, stop, reverse, and as the world looked on, burn up on reentry.

The trouble started when she was cast in the big-budget adventure film, *City Beneath the Sea*. Suzan, naïve and barely nineteen, fell head over heels in love with her quite married and much older costar, Anthony Quinn. Quinn, not renowned for his high moral standards where women were concerned, happily engaged in a yearlong romance with Suzan. Onlookers watched her prance and primp for him, taking just about every opportunity to keep his gaze, no matter what was going on around them. Every one of the onlookers knew it could only end in heartbreak for the beautiful starlet.

That same year, she suffered a series of injuries to her right leg that would eventually lead to a devastating diagnosis. While filming a dance number in *East of Sumatra*, she suffered the first injury, to her right knee. A few months later, she was involved in a car accident that re-injured that same knee. Later that year, she broke off her dead-end relationship with Quinn, but never truly got over him. She decided to retreat to her apartment with her many pets for solace, and while in the kitchen, she tripped on water that spilled from a dog dish. Her right leg was broken. Clearly, something was terribly wrong.

Suzan was taken to the hospital, where she received the news that she had developed tumors in her leg: cancer. The doctors said they would have to amputate the limb to save her life. By this time, she had been dating Richard Long (who would also die of cancer two decades later), and they were engaged. Their marriage had to be postponed, however, due to the impending operation.

The procedure appeared successful, and Suzan moved on with her life, marrying Long, and starting on her next film, *Chief Crazy Horse* (wow, typecast much?). By the end of the film, however, it was clear she was very ill. She had lost fifteen pounds, and looked exhausted. The cancer was not only back, it had progressed. There would be no more movies for Suzan. Undaunted, she immediately embarked on a grueling nightclub tour, and a series of television appearances, as if pretending her cancer wasn't there would make it go away. It didn't.

She collapsed while rehearsing a scene for an appearance on the television drama *Climax,* and was rushed to the hospital. The news was bad. The disease had spread to her lungs. Suzan had just weeks to live. She and Long retired to the comfort of the rented mansion that Universal had graciously offered to allow her to spend her final days in. It was there that she passed away, on August 5, 1955, two weeks past her twenty-first birthday. Her last word, whispered hoarsely as her devoted husband strained to hear, was rumored to have been "Tony."

Vivien Leigh

The fire raged higher and higher up the distressed building's fragile walls, as producer David O. Selznick heard his brother, Myron, come up behind him. He was busy of filming one of the most iconic scenes in movie history—the burning of Atlanta—for one of the most anticipated films of all time: *Gone with the Wind*. He had spent nearly two years searching for his heroine: the incorrigible, dazzling, and unforgettable Scarlett O'Hara. He had tested almost every actress in Hollywood in full view of a diligent public, wasting countless hours and funds in delayed production costs. Still, the part remained maddeningly difficult to fill. "Hey genius!" Myron said as he walked up to the set with two other people. "Meet your Scarlett O'Hara!" Selznick turned, and found himself staring into two of the deepest blue eyes he'd ever seen, set in a face so lovely it took his breath away. "Hello Mr. Selznick. I'm Vivien Leigh." Selznick recalled the encounter later, saying "I never recovered from that first look." Finally, his Scarlett O'Hara stood before him in the flesh, somehow far more beautiful and imposing than he'd ever imagined.

Vivien was born in 1913, in Bengal, India. Her father was an officer in the British-Indian Cavalry, and her mother was an aristocrat. This setting alone was such a rich and exotic beginning for an only child, but she was also spoiled and doted on by her parents. The path to being an actress began began with studying and performing at a convent boarding school in London, at the ripe old age of...five! There, she met and became fast friends with Maureen O'Hara, a fellow waif. Vivien spoke of her dreams of becoming a great actress someday often, and Maureen listened, adoring her passion and purpose.

*Olivier and Vivien as Romeo and Juliet*

After a dream childhood filled with tours of all Europe, and elegant garden parties, the dawn of adolescence brought with it a renewed love for the theater, so she found roles in small stage productions. In 1931, she wed barrister Herbert Leigh Holman, giving birth to a daughter the following year. The wedding was a grand affair, attended by all of London society. The marriage, however, was a disaster almost from the start. They were a poor match, and this could not have been made any clearer than it was in Herbert's disdain for the people involved in the stage and screen environments his new wife so adored. Herbie didn't care for the "theater people", as he called them, not seeming to notice that one of them was sharing his bed and his bath towels.

Vivien had, of course, known of Laurence Olivier long before they actually met. He was one of the most popular and gifted actors on the British stage, and had just begun to make his mark in movies. They became friends, and when they were cast together in the British film, *Fire Over England*, the heat transformed the friendship into a passionate affair that would become known throughout the world as the romance of the century. Their relationship would ultimately prove destructive for Vivien, who began to develop the first signs of mental illness shortly after her involvement with Olivier.

Vivien and Olivier kept working together in several stage productions. They were each striking in appearance, and audiences loved them together. It was during one of these performances that Vivien began to exhibit disturbing behavior. Out of the blue and without cause, she began screaming at Larry backstage one day. Just as suddenly, she fell silent...almost catatonic. She was able to pull herself together, and go on with the performance. The next day, she didn't remember the incident at all; a dark portent of things to come.

By the time she was cast as Scarlett O'Hara in *Gone with the Wind*, she was already emotionally fragile. Vivien was living in a foreign country, working seven long days a week on a major Hollywood production, while Olivier was banished to New York by the studio out of fear that their "illicit" relationship would be discovered by the prudish American press. Rumors flew of wild mood swings, temper tantrums, and the resulting expensive delays as scenes had to be reshot again and again. Leigh was burning mad at Selznick for firing George Cukor, and hiring Victor Fleming, whose vision of a tougher, angrier Scarlett matched his own. Ironically Vivien, being delicate of health and ladylike in temperament, was closer to Melanie Hamilton than Scarlett, whereas Olivia de Havilland, who played Melanie Hamilton, was a hardened Hollywood pro, and therefore closer in temperament to Scarlett than her own role.

Vivien became despondent, hysterical, and had a wee nervous breakdown before that four-hour film was in the can. She was in nearly every scene, wore colored contacts that turned her lovely blue eyes

"Scarlett O'Hara green", tight corsets, heavy costumes...often in sweltering heat (curtain dress, anyone?). One day, Olivia walked past her on the set and didn't recognize her: "She looked so diminished by overwork, her whole atmosphere had changed. She gave something to that film which I don't think she ever got back."

*Gone with the Wind* was a phenomenon. The premiere in Atlanta nearly turned into a riot. Three hundred thousand people lined seven miles of streets to watch the limousines ferry the stars from the airport, and a million people came to town to see the film. It quickly became the highest grossing movie of all time, winning ten Academy Awards, including an Oscar for best actress for this young foreign-born beauty in her very first American movie.

In 1940, both Vivien and Larry were free to marry, so they did. After being prevented from working together in several films, they were finally cast in *That Hamilton Woman*, which was a moderate success. During the war, Vivien entertained troops in North Africa, and developed a persistent cough there. Later, she was diagnosed with tuberculosis; the disease that lead to her early death. Her episodes of mental illness occurred more frequently, making it difficult for her to work regularly. In 1944, she miscarried after falling on stage, sinking further into the darkness. Her moods began to fall into a pattern. She would be very hyperactive, then violently angry, and have to be physically restrained. This would go on for days and/or weeks, and afterwards she would return to normal, and claim no memory of the incident.

During this time, she gave what is considered the best performance of her career—as Blanche Dubois; the tragic, faded southern belle struggling against insanity, in the Tennessee Williams classic, *A Streetcar Named Desire*. Director Elia Kazan said of her ability, "She would have crawled over ground glass if she thought it would help her performance." Vivien said of her role, "The year I spent as Blanche Dubois tipped me into madness." Some would say that ship had already sailed. She won a second Academy Award.

In 1953, she began a grueling, torturous location shoot in Ceylon(now Sri Lanka) for the film, *Elephant Walk*, for which she was ill-prepared. She quickly fell apart, becoming completely delusional on the set, and had to be flown back to England, to the care of her husband. It was around this time that David Niven famously remarked that Vivien was "quite, quite mad."

In the ensuing years, Vivien swung between periods of lucidity and mental delirium. When she was well, she appeared on the London stage in several productions, but those moments grew fewer and fewer. In 1960, her marriage to Olivier was over, and she turned to actor Jack Merivale for solace, apparently with Olivier's blessing. Olivier had become emotionally exhausted, and just couldn't do it anymore, but he remained extremely close to Vivien. For her part, Vivien confided to a friend that she would rather live a short life with Olivier, than a long one without him.

Though Vivien seemed to perk up in the early '60s, it was just a mirage. She earned her first Tony award for the play *Tovarich*, and turned in stellar performances in two films, *Ship of Fools* and *The Roman Spring of Mrs. Stone*. In May of '67, however, her old nemesis, tuberculosis, came calling. Suffering a serious relapse that year, doctors ordered strict bed rest at home (as she refused to be hospitalized), and she was to refrain from smoking, drinking and socializing. Vivien didn't listen. She never did.

On July 7, she watched tennis in bed with Merivale, before he left to perform in a play that evening. She had seen several of her old friends in the preceding days, and was still chain smoking. When Merivale phoned from the theater to check on her, she seemed tired, but content. When he returned at 11:00 PM, he looked in on her, and she was sleeping peacefully; her cat, Poo Jones, resting at her side. He went into the kitchen to prepare a late night snack. When he checked on Vivien again, he found her lying on the floor halfway to the bathroom—still warm—but very dead. Her lungs had filled with fluid, and she had suffocated. She was fifty-three.

Blanche Dubois, in *A Streetcar Named Desire*, said "Oh look! We have created enchantment!" She could have been referring to Vivien Leigh. She was everything a movie star should be: lovely beyond belief, and possessed of a rare quality which transcended the screen, and touched audiences in a way rarely experienced today. She was as talented and unique as she was flawed and doomed. It seems she was just too special for this world.

# Clara Bow

Before the mega shoulder-padded vixens of the '40s, and the bodacious, full-figured '50s goddesses, was the flapper of the '20s. She was a thoroughly modern girl, with a slim figure, shockingly short (bobbed) hair, and a flat chest. She wore her dresses far shorter than was "decent", and she was not shy about her vices, which included smoking, drinking and cavorting with multiple members of the opposite sex. F. Scott Fitzgerald, who helped create the phenomenon, referred to her as "lovely, expensive and about 19." Of course, Hollywood recognized the appeal of this type of woman immediately, and set about finding her very embodiment, which they did, in Clara Bow.

Clara was bright, sweet and perky, which is hard to account for given her miserable, impoverished upbringing in the slums of Brooklyn. She was born in 1905, a time when the infant mortality rate for the poor was eighty percent. Her grandfather went completely insane after regularly beating her grandmother for decades. Her mother, Sarah, had epilepsy and severe bipolar disorder, or schizophrenia, depending on who you choose to believe. It fell to Clara to take care of her mother during the many violent, psychotic episodes. Sarah was a pathetic shadow of a woman, who had once been a lovely thing with delicate features and big dreams; things that stark poverty and mental illness had erased. One day in 1920, Sarah attacked Clara with a knife. Frightened and fed up, Clara locked her in a charity hospital, where she died three years later. This ugly childhood would haunt poor Clara for the rest of her life, and no amount of fame or accolades would be able to wash away the trauma that was buried deep inside her psyche.

Bow struggled, working in small pictures at first, but won critical acclaim and recognition in the film, *Down to the Sea in Ships*. Critics praised the newcomer with copious accolades. *Variety wrote*, "Clara lingers in the eye long after the picture has gone." Louella Parsons said, "She hasn't any secrets from the world. She trusts everyone. She is almost too good to be true. I only wish some reformer who believes the screen contaminates all who associate with it could see this child. Still, on second thought, it might not be safe. Clara uses a dangerous pair of eyes." Shortly after this, she performed the typical flapper dance, mostly nude, atop a table, in a film called *Enemies of Women*. She was not credited in the role, which probably saved her career.

She was soon playing small, but memorable, roles in *Maytime* and *Black Oxen*. It was in *Black Oxen* where the first face-off occurred between flapper types: Bow's "horrid flapper" versus Colleen Moore's more demure, dreamy take on the archetype. The dueling flappers duked it out in a series of films, until Moore withdrew from the contest, and moved on to other roles, proclaiming "No more flappers. They have served their purpose." Now the field was Bow's for the taking, and she did not hesitate. She starred in one exploitation picture after another over the next several years; charlestoning, vamping and gleefully swinging her way toward immortality as the screen's purest example of uninhibited, unbounded sexuality.

She pulled a fair amount of offscreen mischief as well, gaining a reputation as a "party girl" and a drunk. She got engaged, and disengaged, as often as the day becomes night, and apparently really liked the boys in the USC football team. Bow said of her reputation, "All this time I was 'running wild' I guess, in the sense of trying to have a good time. Maybe this was a good thing because a lot of that excitement, that joy of life, got onto the screen."

Around this time, a rather scandalous book was published called *"IT" and other Stories*. The author was Elinor Glyn, who is best described as the first modern romance novelist, and the book had a huge impact on popular culture in the '20s. In the book, Glyn wrote, "To have 'it' the fortunate possessor must have that strange magnetism that attracts both sexes. In the animal world 'it' demonstrates in tigers and cats—both animals being fascinating and mysterious and quite unbiddable." When the movie based on the novel, It, was released with Clara in the starring role, a catch phrase was born. Forever after, she would be known as the "It" Girl. She was definately "It".

Clara was at the top of her game; the most popular star in Hollywood. Yet the Hollywood elite thought she was crude and unpolished, and shunned her. Her thick Brooklyn accent, accompanied by salacious stories of her less than tactful behavior, caused the "in" crowd to pretend she wasn't there. Clara, ever the non-conformist, refused to bend to the hypocritical standards demanded of her by these people, whom she called "frightful snobs", and who no doubt did worse in secret, safe inside their gated homes.

Unfortunately, by the late '20s, Clara had begun to show signs of exhaustion, as well as some mental instability. She signed with Paramount Pictures, and made several memorable films including Wings, the first film to win an Oscar for Best Picture. By October of 1929, however, she was burned out and exhausted. Despite this, she transitioned to talkies effortlessly, in such films as *The Wild Party* (how appropriate), and *Dangerous Curves*. In 1931, a vicious series of articles ran in *The Coast Reporter* that attacked Clara as a wanton woman, who had

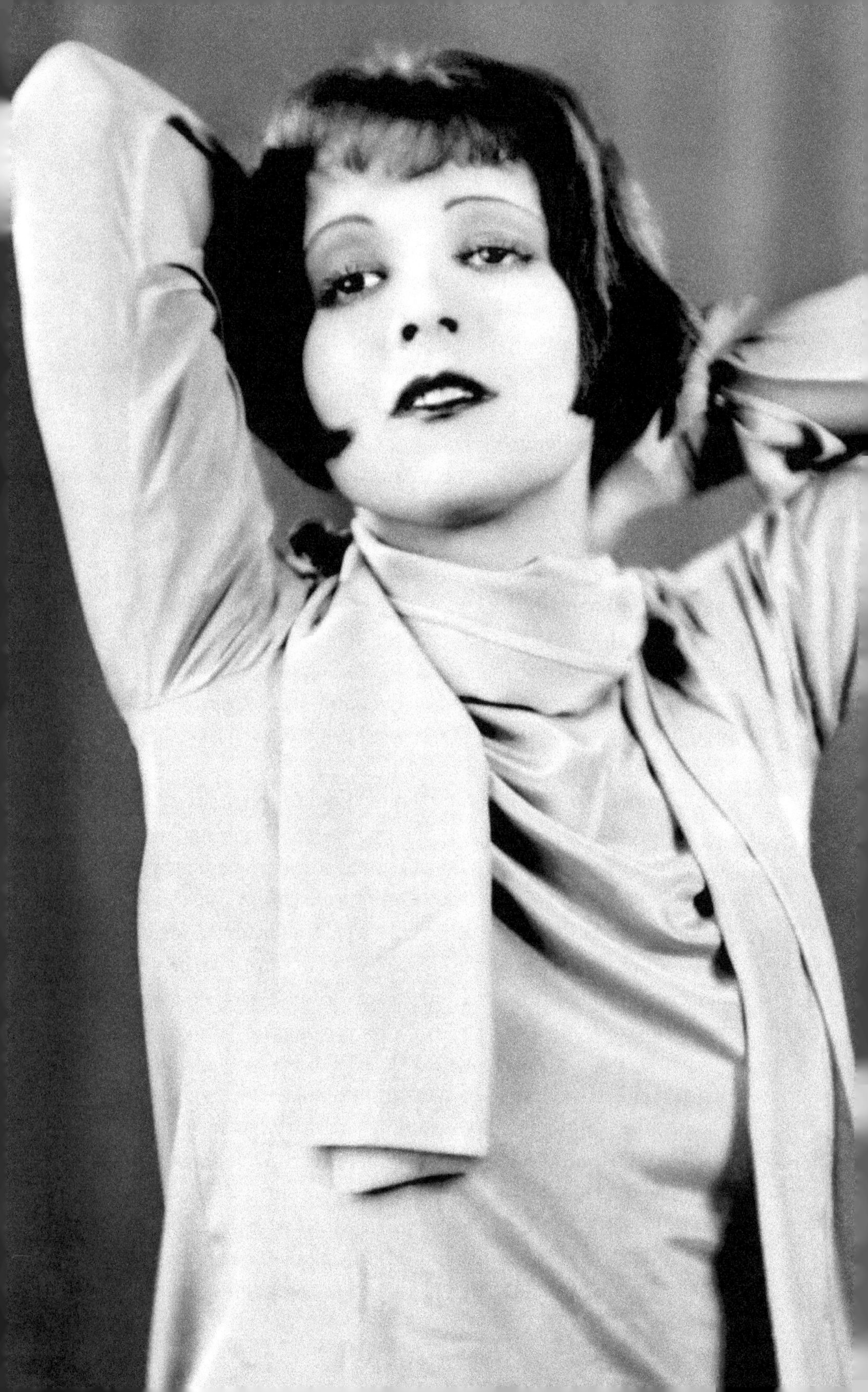

sex in public, and engaged in threesomes with prostitutes and animals at the same time. This was devastating stuff at a time when the fascist, self-appointed censorship monster, the Hays office, had begun to dig its claws into freedom of expression in movies. The days of glorifying wickedness and shamelessness were fast coming to an end. The public went along with it, and just like that, Clara Bow, the first flapper, America's "It" girl, was finished.

Clara didn't seem to care. She married genuine cowboy and western star, Rex Bell, settling with him on his sprawling Nevada ranch. She had two sons, who would grow up to beg her to return to making movies, and in 1932, she gave in and made her last two films: *Call Her Savage* and *Hoop-la*. She began a slow decline into madness afterward. Alone on her Nevada ranch, she attempted suicide while her husband was away running for the US House of Representatives. Becoming a paranoid recluse, she refused to leave the house, and was terrified of letting her husband and children out of her sight. Moving into a "rest hospital" in 1949, supposedly to treat her chronic insomnia, she was given several old school shock treatments. Who knew electrocution was a cure for insomnia? Doctors said she displayed delusional, bizarre behavior, and they diagnosed her as schizophrenic. Bow told them they were full of shit, and left. She lived the rest of her days in a modest home in Culver City, away from her family, and died alone there, save for a professional nurse, in 1965. She was sixty.

Clara was just about everybody's naughty, secret desire: men and women alike. Yet there was a doe-eyed innocence about her that makes details of her life seem all the more poignant. There would be many imitators, but never again would there be another "It" Girl.

# The Forgotten & The Forsaken

*The Grand Theater, Chicago, shortly before being razed.*

Once you make it in Hollywood, you have it made. Until you don't, which is what happened to so many stars throughout the years. Some were unable to adapt to the technological changes that the passing of time always brought. Others allowed their personal demons to consume them, pulling them down the rabbit hole to cold oblivion, and still others were simply discarded like last year's fashion, coldly consigned to the back of the closet in favor of the latest style. After all, it's called show business for a reason.

# Yvette Vickers

Few people who saw the 1958 horror B movie classic, *Attack of the 50 Foot Woman*, could forget leggy blonde actress, Yvette Vickers. She was the perfect foil for the star, Allison Hayes, as the femme fatale who openly slept with the protagonist's alcoholic husband. Adolescent males everywhere drool-ed all over themselves.

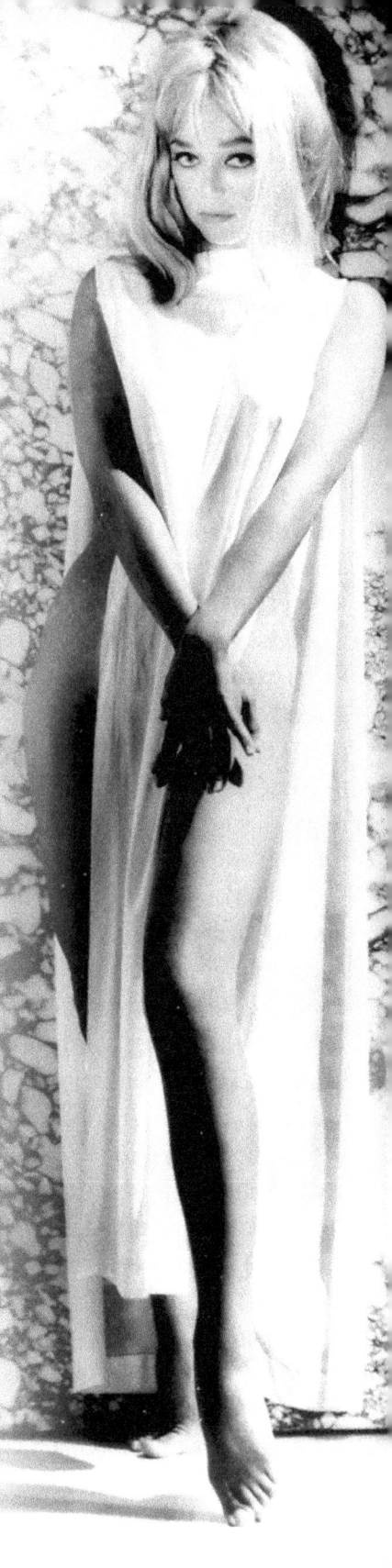

She was an intelligent girl, who studied at UCLA majoring in journalism, and took an acting class on a whim. She loved the attention she received while pretending to be someone else, and decided to change her major. Soon, she said, "The heck with it!" and dropped out of college altogether to pursue an acting career. Getting her start in commercials, she was the White Rain Girl for White Rain shampoo. She eventually snared the role that would make her a cult movie icon, that of Honey Parker in *Attack of the 50 Foot Woman*. Despite its low budget and high camp, the movie was a big hit with the drive-in theater crowd, and continued to entertain subsequent generations late at night on cable television. *Attack of the Giant Leeches*, her only other co-starring role, was as well-received. Yvette quickly capitalized on this exposure, posing nude in 1959 for the controversial new men's magazine, *Playboy*, a move which may have contributed to her stunning career decline. This was, after all, the age of *Ozzie And Harriet*, when America still frowned upon such displays of relaxed morality. Interestingly, her centerfold shoot was photographed by Russ Meyer, who would go on to reign as king of the B horror film directors during the '70s.

After her *Playboy* stint, she dropped out of sight. The movie offers dried up, and her ascent to mainstream film success became a descent into the world of fringe, has-been celebrity status, where living off of thirty-year-old royalties was the norm, and film convention appearances were a rare ego boost to look forward to. She began to drink...a lot. Paranoia set in, and she gradually barricaded herself inside her modest Benedict Canyon home, behind mountains of garbage. Yvette had become that sad creature upon whom reality TV has recently shone an unforgiving spotlight: the hoarder. Her public appearances grew fewer, and her self-imposed isolation, fueled by alcohol and mental illness, grew deeper. She gained a tremendous amount of weight, and behaved erratically. She felt that people were stalking her. Cars innocently parked on her street seemed to be stalkers. Even those closest to seemed to be after her, and her defenses thickened. It's a shame that Yvette did not have anyone in her life who cared enough to get her the help she needed. Perhaps if they had, she could have escaped her grisly fate.

On the morning of April 27, 2010, having not seen Yvette in over a year, her neighbor, Susan Savage, thought something was wrong. She saw cobwebs in Yvette's mailbox, her yard was overgrown and neglected, and through the windows she saw lights lit, and garbage piled almost to the ceiling. The house itself was practically falling down, with a fruit picker out back set up to support a section of its frame. She broke in through the front door, and found what was left of Yvette in an upstairs bedroom next to a running electric heater. She had been dead for a very long time, and her state of decay was staggering. Her body was essentially mummified, her skin black and brown and leather-like. Colonies of insects had taken up residence and were enjoying life inside her body. In all likelihood, she was partially melted into the floor, as this is common for bodies in such an advanced state of decomposition. There was no trace of the golden-haired beauty who once graced the pages of *Playboy* and pranced across the screen stealing husbands, leaving outraged wives and broken hearts in her wake. Indeed, it was hard to recognize a human form in those remains at all.

The coroner, who shockingly was not shocked, claimed several of these types of deaths crossed his path every year, and estimated that Yvette died about a year earlier from a heart attack brought on by coronary disease. A year earlier! How does someone, once so well-known, lie dead in her home for a year without anyone noticing? Savage was clearly distraught. "We've all been crying about this. No one should be left alone like that," she said.

No. No one should be left alone like that; especially not someone who had been a beautiful star. Once, Yvette was a dream of pure desire, a wicked fantasy creature fueling millions of adolescent fantasies, yet when she died, a year went by before anyone even noticed. It's hard to imagine a harder, longer, lonelier fall than that.

Linda Darnell

Few remember beautiful Linda Darnell today, but one look at her alabaster face, framed by that improbably thick black hair, was enough to bring GIs to their knees during WWII. She was a screen goddess, who came down off her pedestal to dance the night away with lovesick soldiers, at the famous celebrity-filled club for enlisted men, The Hollywood Canteen. She had the face of an angel, and the sensitive nature of a child. From childhood on, she was tormented by a recurring nightmare of being trapped in a blazing inferno, and she was terrified of fire her entire life. That she could project such a graceful and alluring presence onscreen while experiencing such inner turmoil is surprising. Moreover, in a world of candles, pilot lights and campfires, on the set and off of it, the courage necessary to venture out from home would be great. Yet sadly, Linda was not quite tough enough for Hollywood.

Born Monetta Eloyse Darnell in Dallas, Texas, in 1923, to a postal clerk and his wife, she was the fourth child in a household that already was home to three, and would sprout two more after her. Her mother Pearl's own dreams of stardom had been buried under the hard facts of a rough life, so she sought to live them vicariously through her daughter. She had Monetta modeling at eleven, as well as entering and winning local talent contests, both while representing Monetta as being several years older than she actually was. In 1937, she won the "Gateway to Hollywood" contest, and with it a contract at RKO Radio Pictures. RKO signed her, yet felt she was too young to use just yet, so they kept her on the bench. Pearl grew more impatient with each passing day.

In 1938, Twentieth Century Fox came to town, on an open call for talent, and Pearl got Monetta a tryout. The scouts loved her, and wanted to get her signed, but they had to pry her out of her existing contract with RKO. They sprang her from that dead-end contact, signed her, and set her on a schedule of classes and preparation to ready her for her first role. Pearl's pursuit of her daughter's fame was relentless, even when at the expense of her other children. It was all about to pay off in a big way.

Monetta became Linda, and at last made her debut in the 1939 film, *Hotel for Women*. At only fifteen years of age, this role made her the youngest leading lady in Hollywood history at the time, but no one knew it. The studio had been told she was seventeen by Pearl (true to form), and they in turn led everyone else to believe she was nineteen. Her real age was revealed a few years later. Her real age aside, she cer-

*Darnell in Blackbeard*

tainly was a vision, with that flowing raven hair, dark sultry eyes, and a radiant innocence that seemed to permeate, even transcend, her sexual allure.

Over the next decade, she went from costar in such films as *Star Dust* and *The Daytime Wife*, to starring roles in big-budget Technicolor projects like *Forever Amber*, *Blood and Sand*, and *The Mark of Zorro*. She was one of the highest paid stars of the time, and her beauty was exceptional, rivaling even the most beautiful actresses around. Life called her the most physically perfect girl in Hollywood. *Look* magazine voted her one of the most beautiful women in films, alongside Gene Tierney, Ingrid Bergman and Hedy Lamarr. Linda herself described this period as being "like a fairytale. I stepped into a fabulous land where overnight I was a movie star." She lived an enviable life, costarred with legends such as Tyrone Power, Lillian Gish and Henry Fonda, and lived in a lavish mansion in Bel Air. She married a much older man, cameraman J. Peverell Marley, who taught her how to drink and be difficult. Unfortunately, her meteoric rise would only be surpassed by her even more rapid descent into obscurity, and in just ten years, Linda found herself a living example of that saddest of Hollywood clichés—the has-been.

Her decline began when her mentor, Darryl Zanuck, lost interest in her. He promoted others over her, leaving her inferior parts. By 1952, her contract with Fox expired, and Linda could not find good paying roles. She had started drinking while still on top, as a way of coping with the emptiness of her private life. As her career sank, her drinking increased, as did her weight. "Suppose you were earning $4,000 or $5,000 a week for years. Suddenly you were fired, and no one will hire you at any figure remotely comparable to your previous salary." she said later. She was washed up at twenty-nine. By thirty-nine, she had lost her mansion, a second marriage, and her father. Her once-tireless mother wasted away in an expensive nursing home. To pay the bills, she worked small stage productions and nightclubs. Exhausted, and probably ill with liver disease, she sank deeper into the bottle.

In April of 1965, after two grueling months on the road with a theater group, Linda went to Glenview, Illinois, to see her friend Jeanne Curtis and breathe. She was weak and frail, but still had her famous spunk. On the night of April 8, Linda, Jeanne and Jeanne's teen daughter, Patty, had just watched one of Linda's earliest films, *Star Dust*, on television. Linda was in great spirits, laughing and giggling throughout the movie, and even getting a bit nostalgic. *Star Dust*, ironically, borrowed heavily from Linda's early experiences in Hollywood, showcasing her when she was as yet untouched by the ugly disillusionment that would later be etched onto her beautiful face.

After the movie, two full ashtrays were dumped into the kitchen sink, and all three women went upstairs to go to bed. Sometime before dawn, a fire broke out downstairs, trapping the women upstairs. Panicked, Jeanne shoved her daughter out of one of the bedroom windows, and squeezed herself out. She reached out her hand to help Linda out of the window, but there was no hand to meet hers. She screamed for Linda, but heard nothing, so she went back into the smoke-filled bedroom to try and find her. The smoke and heat beat her back before she was able to take a step, and she retreated back through the window and onto the roof.

A comedy of errors that would have made Buster Keaton proud, and a Keystone audience roar with laughter, if it weren't so horrible, then ensued. The fire had completely engulfed the home by the time the fire department arrived on the scene. Jeanne was hanging onto the windowsill, and screaming that there was still a lady inside, but the firemen thought she said baby, and when they entered the house, they were crawling on their hands and knees, looking for an infant. There was general pandemonium in the streets, as people rushed around in all directions, trying to figure out what to do. Meanwhile, a neighbor saw a chilling scene right out of movie. He had gone over to help, and noticed the figure of a woman in a living room window, standing right in the middle of the inferno, silhouetted against the flames. As he smashed the window with a snow shovel, oxygen swept in, and the resulting fireball engulfed the figure.

They found Linda on the living room floor, barely conscious. She had been too terrified to climb out of the second story window and jump from the roof. Instead, she walked down the stairs and straight into the inferno, covered in just a few blankets. She was trying to make it to the front door, but became disoriented, then collapsed in the living room. They rushed her to the hospital, cussing and screaming all the way. She had no intention of dying, and was even quoted as saying, "Who says I'm going to die! I'm not going to die!" But she was burned over 90% of her body, and succumbed to her injuries the following afternoon. She was forty-one. Rumors sprung up that Linda, in drunken carelessness, dropped a lit cigarette in a chair, causing the fire. There is no proof of this, and the true cause of the fire was never determined.

Linda was a sweet, gentle girl who found out that the fairytale life of being movie star has a dark side—slide just a little to the left of perfection, and suddenly you're performing way off Broadway, and wondering how it all went so wrong. Don't forget that she did accomplish her mother's dream, and faced down her lifelong nightmare, nearly surviving it. She was down, but not broken, all the way to the end.

# D.W. Griffith

*The Knickerbocker Hotel in Hollywood, circa 1938.*

On any given night, during the '40s, the lone shadow of a man could be seen hunched over the gleaming, paneled bar of the glamorous Knickerbocker Hotel, quietly sipping his drink, or bending the ear of a nearby stranger, until indifference led to familiar isolation once again. This once great and powerful Hollywood player was living out his life in obscurity, alone and forgotten. The strangers he spoke with would probably not believe that they were talking to the person who held the title: "The Man Who Invented Hollywood". They would be stunned to learn that this man was one of the greatest pioneers, and most influential directors, in the history of film. He also carried the dubious title of "The Greatest Racist in Show Business", a stigma that would follow him to his early grave. His name was D.W. Griffith, and his importance to modern film cannot be overstated.

He was born in Kentucky, on a plantation, ten years after the end of the civil war. His family was impoverished, having lost everything during the war, and struggled to eke out a living on the farm. With the death of his father, a former colonel in the Confederate army, the family moved off the farm and into the city of Louisville, where their situation went from bad to worse.

Eventually, Griffith began acting as an extra in several small theater productions as a way to escape his desperate poverty. This led to an early interest in show business, and he moved to New York to further his career. Before long, he landed small roles in the new medium of movies. He was soon writing them as well, a talent that ultimately led to the Biograph Film Company hiring him to direct. Over the next few years, he directed more than four hundred short films for the company, but he had also become aware of a new way of telling stories in film: the feature. He had spent his early years at Biograph inventing, or perfecting, many of the techniques that later became intrinsic parts of the language of film, such as intercutting scenes to raise tension, and could see the potential of the longer format.

However, Biograph did not share his vision, and he made only one feature for them before taking his actors and crew to California, to form a third of what would later be known as The Triangle Film Corporation. His first project was a film version of a post-Civil War novel, *The Clansman* by Thomas Dixon. The novel had been made into a play, and was very popular in the South, as it fed beliefs that blacks were not only inferior, but also dangerously clever, and capable of great evil; a contradiction that did not seem to trouble the droves who bought the book and saw the play. An audience was already primed for the story when Griffith set out to make a film that would change the industry forever: *Birth of a Nation*.

Promising to be a sweeping epic on an unseen scale, it boasted thousands of extras, elaborate special effects, hundreds of stunts, and buckets of drama: in short, something for everyone...as long as you weren't black. It was the civil war with a sledgehammer skew favoring the confederate point of view, portraying freed slaves as wild animals out to steal the virtue of white women and the rightful place of the white race. The Klan were "white knights", saving women and society from the ruin inflicted by the evil scourge set by the Union Army upon their gentle, beautiful, white world.

*Birth of a Nation* was a filmmaking masterpiece, using innovative techniques such as color tinting, moving camera, and the long panning shot. It was one of the first films to have multiple interwoven plots and storylines. It was over three hours long, three times as long as a one reel, and it was a stunning success, smashing all box office records and holding its position as the most profitable film of all time for the twenty-five years. It took *Gone with the Wind* to steal its spot. D.W. Griffith had just directed the first blockbuster.

There was just one problem. It was a huge, gaudy, bald-faced, shameless lie. The old South was shown in all its magnolia-scented, mimosa-soaked magnificence, with contented slaves enjoying their lives of servitude to gentle masters who patted them on the head, and made sure they were well cared for. The ungrateful wretches repaid this kindness by taking their new found freedom and marauding through the streets like dogs, leering at white women, and staging corrupt elections in order to seize power, for the sole purpose of getting drunk inside the voting chamber and passing interracial marriage laws. Enter the boys in white, perched on hooded steeds, ready to save the day! The bullshit was piled so high in this movie that it would take decades to clean up.

*Klan members abuse a victim in Birth of a Nation.*

    The Ku Klux Klan was, prior to the release of this movie, an organization that had essentially died out, after being declared a terrorist group in 1870. After the film was released, however, a renewed Klan was born again, fired up over both the movie, and the public's positive fervor over the role the Klan played in it. They saw *Birth of a Nation* as the most effective recruiting tool they had ever had! Millions of new members swelled their ranks, bringing this once-dead organization to back to life with a vengeance, to wreak havoc and terror again for decades to come.

*Soldiers retreat from advancing Klan horsemen in Birth of a Nation.*

African-Americans had a different view of the film, and riots broke out in Boston and Philadelphia when it premiered. The NAACP tried to ban it in several cities, staging organized protests wherever it opened, to no avail. White America was still firmly in charge, and white America loved this movie.

Griffith, not one to rest on his laurels, launched right into his next big epic. It would be at an even more colossal scale than *Birth of a Nation*. Titled *Intolerance,* the concept was so complex, so ambitious, that many in the industry doubted both Griffith's judgment and the project's commercial viability. The doubters did not trouble the great and powerful Griffith, who proceeded to commit to film the most spectacular example of movie making in the field's short history. *Intolerance* portrayed the historical oppression of the poor and downtrodden at the hands of brutal kings and modern capitalists, through the eyes of four protagonists in four distinct time periods. These periods were ancient Babylon, 15th century France, ancient Judea during the time of Christ, and present-day America. Astonishingly, these stories were not told in chronological order, but in parallel, each building to a dramatic climax alongside the rest, and slowly building tension leading to that crescendo of emotional resonance. It was like four great films in one! Production costs were through the roof. The magnificent ancient Babylonian scene alone, with its massive columns and three thousand extras, was the most elaborate and expensive scene yet filmed, remaining so for two decades.

The impact of Intolerance was not nearly as dramatic as that of *Birth of a Nation*. The pacifist theme was popular in pre-WWI America, but quickly became dated as the country geared up for war with Germany, a year later. In addition to the huge production costs associated with the film, Griffith spent millions more on an elaborate road show that accompanied the movie wherever it premiered, plunging the project even further into debt. The film began to hemorrhage money, and eventually failed at the box office. Still, *Intolerance* is considered by many to be the greatest silent film ever made. In 2007, The American Film Institute ranked it 49th of the 100 best movies of all time. David Kehr, film critic for *The Chicago Reader,* wrote "One of the great breakthroughs. The *Ulysses* of the cinema—and a powerful, moving experience in its own right." Jon Fortgang wrote in his review for *Film4*, "...It's still the most spectacular undertaking in film ever seen"

*The set of Intolerance.*

In 1920, Griffith co-founded United Artists, along with Charlie Chaplin, Mary Pickford and Douglas Fairbanks, and continued to direct films. However, by the mid-'20s, tastes had changed, and Hollywood grew increasingly tired of Griffith's outdated approach, and his lavish, expensive productions. It would not be long before he found himself shut out of the business he had almost singlehandedly created. The once-great director retired to the elegant Knickerbocker Hotel, and spent his days drinking and jauntily walking down Hollywood Blvd., swinging his cane and reliving his glory days with anyone who would stand still long enough to hear his stories. Much of the time, he could be found hunched over the Knickerbocker bar, soaking his sorrows in booze, until he staggered back to his hotel room, all alone. He was a silly old drunk, ridiculous with his hat and cane, a gaudy relic from a past that no one cared to remember anymore.

On the afternoon of July 23, 1948, Griffith was walking under the great chandelier in the lobby of the Knickerbocker, when he suddenly fell to the floor, unconscious. He had suffered a massive cerebral hemorrhage, and was dead before he reached the hospital. He was seventy-three.

A memorial service was held in his honor at the Hollywood Masonic Temple, but few in the industry bothered to come. Still, there were some left who remembered the genius he once was. Charles Chaplin referred to Griffith as "The teacher of us all!" Orson Wells put it best when he said, "I have never really hated Hollywood except for its treatment of D.W. Griffith. No town, no industry, no profession, no art form owes so much to a single man." He was laid to rest in a modest grave, in his home state of Kentucky, a long way from Hollywood, the town he helped to invent.

# Charlie Chaplin

The image of the Little Tramp, with his baggy pants and swinging cane, sauntering jauntily down a dirt road, is as endearing today as when Chaplin first committed the character to film, nearly a century ago. Chaplin overcame a soul-crushing childhood that would even stretch the imagination of a Dickens reader. He would become the most famous actor in history. He could take his pain and with it, paint a masterpiece in celluloid, unparalleled in its influence on modern films. How did America and Hollywood honor this? At the first hint of scandal, Hollywood and the US shut him out. He was forced to flee in fear and disgrace, back to his native England, never to return.

In 1889, Charlie was born into poverty—and South London—to parents who eked out a living performing in the gritty music halls popular with the working class then. Hannah, his mother, was promiscuous, and birthed an illegitimate son, Sydney John, four years prior to Charlie. Chaplin said many times that he was not entirely sure the man presented to him as his father, whose name he bore, was his biological sire.

Chaplin's parents split up when he was only two. Hannah tried to make ends meet by sewing and scrubbing floors, with no help from her husband. Her career as a music hall singer faded with her voice. One night she was booed offstage by the crowd, as five-year-old Charlie watched from the wings. Desperate, the theater manager shoved the little boy onstage, and told him to sing. Terrified, he stammered out a song that delighted the crowd, and was pelted with pennies. The debut of Charlie Chaplin was a success!

Life at home went from bad to worse for young Charlie. The crushing poverty, malnutrition, and syphilis took their toll on his mother, and she went insane. Charlie and Sydney were sent to The Central London District School For Paupers when Charlie was just seven. This "school" was actually a brutal sweatshop for waifs, where the brothers toiled for two years. Hannah took the boys back briefly, but gave them up again to another wretched workhouse. Meanwhile, Charles Chaplin Senior drank himself to death by cirrhosis of the liver in 1900, at thirty-eight. Hannah—in and out of institutions for five years—went permanently insane in 1905, and stayed locked up for the rest of her life. Thirteen-year-old Charlie fended for himself, until Sydney returned from the Navy.

*A young Charlie Chaplin, photographed by a carnival worker.*

Through all of it, Charlie never forgot the night he set foot on a smoky stage, and conjured song for a rowdy, inebriated crowd that pelted him with pennies. He returned to the music halls, and soon was cast in a London stage production of *Sherlock Holmes*. His professional acting career was launched.

He later won national recognition for the comedy routines he performed with the Fred Karno players. When the Karno troupe played New York in 1910, Charlie was a featured player. It wasn't long until he was noticed by the New York Motion Picture Company, the producers of popular Keystone slapstick comedies, and he was invited to audition. Charlie was soon working for Keystone in the fledgling industry that had only just begun to change the world.

*Motion Picture Magazine, July 1915*

*Chaplin in The Little Tramp*

Initially, Charlie was put off by the gag-centric physical comedy comprising most of the Keystone shorts at the time. He felt they lacked subtlety and innocence, gaining laughs at the expense of beauty and deeper, subtler emotions. His second film for Keystone debuted the character that would forever shadow his life—*The Little Tramp*. Charlie described, years later, how he designed the character's costume: "I wanted everything to be a contradiction; the pants baggy, the coat tight, the hat small, the shoes large." He went on to say that he did not understand the character, until he put on the costume, and then became the tramp.

The tramp started out as just another sight gag routine, common in the one-reel shorts of the time. Chaplin had bigger plans for him, and when finally he won directorial control over his work, he began borrowing situations from his childhood experiences to incorporate into his films. The tramp became a tragically pitiable tragic figure—the ultimate outsider—an innocent whose life experiences are both funny and poignant. Sublime themes of alienation, poverty and oppression wound their way through his work. Audiences found themselves laughing one minute, and dabbing tears the next. This type of comedy had never been done to the degree that it was accomplished in the Little Tramp features. Pre-depression, pre-WWI America was in love. Chaplin was a huge star, and the Tramp the most recognized character in film history.

Throughout his late teens and early twenties, Chaplin could do no wrong, at least not on film. He crafted his greatest masterpieces during this period, including *The Kid*, *The Gold Rush*, and *A Woman of Paris*.

His personal life was another thing entirely. People were talking about his fondness for young girls. In 1918, he married sixteen-year-old Mildred Harris, thinking she was pregnant, but she wasn't. He was angry when he found out, as didn't love her, and felt she stifled his creativity. When the child was born in July of 1919, it was horribly deformed, surviving only three days. Charlie and Mildred separated eighteen months of wedlock, and she went after his fortune with a vengeance. Charlie was inspired by the relationship's end and the death of his child, and poured those emotions into his first masterpiece, *The Kid;* a heartbreaking story of a homeless tramp who struggles to care for a small, abandoned child.

His next disastrous relationship was with *The Gold Rush* costar, Lita Grey. Impregnated by the then thirty-five-year-old Chaplin at the age of sixteen, Lita seemed to be forcing him yet again into a loveless marriage

*Chaplin and Jackie Coogan in The Kid*

to avoid scandal. He kept his new son and new wife hidden for months, as the birth was too obviously soon after the marriage to not seem related. Once the press had done the math, it was obvious to the public that he had been sleeping with an underage girl out of wedlock, a crime punishable by serious jail time in California. Is it any wonder, with such an inauspicious beginning, that the marriage was never more than a complete failure? Chaplin avoided Lita as much as possible, spending long hours at the studio. Giving birth to a second Chaplin son in 1927, Lita left him as was filming *The Circus*, taking the children with her. She filed a divorce complaint through her lawyers that read like a dirty novel, accusing Chaplin of onerous sexual perversions and mental cruelty. Copies were leaked to the press, and the tabloids threw a Chaplin skewering party that would have made Rupert Murdoch blush. Conservative groups across the country called for the boycott of all Chaplin films on moral grounds. Chaplin handed Lita six hundred thousand dollars to make her go away—the largest divorce settlement of its kind at the time. Ultimately, The Tramp proved too popular to be snuffed out even by this controversy, and Chaplin's career continued without much negative effect.

By the time talkies rolled around, Chaplin was still clinging to the artistry and beauty of the medium he had fully commanded for fifteen years: silent movies. He was skeptical of sound, and had an intuitive sense that giving The Tramp a voice would ruin the image he had so carefully

*Charlie Chaplin in Modern Times.*

crafted for over a decade. He would go on to produce two of his greatest masterpieces in the next decade, silent anachronisms amid a cacophony of talkies. The first was *City Lights*, in 1930, which told the heart-wrenching story of a down-and-out drifter who helped a blind girl regain her sight, falling in love in the process. The film won critical praise, and is considered by some to be Chaplin's finest work. The final scene in *City Lights*, in which the tramp realizes the girl can see his face for the first time, has been called the greatest moment on film. Six years went by before he released another movie.

Charlie was distressed and aimless in the world of sound pictures. He knew his Little Tramp would never make the transition, and he did not know how to proceed without him. In 1932, he met twenty-one-year-old actress Paulette Goddard, and entered into the first positive relationship of his life. The depression was raging, and Chaplin, who had always had a distrust of unbridled capitalism and industrialization, began to formulate the concept for his next film. The movie was *Modern Times* and shockingly, Charlie chose to make it silent six years after silent films had virtually disappeared. It was the story of a hapless industrial worker, a mere cog in the wheel of a giant evil machine that destroyed humanity in the name of progress. It was to be the last time the Little Tramp appeared before the cameras. Paulette costarred as The Gamine, an innocent child/woman who joins the Tramp in his "us against the world" adventure. The movie received mixed reviews but has since been recognized as the masterpiece that it is. Goddard and Chaplin divorced soon after *Modern Times* was released. Rumor has it that the couple were never legally married to begin with.

Chaplin's next film proved to be his most controversial. It was called *The Great Dictator*, and it was a thinly disguised parody of Hitler and his Third Reich, which was raging atrocities over Europe at this time, but was still at peace with the United States. This was Chaplin's first real talking picture, and though the Tramp does not make an official appearance, he is clearly present in the character of the Jewish barber. The film was well-received, and proved to be Chaplin's most commercially successful film. A persistent rumor circulated that Hitler himself viewed a copy of the film before it was released, but his opinion was not recorded.

Chaplin's life then entered a turbulent period, due in part to his leftist politics, and his inability to stay away from unstable young (some would say too young) women. Such as twenty-year-old actress Joan Berry, with whom he had a brief affair before realizing she was crazy. He broke off the relationship, but Berry stalked him, breaking into his home, and threatening suicide while alternately aiming a gun to her own, then his head. She eventually took him to court, claiming he was the father of her illegitimate daughter. Chaplin was indicted on charges that he violated the Mann Act, for transporting Berry across state lines for sexual reasons. He could have received twenty-three years in prison. Scandal again rained down on Charlie, and he went into hiding. He was acquitted of the charges, and blood tests proved he was not the father of Berry's child, but the judge refused to admit the test as evidence, and he was ordered to support the little girl anyway. Wow. Berry lost custody of her daughter when she lost her mind completely, and was found wandering around the streets carrying baby booties and mumbling that they were magic.

Demonstrating astonishingly poor judgment yet again, Charlie married eighteen-year-old Oona O'Neill only weeks after he was acquitted. He was fifty-four at the time, and the public once again rolled their eyes. This marriage turned out to be the most stable and positive of all. Oona O'Neill was wise beyond her years, and provided Charlie with a loving home and six children. She stood by him during his most difficult period and went into exile with him, along with their brood, giving up her home and family for him.

Chaplin's real problems started with *Monsieur Verdoux*, an unabashed, openly left-leaning, political commentary about a serial killer (representing society) who wreaked mass murder on the most innocent victims (representing the innocence lost during war). The public was not amused. Chaplin was booed at the premiere, and the film flopped. United Artists had to pull and re-release it, but it still failed miserably. The public had grown tired of their Little Tramp, once such an enduring figure, as he turned into this ranting political chastiser they did not recognize. Charlie did not help things by associating with communist organizations, and cozying up to the Soviet Union at a time when The House Un-American Activities Committee was on a rampage, tearing through people's lives in their relentless pursuit of communist infiltrators. There were public protests, and calls for him to be deported. He was called before the committee, but not asked to testify. He denied he was a communist. but he would not compromise his principals, which always held that unbridled capitalism was evil. Shock. Charlie would have been a proud member of the 99%!

Charlie shook off his first failure, and started working on *Limelight*. This film would be a family affair, including four of his children and his half brother. It was set in London, so Charlie decided to hold the premiere there. He, Oona, and their six children set sail on the Queen

Elizabeth for England on September 18, 1952. Charlie Chaplin did not see the United States again for twenty years. While out at sea, Charlie's re-entry permit was revoked by the Attorney General of the United States. It was made clear in a telegram to the director that to re-enter the country, he would have to submit his answers to several pointed questions regarding his political and moral views. Chaplin declined, choosing instead to live out his days in Switzerland, with Oona and their kids.

His final two decades were spent tinkering with various film projects, including *A King of New York*, a scathing parody on The House Un-American Activities Committee (Go Charlie!). His last complete film was *A Countess from Hong Kong*. It was a tender, romantic love story released in a 1960s world full of rebellion and free love, and was a commercial and critical failure. Gradually, over the course of this decade, America woke up from its commie/witch-hunting hysteria with a bad hangover, and a disquieting sense of regret. The film industry began to rediscover Chaplin's older work, and with this came a renewed sense of the tremendous genius they had let slip away.

Finally, in 1972, the Academy Of Motion Picture Arts And Sciences bestowed on Chaplin an honorary award for his "incalculable effect in making motion pictures the art form of the century". Charlie was invited to America to accept the award. He had not set foot on American soil in twenty years. In one of the most emotional scenes in the Academy Awards Show's forty-three year history, a frail Charlie shuffled slowly onto the stage of the Dorothy Chandler pavilion, to a crescendo of thunderous applause, and shouts of "Bravo! Bravo!" The star-studded crowd rose to its feet, and stayed there for a full five minutes, the longest standing ovation in the show's history. Chaplin was in tears as he gazed in awe at the tribute. "Such sweet people," he mumbled. Jack Lemmon suddenly appeared, handing him the hat and cane of the Little Tramp. The effect was complete.

It took twenty years for Hollywood, and the country, to come to its senses and honor the man that had first dared to take comedy to a deeper place, and in doing so, change our view of ourselves. Chaplin once said, "More than machinery, we need humanity. More than cleverness, we need kindness. Without these qualities, life would be violent and all would be lost." In the end, a world that had shown nothing but disdain for this gifted genius for twenty five years finally came around, and showered him with the love and recognition he so richly deserved.

Charlie Chaplin died on Christmas Day in 1977, his beloved Oona at his side. He was eighty-seven. In a macabre turn of events, his coffin was stolen a year later, and held for ransom. The Swiss police eventually tracked it down and arrested the perpetrators, who had demanded £400,000 for the safe return of the body. It sounded like something right out of a Keystone comedy. Somehow, I think Charlie would have been amused.

*Charlie Chaplin's Coffin after it was recovered.*

CHARLES CHAPLIN
1889 + 1977

# Dorothy Dandridge

Entertainment agent Earl Mills finally broke into the once-grand apartment, having knocked for several minutes without response. As he stepped in, he called for "Angel Face"—the young woman he'd come for—but there was only silence. On reaching the bathroom, he saw why. Lying on the bathroom floor in only a blue scarf, was the body of lovely actress, Dorothy Dandridge. She had been dead for several hours, and was showing signs of rigor mortis. Earl was overcome with sadness, and when the world found out, it was right there with him.

Dorothy was born in 1922, in Cleveland, Ohio. Her mother, Ruby, left her father while still pregnant with Dorothy. Soon, another woman came into their lives, Geneva Williams, and she soon became the disciplinarian of the household, brutalizing and intimidating Dorothy and her sister, Vivian. The nature of lesbian relationship between her mother and Geneva would not be clear to Dorothy until decades later, however. Ruby Dandridge was an aspiring actress herself, and saw potential in promoting her darling daughters as a singing/dancing duo known as "The Wonder Children". They joined the National Baptist Convention, and toured for three years, performing at various churches throughout the South. Their act was part of a collection of similar acts and venues known as "The Chitlin Circuit", where black entertainers could safely perform in the heavily racially-segregated south. The girls performed day-in and day-out, harassed by Geneva's relentless "tutoring" to improve their performances. They rarely attended school, or enjoyed normal childhood activities.

Early in the Great Depression, Ruby moved the family to Hollywood hoping to get the girls into films. Etta Jones was added to the duo, and the act was renamed "The Dandridge Sisters". They toured the United States, even performing at the famous Cotton Club in Harlem. The Cotton Club was the first successful nightclub to showcase only black entertainers, who performed in front of an all-white audience. Soon, she was playing uncredited bit parts in films such as *Teacher's Beau*, and *A Day at the Races*. Her first credited film role was in *Four Shall Die*. In 1941, she was paired with Harold Nicholas, of the famed Nicholas Brothers tap-dancing duo, for the film *Sun Valley Serenade*, where they tap-danced together. This scene was cut from the film when it played in the South. She fell in love with Nicholas, and they married in 1942. The marriage was a disaster from the start. Dorothy was desperate to get away from her controlling mother and her mother's cruel girlfriend, Geneva, and marriage to Nicholas provided that opportunity. Unfortunately, Nicholas was fond of drinking, womanizing, and staying away from home. She got pregnant in 1943, and was home alone when she went into labor. The birth was difficult. The baby girl, named Harolyn, was deprived of oxygen, and suffered from severe mental retardation as a result. Dorothy was devastated, but tried to care for the girl at home, with little or no help from her husband. At one point, she even sent her to live with Geneva and her mother, as she could no longer control her frequent outbursts. Finally, in desperation, she placed Lynn in an expensive institution under the care of a private nurse. By this time, Dorothy'd had enough of her absentee husband's philandering ways and filed for divorce.

Distracted by her personal life, she had neglected her career, and found it extremely difficult to get any film work. The parts she did get were meager, small roles not worthy of her beauty, experience or talent. In 1951, she met Earl Mills, a Hollywood agent, who realized the rare and talented gem that she was, and set out to revive her career. Mills booked her at some of the most prestigious nightclubs in the country, including the Mocambo, and the famed Waldorf Astoria's Empire Room.

It was during her tours of Miami and Las Vegas that Dandridge encountered some of the most blatant racism to which she had ever been subjected. How extreme was it that it could exceed anything she encountered on the Chitlin Circuit? It was beyond extreme. While performing in Miami, she was not able to stay within the city limits due to her race. At one of the venues, she was handed a plastic cup when she asked where the restroom was. While headlining at a major casino in Las Vegas, she was treated like an infectious disease instead of the star she was. She was not allowed to mingle with the guests, eat in the public dining room, or use any of the hotel's public facilities, including the front door. Despite it all, she and Earl decided to take a little dip in the pool, in direct defiance of the rules. Before she even had a chance to slip into the water, the manager came running out. He created a huge scene, screaming and yelling that she was not allowed to do that. Humiliated and angry, Dorothy dipped her foot in the pool in righteous indignation. Later that evening, she walked past the area again, and saw that the pool had been drained, and was being scrubbed clean top to bottom, by black employees.

The nightclub tour did the trick, however, and Dorothy was soon cast in MGM's *Bright Road*, opposite up and coming actor Harry Belafonte. Her face began to appear on major national magazines, and her future looked bright. She was then cast in the role that would catapult her to major stardom, the title role in Otto Preminger's *Carmen Jones*. The film was a modern take on the French opera, *Carmen*, and was a perfect vehicle for Dorothy. The role was challenging, containing numerous musical numbers and dance sequences. Despite being a professional singer, Dorothy's voice was dubbed, as were all her costars'. The film was a huge success, both critically and at the box office, and Dorothy was suddenly a hot commodity. Dorothy Dandridge became only the third African-American actress to be nominated for an Academy Award, and the first to be nominated for Best Actress. The ice cream blonde from Philadelphia, Grace Kelly, took home the statue for her performance in *The Country Girl*, much to Dorothy's abject and bitter disappointment.

It was on the set of *Carmen Jones* that she became romantically involved with the married director, Otto Preminger. He gave her career advice, telling her to turn down roles that were beneath her new stature as a leading lady, and she complied. Thus began the slow descent of her career, after only a brief period of upward momentum. She again scored a major success with the film *Island in the Sun* in 1956, and critical acclaim for her performance in *Porgy and Bess*. The latter film was highly unpopular with blacks, as they felt it perpetuated negative racial stereotypes. It seems the white audience didn't care much for it either, and the film was a flop.

Dorothy realized Preminger would never leave his wife for her. Bitter and lonely, she married Jack Denison—a white restauranteur who brutalized, beat and bankrupted her over the next several years. He also forced her to cut ties with her close friends, including Earl Mills, the man who had helped make her a star. She discovered that she owed one hundred and thirty thousand dollars in back taxes, and had also lost a great deal of money in an oil investment scam. Financially and professionally ruined, she was forced to give up her glamorous home, and put her mentally challenged daughter in a state-funded institution. Wracked with guilt, alone, despondent and rejected by Hollywood, she drank and took prescriptions. In 1963, she declared bankruptcy.

By 1964, some of her old spirit returned. She rekindled her friendship with Earl Mills, and went to a spa in Mexico to try and get healthy again. While touring with her nightclub act, she twisted her ankle, and couldn't work. On the afternoon of September 8, 1965, Mills came to drive her to have a cast put on her ankle. He discovered his "Angel Face" lying nude on the bathroom floor, dead for hours.

The coroner's report listed the cause of death as a rare embolism that occurred when fragments of bone marrow left her fractured ankle and lodged in her lungs and brain. Interestingly, the toxicology report painted a different story. Accidental overdose of the anti-depressant Tofranil was listed as the cause of death. Whatever the cause, beautiful Dorothy Dandridge was gone at forty-two. When Mills searched the apartment, he found a note that read, "In case of my death, Don't remove anything I have on—scarf, gown, or underwear. Cremate me right away. If I have anything—money, furniture, get it to my mother Ruby Dandridge. She will know what to do." Right to the end, it seems Dorothy was unable to completely break the cord.

She said, "If I were white, I'd rule the world." She was probably right.

*Police carry Dorothy's body away from the El Palacio Apartments in Los Angeles.*

Tom Neal

A bad relationship will ruin your life and few knew this better than Tom Neal. Born in 1914 in Evanston, Illinois, he became the quintessential jock at Northwestern University, serving on the Boxing team where he scored a record forty-two wins. Moving on to Harvard, he earned a law degree. He was smart, good-looking, ambitious, and came from a supportive, wealthy family. He could have had a very successful law practice, but Tom had stars in his eyes, or rather, the lights of a Broadway stage.

Tom worked in a handful of plays before making the leap to Hollywood in the late '30s. Once MGM had him on contract, they shuffled him around from one mediocre B movie to the next. In 1941, he starred with Frances Gifford in the fifteen-series serial, *Jungle Girl*, and in 1945, his career peaked with the film noir classic, *Detour*, co-starring Ann Savage. Tom garnered the best reviews of his career for his portrayal of doomed piano player, Al Roberts, and hoped the praise would bring a serious career boost, but it didn't happen. Fascinated by the Black Dahlia murder, Tom claimed to have inside information on it from a private detective hired by the family. He tried to secure funding for a film project where he would costar as a hard-boiled detective who falls for the murder victim as he works her case, but failed. Too bad. It would have made for a great movie. Oh wait, wasn't that called *Laura*?

By the 1950s, still relegated to B movies, he grew increasingly frustrated. In 1951, he met the woman who would help him destroy his career for good, film noir blonde bombshell, Barbara Payton. He fell hard for Payton, and they had a passionate affair. The only problem was, she was already engaged to a major star, Franchot Tone. When Tone found out, he went straight to Barbara's home and confronted the lovers (rumor has it he caught them in the act).

*Tom Neal and Ann Savage in Detour.*

Confronting Tom was probably not Tone's best idea, considering Neal's extensive background as a champion amateur boxer with forty-one knockouts to his credit. Tone and Neal got into a brawl right there, in front of Barbara's Beverly Hills house. Tom punched Tone so hard he was literally knocked back twelve feet. Tom pounced on Tone, pummeling his head and face with his fists repeatedly. When Barbara tried to pull him off, he slugged her in the eye. Needless to say, Tone came away the loser physically, with a broken nose, shattered cheekbone and bruised brain. He was in a coma for eighteen hours, and required plastic surgery to fix his once-perfect features. It would be Neal and Payton who would be the losers in the long run, however.

The tabloids lapped this up, siding, of course, with the legitimate fiancé, vilifying Tom as a home wrecker. Public outcry and sympathy for Tone drove Payton away from Tom, and back to her fiancé, and they married two weeks later. The marriage lasted exactly fifty-three days, most of which she spent cheating on Tone with Neal. The impact to Tone's career was not serious, but Payton and Neal were officially blackballed from Hollywood. Unable to make a living in films, they capitalized on their notoriety in a series of plays, such as *The Postman Always Rings Twice*. Their marriage lasted four years, until Barbara chose booze over Tom, and they divorced in 1957.

*Barbara Payton and Tom Neal*

Neal had to resort to gardening to pay the bills. He married a second time, to Patricia Fenton, and fathered a son. Unfortunately, she died tragically from cancer the following year. By all accounts, Tom considered her the love of his life. His landscaping venture failed, and he filed for bankruptcy. In 1961, he married a third time, to a twenty-five-year-old receptionist named Gail Bennett. Wedded bliss, however, was not to be.

On the evening of April 1, 1965, Tom entered a restaurant in the mountain village of Idyllwild, near Palm Springs, and told the owner that he killed his wife in her sleep. Police were called to the home, where they found Gail's body lying on the couch, dead from a .45 caliber gunshot wound behind her right ear. Neal was indicted for murder, and a public defender appointed to defend him. The public defender never showed up to meet his client. He later claimed this was a strategy to force Tom's former Hollywood friends to come to his aid. Seems it worked. Mickey Rooney, Blake Edwards and even his archenemy, Franchot Tone, all helped raise money for his defense.

It was revealed at the trial that the couple had been separated for months, and Gail was planning to file divorce papers. A mysterious mens wallet and suit were discovered in Gail's bedroom closet that the defense argued did not belong to Neal. It turned out they belonged to a salesman who was renting the spare bedroom. What they were doing in Gail's closet was never fully explained. Hmm. Tom took the stand and said the whole thing had been in self-defense, and started when Gail pulled the gun on him first. He claims he went for the weapon and a struggle ensued. Somehow she ended up getting shot in the back of the head, while lying on the couch, in a position as if she were taking a nap. That sounds logical.

Follow-up testimony revealed that Gail had been terrified that Tom would kill her once he found out she was filing for divorce, and complained that he had threatened her with a .45 caliber gun in November. Barbara Payton came to the trial, and she and Neal would often wave at each other like middle-schoolers in study hall.

After the trial ended, they never saw each other again. Unbelievably, the jury bought the defense version, and Tom was convicted only of involuntary manslaughter. His lawyer was elated, and went around saying that, with time served, and in consideration of his clean record, his client could be out by Christmas. The sentencing judge disagreed. "The fact that the jury brought only a verdict of involuntary manslaughter is as big a break as Mr. Neal deserves." he said. Tom Neal, B movie star, with over 180 films to his credit, was sentenced to ten to fifteen in state prison.

On December 7, 1971, having served six years of his sentence, he was released on parole. He moved back to the town that had turned its back on him, and died there of heart failure exactly eight months later, on August 7, 1972. He was fifty-eight. In a creepy twist, Tom Neal Jr., a dead ringer for his father, starred in the 1992 remake of *Detour*.

Tom Neal seemed to have everything going for him but it was just an illusion. As he so prophetically pointed out, through the words of a screenwriter, in his only major film, *Detour*, "Fate or some mysterious force can put the finger on you or me for no reason at all." Indeed it can, but there is usually also a clear and unblinking reason, and in Tom's case, it seems to have been an issue with violence along with an inability to admit to his own mistakes. Oh yeah, and getting involved with the wrong woman.

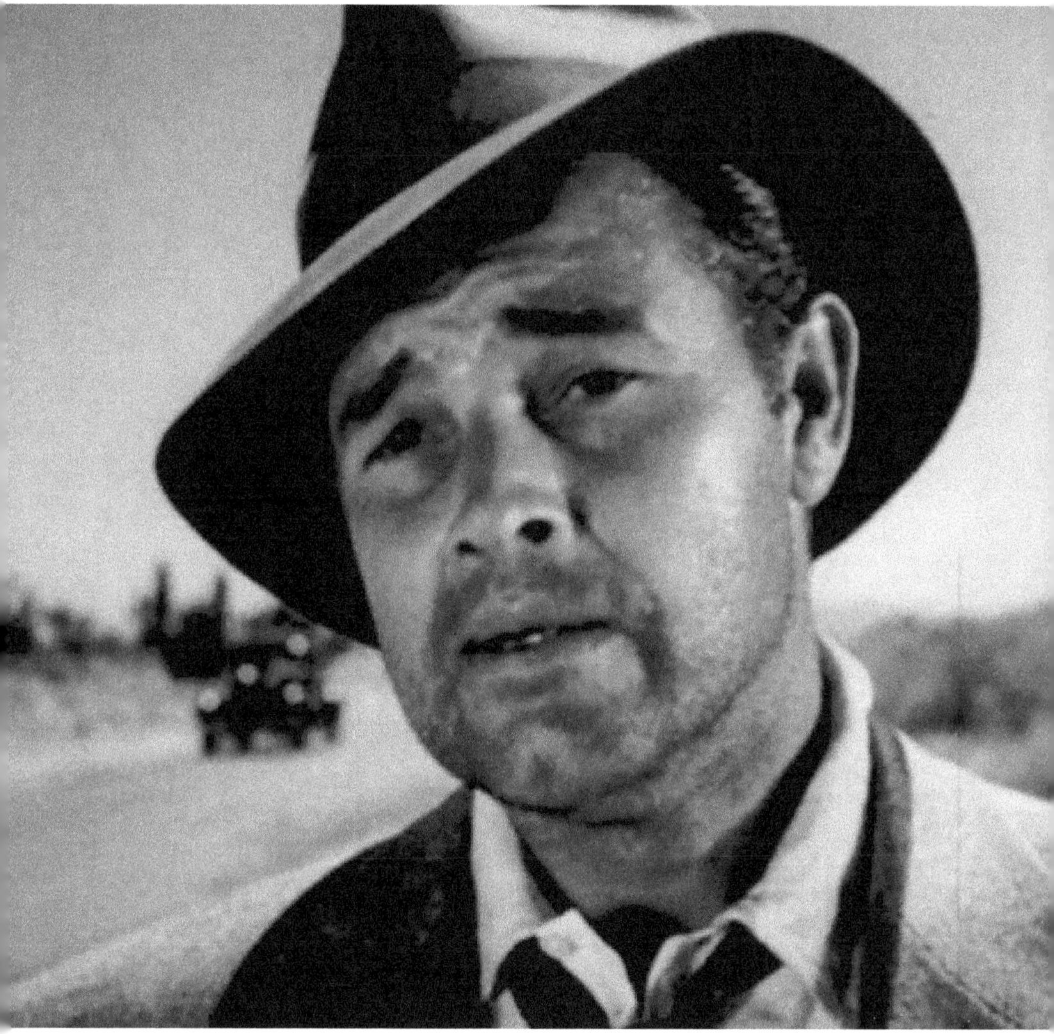

# Montgomery Clift

Kevin McCarthy, known to those who love cult horror classics as the shrill Dr. Miles J. Bennell from the movie, *Invasion of the Body Snatchers*, was navigating his way down a treacherous stretch of winding road in Coldwater Canyon, when he noticed the headlights behind him had disappeared. McCarthy became concerned, because he had been guiding an inebriated Montgomery Clift, who was unused to driving, down the hill as a precaution. He whipped his car around, and went to look for Monty. A horrific sight met him around the second bend. Monty had lost control of his '56 Chevy, careened down a hill, and plowed into a tree. The car was totaled, and Monty lay unconscious, his face nearly torn off, in the crumpled driver's seat. It's been said that this was the start of beautiful, gifted Montgomery Clift's slide into total self-destruction. In truth, he had been trying to kill himself for years, in what famously was labeled "the longest suicide in Hollywood".

He was born in Omaha, Nebraska, to an eclectic, middle class family. His father, William Brooks Clift, was vice president of a bank, and his mother, Sunny, believed she had aristocratic blood, though she was adopted and couldn't actually prove this. She raised her children with this belief, however, and groomed them for their eventual acceptance into high society (think Amanda in *The Glass Menagerie*). They were privately tutored, and schooled in French, German, and Italian. Monty's childhood years were spent lounging in extravagant Victorian mansions, and traveling with his mother and siblings across Europe, while his father toiled away at work, trying to keep up with Sunny's spending sprees.

Monty was bitten by the acting bug at fifteen, and spent the next ten years performing on stage, honing his craft. He earned a reputation for being an extremely competent actor during this time, making his transition to films effortless. During these years, he entered a bizarre relationship with former Broadway star (and infamous bisexual) Libby Holman, who would exert a tremendous amount of influence over his early career choices. This relationship was supposedly Monty's last heterosexual liaison.

*Montgomery Clift in 1948*

He had the Midas touch upon arriving in Hollywood, skipping the hard knocks and toil that beset most actors fresh from the Broadway stage. Stunning good looks may have been a factor. He walked right into a costarring role in the big-budget western, *Red River*, with Hollywood legend John Wayne and directed by Howard Hawks. A riveting debut performance, he held his own alongside Wayne. Rumors flew that Clift was in an offscreen romance with costar, John Ireland, which caused palpable onscreen tension. True or not, the rumor added new depths to the gun exchange scene.

Clift was next cast as a fortune-hunting, would-be gigolo, opposite Olivia de Havilland's rich and lonely plain Jane in *The Heiress*. Only Monty's third film role, he nonetheless felt he knew better than veteran Olivia, or the experienced director, Billy Wyler. Becoming a perfectionist, he insisted that he knew what the movie really needed. This bred animosity on the set, alienating him from cast, crew, and Wyler, who considered him an impudent, disrespectful upstart who hadn't paid the dues to justify his hotshot demeanor. Clift hated the film, and hated his performance in it, leaving the premiere early in disgust. Still, *The Heiress* was a huge at the box office, and it seemed Monty could do no wrong. A legion of rabid female fans swelled, waiting breathlessly for his next movie, and bombarded de Havilland with hate mail for scorning their darling boy in the final scene of *The Heiress*. He seemed poised for greatness, and indeed, his best work was ahead of him.

After Heiress, at the behest of mentor Holman, he turned down a plum role as a down-and-out screenwriter opposite Gloria Swanson's faded silent movie goddess in *Sunset Boulevard*. The part was written with Clift in mind, but he chose instead to play opposite Elizabeth Taylor in *A Place in the Sun,* the film adaptation of the Theodore Dreiser novel, *An American Tragedy*. Elizabeth and Monty would develop a lifelong friendship, and the sight of the two of them together was almost too much for people to take. Taylor was barely nineteen, nearing the full bloom of her incredible physical perfection, and Monty was male beauty personified. To say they lit up the screen with sexual excitement would be a profound understatement. For her part, Elizabeth fell in love with Monty, though she knew he was homosexual. Monty loved her as well, as deeply as he was capable of loving a person in a non-sexual way. They would remain close for the rest of Monty's life.

*Elizabeth Taylor and Montgomery Clift in A Place in the Sun (George Stevens, 1951)*

*A Place in the Sun* was a huge success. Brando was so moved by Monty's gut-wrenching performance in the final scene that he voted for Clift to win the Academy Award for Best Actor instead of his own work in *A Streetcar Named Desire*. Of course, Monty voted for Brando, and both lost to Bogart in *African Queen*. *A Place in the Sun* became a Hollywood classic. Charlie Chaplin said that it was "the greatest movie made about America." Taylor and Clift are considered by many to have been the most beautiful onscreen couple to this day.

Monty turned down the lead in *High Noon*, instead making his first commercial failure, *I Confess*. Director Alfred Hitchcock, usually the master of suspense, seemed more interested in trashing Catholicism and its most cherished values than making a good picture. *I Confess* was neither his, nor Monty's, finest moment, and it bombed.

Monty's next movie, the war epic *From Here to Eternity*, was the apex of his success. *Eternity* was a gritty war drama, devoid of the glory and glamour most war films of that era conveyed, focusing instead on themes of alienation and heartbreak. Monty threw himself completely into the tragic Private Prewitt, an army bugler, who is relentlessly harassed and tormented by a sadistic commanding officer, and beaten nearly to death. Weak and wounded, he dutifully crawled out of bed to join his regiment in defending Pearl Harbor against the Japanese attack, but is shot to death by a friendly sentry. Monty learned to play the bugle, even though the bugling was dubbed, to be sure his lips moved correctly. That scene where he played "Taps" as tears streamed down his face, is held up as one of his finest screen moments. He received a second Academy Award nomination for Best Actor, but again lost to a lesser actor in a less impressive performance—in this case, William Holden in *Stalag 17*.

It became clear that while the Hollywood gods appreciated Clift's talents an actor, his refusal to play ball with their subtle rules regarding social behavior and etiquette displeased them. He did not attend their parties, or stroke their massive egos on command, and they steadily shut him out. He, Brando and Dean represented a new and daring kind of performer, a kind that had a disquieting effect on the status quo. Of his outsider reputation, Clift said, "Look, I'm not odd. I'm just trying to be an actor, not a movie star, an actor." It's hard to believe that just ten years later, Montgomery Clift would be unemployable.

By this time, Monty was already drinking heavily and taking prescription drugs. On the advice of Holman, he turned down *East of Eden*, which Dean happily snapped up, to star in an underwhelming, overly ambitious period piece about the Civil War called *Raintree County*. He was again paired with the gorgeous Elizabeth Taylor, a little plumper, but no less stunning.

On the evening of May 12, 1956, Monty was invited to a dinner party at Taylor's home. Her marriage to Michael Wilding was crumbling, and the couple considered him a neutral third party. Monty initially did not want to go, as he usually shunned these types of gatherings, but Elizabeth would not take no for an answer. The party was dull, and the tension between Wilding and Taylor was palpable. Monty had taken a handful of Seconal before he ever got to the gathering, and drank throughout the evening. When Kevin McCarthy got up to leave, Monty also decided to call it a night, and the two started down the dangerous hill together. McCarthy admitted that he was speeding to avoid any possible attempt by Monty to ram the back of his car as a practical joke. Monty must have desperately tried to keep up, but he failed to negotiate one of the hairpin turns, and his car went off the road, slamming into a tree. When McCarthy saw what had happened, he drove back up the hill to alert Taylor, who then ran screaming down the hillside to where the wreckage was. She climbed in through the back window, into the front seat, and cradled Monty's bloody pulp of a head in her designer silk-draped lap. He began choking, and she reached into his mouth and pulled out two of his teeth, thus clearing his airway. He had a broken nose, a fractured jaw and extreme trauma to the soft tissue of his face and upper lip, which was torn away so badly that his upper jaw line was visible through the gaping hole.

Months of grueling surgeries followed. The producers of *Raintree County* were in complete meltdown mode. If Clift didn't recover enough to return to the set, the entire film would have to be shelved. Amazingly, Monty did return to finish the picture two months later, but he was not the same. The accident caused scarring on the right side of his face, creating a hardness to his once milky, perfect visage, and a slight deformity of his lip. He had become self-conscious and halting in his mannerisms, and seemed uncomfortable in his own skin. It is jarring to watch when pre- and post-accident scenes occur consecutively in the film.

*Clift's mangled Chevy*

Despite the mediocre script and negative publicity, the film did surprisingly well at the box office. Never underestimate the morbid curiosity of the public, who flocked to theaters to see the mid-film changes in Clift's appearance and demeanor. *Raintree* turned a nice profit.

Monty became increasingly dependent on narcotics, to ease the chronic pain he suffered after the accident. While he had always been a pharmacist's best friend, he became seriously dependent after 1956, spiraling down into a haze of addiction and mental instability. In addition to his physical problems, he suffered from profound insecurities, and an overwhelming sense of guilt over his homosexuality, which was still considered a deviant mental illness back then. He crumbled and aged at an astonishing rate, due in part to an undiagnosed hypothyroid condition, as wells as physical and mental stresses.

Only Liz Taylor stood between Clift and complete Hollywood oblivion in the later years. He had become virtually uninsurable, and thus, unhireable. It was at Taylor's insistence that Clift was cast opposite her in the film adaptation of Tennessee Williams' play about latent homosexuality and overbearing mothers, *Suddenly Last Summer*. Was Williams channeling Clift's own childhood? The decision was a mistake. Unable to shoot long scenes in a single take, as a movie adapted from a play often requires, Monty's scenes had to be broken up so he could rest between them. His frail health and chronic alcoholism caused endless delays and extreme frustration for Joseph Mankiewicz, the director, who wanted to fire him after the first month. This roused the mother hen protective instincts of both Taylor and Katharine Hepburn, who both voraciously defended Monty against any attempts at dismissal. Hepburn was said to have spit in Mankiewicz's face over what was construed as his mistreatment of the actor. The film was a flop.

In 1961, Clift was cast opposite Marilyn Monroe and Clark Gable in what would be the final film for both legends, *The Misfits*. Playwright Arthur Miller, then husband to Monroe, had written the script to showcase the actress's fragile, shattered personality, and to highlight her vulnerability—something audiences had sensed for years, but which had never been fully exploited.

Unfortunately, the entire production seemed doomed from the start. The shooting location was extremely difficult, set in the searing one hundred and ten degree heat of the Nevada desert. All relevant parties involved—director John Huston, Monroe, Gable, and Clift—were in their declining years, and barely able to function. Monroe quipped that Monty was the only person she ever met who was in worse shape than she was. Huston spent all his free time gambling and getting drunk, often showing up on the set after having been on an all night bender, then falling asleep in his director's chair. He lost so much money at the craps table that the studio was forced to cover some of his losses. Gable was not a young man, and the endless hours spent in the heat, often waiting for Monroe to stumble through numerous takes, or possibly not showing up at all, began to take a toll on both his patience and health. He remarked that "That girl is going to be the death of me!" and indeed he would die, just two weeks after filming wrapped. Monroe was so far gone by this time that she was barely functional. She would often keep the entire crew waiting for hours before she stumbled onto the set, ill-prepared and looking like hell. Sometimes she wouldn't show up at all. Huston sent her to a hospital for two weeks just to dry out enough to be able to get through the picture. At one point, in an apparent dry run for the real thing, she overdosed on barbiturates, nearly killing herself. Her marriage to Miller disintegrated in a very public way, and Miller turned to drinking. It was as if there was a contest between these dysfunctional (real) misfits as to who would self-destruct first.

Amazingly, Monty proved to be the least troublesome member of the entire three-ring circus. He was professional, punctual and polite throughout the filming. There is a poignant scene where his character, Perce, places a call to his mother in a dusty, desert phone booth, almost begging for her approval. It is profound, moving, and uncomfortably similar to Clift's relationship with his own mother. Monty nailed it in one take.

The movie was a box office bomb, partly due to being a little ahead of its time. The metaphorical nature of the plot, juxtaposed against the stark realism of the scenes, confused the average moviegoer. In hindsight, it has since only grown in stature, and today, it is viewed as a testament to Huston's genius—a man who was apparently a better director when he was hungover then most others were when stone-cold sober. It showcases some of the finest performances of the stars' careers, and reveals, in all their delicate vulnerability, the flickering final moments of two of Hollywood's greatest icons. It is achingly beautiful in its purity, and has withstood the test of time.

Monty's downward spiral continued, despite his standout performance in *The Misfits*. Unable to remember his lines, or get to the set on a regular basis, Universal sued him for breach of contract over the film *Freud: The Secret Passion*. His twelve-minute performance, as a mentally challenged man who had been tortured by the Nazis in *Judgment at Nuremberg*, had to be ad-libbed because he could not remember his lines. Still, he was nominated for an Academy Award for Best Supporting Actor. After *Nuremberg*, Hollywood had had enough of Montgomery Clift. He spent the next three years begging for an acting job, any acting job, to no avail. In 1967, he reemerged in a nondescript film titled *The Defector*, which was his final appearance onscreen. Taylor had badgered the producers of her film, *Reflections in a Golden Eye*, to give Monty a chance, and while they reluctantly agreed, it was not to be.

On the evening of July 22, 1966, Clift had spent the day lounging in the bedroom of his New York apartment. His live-in personal secretary, Lorenzo James, invited him early in the evening to watch *The Misfits* on television with him. "Absolutely not!" Monty replied. He was found dead early the next morning, face up in his bed, glasses on, and stiff with rigor mortis. He had suffered a massive coronary, brought on by decades of self-abuse, some time during the previous night. He was forty-five. In three years, he had rarely had work. Hemingway once said, "All things truly wicked start from innocence." Montgomery Clift, beautiful golden boy with a fragile soul, would never overcome the wicked power of his own debilitating self-doubt.

# Live Fast Die Young

The public has always had a macabre fascination with those among us who seem overly blessed, yet remain pitifully unhappy and restless. After all, if someone who is stunningly beautiful and talented is still miserable, this makes the unhappiness of everyone else's lives seem much more tolerable. There is a certain smug gratification when the rarified and glamorous crash and burn in full view of those who placed them on their pedestal in the first place.

James Dean

*Dean's last known photo*

A man is slumped over a microphone, sitting at a table meant for twenty, in an empty hall that once held a huge crowd. The huge, oblong banquet table dwarfs his slight frame. Two observers silently stand in the doorway at the rear of the hall, listening to his incoherent slobberings. Suddenly, his words become crystal clear, and he shouts loudly, as if giving a rousing speech to an attentive crowd, "What has Texas given to me? Not a god damn thing!" The clarity reverts to mumbling, then to sobs as the man stammers, "Pretty Leslie. Pretty Leslie! Wonderful, beautiful girl bride! Rich...rich Mrs. Benedict. She's beautiful, lovely... the woman a man wants! The woman a man's gotta have too!" The two observers turn and leave. James Dean, as Jett Rink, had just given the performance of his career. He would not live to give another.

It has been almost six decades since Dean was killed in an accident on a lonely stretch of California highway, far from the glitz of Hollywood. His legend continues to overshadow his short legacy. What is it about this troubled young man that continues to fascinate subsequent generations, even those whose parents weren't even born when his life screeched to its abrupt end in 1955? He only made three films, and yet he is more famous today than when those films were released. The myth of James Dean is far more powerful and enduring than the reality; more timelessly engaging than any of his roles. This myth has become a part of the fabric of our collective American identity, and this is why the memory of Dean is as fresh today as it was when he first walked in front of the camera, over half a century ago.

Born on February 8, 1931, in Marion, Indiana, James was extremely close to his mother, Mildred, who died when he was only nine years old. His father was unable, or unwilling, to care for him, so James was sent to live with his sister and her Quaker husband on a farm near Fairmont, Indiana. In his teens, something happened to James that profoundly affected his life. A Methodist preacher named James Deweerd (oh, the irony) befriended him, and the two became inseparable. Deweerd (having a hard time referencing this with a straight face) influenced the young and impressionable James in his future obsessions with race cars, the theater, and apparently other things. Their "friendship" also became Dean's first homosexual experience. This man was well into his thirties when he singled Dean out for "special" guidance. Today, we call it child molestation. Then, it was called "mentoring." Dean confided to Elizabeth Taylor, during the making of *Giant*, that he had been "molested by a preacher in high school." Years later, it would come out that Deweerd was known in Fairmont as the local pedophile. In the biography, *James Dean: Little Boy Lost*, by Joe Hyams, he confessed that they "enjoyed a sexual relationship, but only after Jimmy was eighteen." Really?

After high school, Jimmy moved to California to live with his father and stepmother, where he enrolled in UCLA, majoring in drama. This angered his father, and the two became estranged. He soon left college to pursue acting full-time. These were lean times for James, who would often sleep in his car because he couldn't afford rent, and go on gay dinner dates just to eat. He even worked as a parking attendant at CBS studios. After getting only bit parts in commercials, he decided he wanted to become a real actor. He moved to New York, enrolling in the famous mecca of method acting, The Actors Studio. James betrayed the innocent wonderment of a besotted boy on Christmas morning, in a letter he sent home about his admittance into the prestigious acting school. "It houses great people like Marlon Brando, Julie Harris, Arthur Kennedy. Very few get into it! I am one of the youngest to belong."

While at the Studio, his career began to take off with such vehicles as *The Kraft Television Theater*, *The General Electric Theater* and *Omnibus*. But it was his work in the theatrical production of *The Immoralist* that got director Elia Kazan's attention. Dean's brooding persona and wild energy were perfect for the lead, Cal Trask, in his film adaptation of John Steinbeck's novel, *East of Eden*. Kazan had originally pegged Marlon Brando for the role, but when he saw Dean's performance, he knew he was looking at his Cal. Even Steinbeck agreed, though he disliked Dean personally.

Jimmy gave an astonishing, pure method performance; much of it adlibbed and offscript, something he would do again and again in later roles. In the scene where his father—played by veteran actor Raymond Massey—rejects Cal's gift of $5,000, the script called for Dean to turn and run away. Instead, he cried out in anguish, grabbed Massy, and clung to him in a pathetic, desperate attempt to elicit love from the man. Massey's face betrayed his genuine shock at Jimmy's offscript behavior, and it's priceless. The scene is gut-wrenching to watch, and put Dean in a category by himself. He received an Academy Award nomination for Best Actor for *East of Eden*. It was the first posthumous nomination in the Academy's history. It was the only film he made that was released during his lifetime.

Dean got involved with beautiful—but troubled—Italian actress, Pier Angeli, whom he followed around like a lovesick puppy. Pier's controlling mother did not approve of the relationship, as Jimmy was neither Italian, nor Catholic (and not entirely heterosexual?). In his autobiography, Kazan writes that he was often subjected to them loudly making love in Dean's dressing room on the set. Pier decided to allow her mother to control her destiny, marrying the approved Italian Catholic crooner, Vic Damone. James was not happy. He reportedly parked his motorcycle directly across from the church, watching the ceremony from afar, a la *The Graduate*. Apparently it didn't work out for Pier and Damone, or anyone else for that matter, and she committed suicide fifteen years later.

An unintentionally gayish press release linked Dean with two other stars, in all their hunky, pool-boy goodness: Rock Hudson and Tab Hunter. The release stated that each of these men were "eligible bachelors", who had not found the time to commit to a single woman. Right. All three would later become the darlings of the underground gay cinema set. Of his own sexuality, Dean made only one public comment. "No, I am not homosexual, but I'm not going to go through life with one hand tied behind my back." Nailed it!

James followed *East of Eden* with another Brando castoff, the role of Jim Stark in the aptly-titled, *Rebel Without a Cause*. *Rebel* later garnered a macabre reputation for being cursed, as all three principal stars—Natalie Wood, Sal Mineo and James Dean—died tragically before their time. This is the movie that sealed Dean's image as a restless outsider just too cool for this world. The classic scene where he begs on his knees his unbelievably insensitive parents to stop bickering, is one of the most powerful of his career. "You're tearing me apart!" he wails pathetically.

Natalie Wood came to worship Dean as if he was a god, and believed he had no peer among actors. "He was all she could talk about. Every night, for weeks, she went to see him in *East of Eden* at the Egyptian Theater. She must have seen it fifty times!" recalled Sal Mineo, years later. This was his most famous performance, and another released posthumously. Jimmy never lived to see his leap from 'interesting newcomer' to full-blown Hollywood star.

Dean decided to take the role of the complex Jett Rink in *Giant* to avoid being typecast forever as the rebellious, angst-ridden teenager. This was his first official adult role, and he tackled it with his typical intensity and extreme focus. Whereas he had only toyed with Natalie Wood, just because he could, he genuinely fell for Elizabeth Taylor. It seems anyone with a penis loved Ms. Taylor: gay, straight, young, old, rich, poor, dogperson, catperson, vampire, werewolf, vegetarian, carnivore—it didn't matter. Dean and Taylor would disappear together for hours, showing up only when they had to for their scenes. Dean's relationship with Hudson was another story. They shared a room briefly at the start of the shoot, and the story was that Hudson made an awkward pass at Jimmy, who preferred younger, edgier lovers. Spurned, Hudson felt an intense dislike of his young costar, complaining to director George Stevens, that he was being upstaged by the little asshole (which he was).

Had he known this would be his final performance, Dean could not have done more justice to the character. As Jett Rink, he is at once both hateful and pitiable, both an insecure child and a cunning tycoon. The subtleties of his performance are astonishing. In one of his most memorable scenes, he does not even speak, but is shown only in silhouette, pacing off the boundaries of his newly-inherited patch of scrub brush. Finally, at the end, he scales a windmill and plunks down, surveying his prize in complete contentment as the sun descends behind him. Without speaking a word, Dean perfectly conveyed Jett Rink's joy at finally possessing something of his own. He was nominated posthumously for a Academy Award again, and that was the only time in history that had happened.

Dean developed a love for racing early on, purchasing a motorcycle and MG sports car as soon as his finances covered more than his basic needs. He had raced in several competitions, placing first and second in his class. In 1955, while still filming *Giant*, he purchased a Porsche 550 Spyder, which he had custom-painted with the number "130" and "Little Bastard". The studio had barred him from all racing events for the duration of the film shoot, which made him restless, as racing was his way of releasing stress and relaxing between projects. As soon as the final scenes were in the can, and the ban lifted, he took off in his new sports car for a race in Salinas, California. Just before he left, he took the time to film what is now an eerie public service message about speeding, in which he looked straight into the camera and said, "Take it easy driving. The life you save might be mine." Those were the last words he ever spoke on film.

Actor Alec Guinness recalled feeling a sudden unease when Dean proudly showed him the car a week before. He looked at Jimmy and said "If you get in that car, you will be found dead in it by this time next week." Jimmy laughed. This was on September 23, a week before the fatal accident.

On the morning of September 30, 1955, Dean picked up the Porsche from his mechanic, Rolf Wütherich, who had been fine-tuning it for the race. Both men headed out to make the four-hour trip up the coast. At the notorious Grapevine, a steep mountain grade south of Bakersfield, Dean's Porsche began to whiz down the highway a little too fast, prompting CHP officer Otie V. Hunter to pull him over and cite him for speeding.

Two hours later, as he neared the bump in the road known as Cholame, the sun was sinking below the horizon. He closed in on a Y-intersection where highways 466/41 and 46 meet, usually free of traffic. Donald Turnupseed (no, that is not a misprint), driving a 1950 Ford

Coupe, was coming east from 466, and turned left onto 46. The sun was low, and Turnupseed later claimed that he never even saw the Spyder as he entered the intersection. Dean was going 63 mph, saw the Ford approaching without hesitation, and asked Wütherich, "That guy's gotta see us, right?" He didn't. The Ford pulled directly in front of the Porsche. Dean had very little time to react, so instead of slamming on his brakes, he sped up and swerved to try to avoid the other car. This was a classic racing move taught to drivers to avoid collisions on the track, but there was simply not enough time to pull it off. Dean's left front bumper slammed into the left front bumper of Turnupseed's car. The driver's side of Dean's Porsche Spyder bore the brunt of the impact, crushing him inside the mess of twisted metal. Neither Rolf nor Dean was wearing a seat belt, but luck saw the mechanic thrown clear of the accident when the car spun violently on impact. Dean had a broken neck, crushed pelvis, broken legs and severe internal injuries. Wütherich suffered a broken jaw, hip and legs. Amazingly, he survived, living to tell the world of his experiences for decades. Jimmy wasn't so lucky. He was twenty-four years old when they pronounced him dead on arrival at Paso Robles War Memorial Hospital. He was twenty-four.

They sent him back to Indiana to be buried; back to where his mother died, back to where he had been molested by a creepy Methodist min-

*James Dean crash scene. Man lying on the ground (Dean?)*

ister, back to the place he'd left as soon as he humanly could. I guess they thought that's what he would have wanted. The wrecked Porsche made the rounds as a novelty act, its cannibalized parts wreaking doom and destruction on those brave enough to incorporate them into other automobiles. The car finally disappeared for good sometime in 1960, from a sealed train car. At least two female fans committed suicide when Jimmy's death became public. Elizabeth Taylor flirted with a nervous breakdown, and had to be hospitalized briefly.

All this over a man who made just three films, two of which had not yet been released. Today, a casual stroll down Hollywood Boulevard reveals Dean's continued impact on current trends. His image is everywhere, on billboards, murals, peering from store windows, hands jammed in his pockets, staring moodily from a cardboard cutout, and looming from giant posters. If his life and death were not as famous as his legend, visitors could be forgiven for assuming he was a contemporary star, alive and still making pictures. But that would be wishful thinking. Come back to the five and dime Jimmy Dean, Jimmy Dean. And this time, stay a little longer.

# James Dean
## MEMORIAL JUNCTION

*(Previous) The intersection where James Dean died, as it appears today.*

# River Phoenix

The panicked young man on the phone with the 911 operator could barely keep his emotions in check. "He's having seizures on Sunset and Larrabee! Please come here!" he pleaded. His voice pitched into a sob. "He's having seizures! You must get here please! Please 'cause he's dying! Please!" The young man was the Academy Award-winning actor, Joaquin Phoenix, a decade before he became famous, striving helplessly to save his older brother, River, who lay dying from a drug overdose outside a Sunset Strip nightclub. How had it come to this for River, one of the brightest, most talented young actors in Hollywood?

He was born River Jude Bottom in 1970, to a pair of genuine hippies, Arlyn Dunetz and John Lee Bottom. They met when Bottom saw Dunetz hitchhiking in Northern California, and gave her a ride. No kidding. Five children would follow, including River, Rain Joan Of Arc Bottom, Joaquin and Summer. River was named after the river of life in Herman Hesse's novel, *Siddhartha*.

In 1973, everyone thought it would be good idea to join a religious cult, because that's what everyone did. River's family joined the Children Of God cult, and spent the next several years starving as missionaries in South America. The family was so poor that young River and his sister, Rain, would have to go onto the streets as a musical duo, with River on guitar, and Rain on vocals, to solicit change for food. The Children Of God were well-known for their, shall we say, broadminded social practices, which included free love, polyamory, and allowing children to sleep with their parents while they had sex. There's nothing like that good ole time religion. Eventually, starvation and poverty overpowered Arlyn and John's devotion to the cult, and they stowed everyone away on cargo freighter bound for the States. Some people have all the interesting childhood experiences. River was scarred for life from the horrendous experiment that was his early life, and he would draw on these emotions later in his work.

Eventually, this unconventional family made its way to Hollywood, where the ever-diligent Arlyn set about trying to get her brood into the entertainment industry. She said she wanted to change the world for the better, and this was the only way she could think of to accomplish that. How noble. The family could often be found jamming on the streets of Westwood Village to an enthusiastic street audience that would shower them with pocket change. They weren't exactly the *Brady Bunch*. They were close enough for talent agent, Iris Burton, who agreed to represent all five children. By this time the family had changed their name from Bottom to Phoenix, (thank God, though I suspect some diligent studio executive would never have allowed the budding star to perform with the byline of River Bottom). The new name was a symbol for their new lives.

River was the standout star from the beginning. There was just something about this kid, an aura that screamed movie star. He had long, soft, sandy hair and deep set, fiery eyes that fixed people with a "You can't bullshit me" look. He was immediately cast in the short-lived television series, *Seven Brides for Seven Brothers*. He was then cast in a series of small, but memorable, roles in made-for-TV movies, until his big break in 1986, when he was cast in the offbeat, sci-fi movie *Explorers*, along with a young Ethan Hawke. He caught the attention of Rob Reiner, who cast him in his coming-of-age film, *Stand By Me*. River played Chris Chambers, the doomed tough kid with a heart of gold, and he knocked it out of the park. His performance was incredibly sophisticated for such a young actor. *Stand By Me* made River a star.

River made hit after hit for the next three years, rapidly becoming the primary breadwinner for his large family. He followed *Stand By Me* with an intense part as the son of Harrison Ford in *The Mosquito Coast*. That was followed by *Little Nikita*, *Indiana Jones and the Last Crusade*, *A Night in the Life of Jimmy Reardon*, and *Running on Empty* (which he was at this point)—all in rapid succession. He felt the pressure of keeping his family in the style to which they had now become accustomed, and became withdrawn. It didn't help that his mother continued to insist that they live like gypsy fugitives, moving every few months, often to different states. They moved more than forty times before River turned eighteen.

In 1991, he starred in his first adult role, as a gay street hustler aching with unrequited love for Keanu Reeves, in *My Own Private Idaho*. The two had become fast friends in real life, and the chemistry was amazing. River proved with this difficult role that he was more concerned with becoming a good actor than maintaining his squeaky clean image as America's heartthrob. He immersed himself in preparation for the role, even hanging out with street hustlers or "rent boys" on the streets of Portland, Oregon, and interviewing them about their lives. It was during the filming of *Idaho*, during endless, frat boy-style sleepovers at director Gus Van Sant's rented home, with Flea (bass guitarist for The Red Hot Chili Peppers and River's close friend) and the rest of the cast, that River developed a real drug problem. It seems any drug imaginable was freely available, and freely ingested, by all. Despite this, River's hard work paid off. *Idaho* was his finest moment.

River was a sensitive soul, and the pressure to not disappoint those who had grown dependent on his success weighed on him. He would often escape into his first love, music, locking himself in his room for hours to jam away on his guitar, until falling asleep from exhaustion. He also sought escape through drugs, though he followed a strict vegan diet, and was otherwise extremely health-conscious. This is your brain on McDonalds, kids. He longed for the stability of a normal family, and once said "When you're making a film, you're a family, but when the film is over, the family is over." As Hermann Hesse wrote so perfectly in his *Siddhartha*, "Dreams and restless thoughts came flowing to him from the river, from the twinkling stars at night, from the suns melting rays. Dreams and a restlessness of the soul came to him."

Such a good musician was River, that he secured a two-year development deal with Island Records. His band, Aleka's Attic, which featured sister Rain as well, released their first single titled "Across The Way" in 1989. Another song, "Too Many Colors", appeared in *My Own Private Idaho*, and was also released separately under the band's label. River always maintained that his family originally came to LA so that he and Rain could become recording artists, and that the acting thing just happened out of financial necessity. He was dead set on making his music a success without the help of his star power, and refused to allow his band managers to book gigs using his name. Of course, people always found out anyway, and packed Aleka's Attic events just to see River.

*River at the 61st Academy Awards Governor's Ball, photo by Alan Light*

He was also a passionate animal rights activist, due to the atrocious treatment of animals he witnessed as a youth living in Venezuela. He appeared frequently as a spokesperson for PETA, and was honored with their highest award, the Humanitarian Award, in 1992. He loved nature and animals, and these were the guiding inspirations for his political activism and lifestyle.

River's last film, Peter Bogdanovich's *The Thing Called Love*, co-starred Samantha Mathis and Sandra Bullock. He gave a touching performance as an aspiring, idealistic musician, who found love in a Nashville honky-tonk. He dated Mathis, treating her with boyish innocence, and proclaiming his heart beat wildly just holding her hand. But by then, his boyish glow had dimmed, and darkness had begun to descend on his personality. His skin grew sallow, and his hair—once his flaxen pride and joy—began to look listless and dull. He started to lose weight, and his eyes had a haunted glaze. He just looked like a junkie. He tried to get a handle on his addictions, and was one of those "weekend addicts" who would stop for long periods of time, then start up again when he was surrounded by the wrong crowd or under too much stress. This behavior can be more dangerous than the behavior of a full-time addict. A consistent drug user will build up a tolerance for the substance, and it becomes harder to overdose, but a person who starts and stops all the time can easily throw his clean body into shock with a dose that he thinks is safe.

River spent his last day alive on the set of his latest movie, *Dark Blood*. He managed to kick his drug habit during the two months they shot on location out in Utah. Back in LA, however, where drugs were more plentiful than money, he relapsed, and ingested something before showing up on the set that morning. He was oddly quiet and still, spending most of the day motionless on a chair, while the elaborate love scene was carefully set up. There was tension between him and his co-star, Judy Davis, who seemed to intensely dislike River for no apparent reason. River was never good at faking it. He asked the director to put off shooting the tender love scene for as long as possible, as he was unusually intimidated by Davis, and worried about his ability to pull it off.

The very last images of River Phoenix on film are chilling. According to the show *The Last Days of River Phoenix*, the love scene took four takes to complete and then was done. The director called cut, the lights were extinguished, and River just stood there, silhouetted against the still burning candles, as the camera continued to roll. He turned and walked towards the camera, staring silently into the lens for nearly five minutes, as the candles burning eerily behind his dark visage. Finally, someone realized that the camera was still running, and switched it off. After River's death, this last penetrating image would haunt the cast and crew for years.

Upset and stressed out by the bad vibes on the set, River decided to blow off steam that night, joining his family and friends at The Viper Room; a popular West Hollywood nightclub owned by River's pal, Johnny Depp. It was the night before Halloween, and everyone was in a good mood. The party began in River's suite at the Hotel Nikkon, where his girlfriend Samantha, his sister Rain and brother Joaquin joined him. There is debate as to whether or not River drank anything before going to the club. Most sources say he didn't, as he was very excited about jamming with Depp and Flea on stage that night, and wanted to stay focused.

Around midnight, everyone was at the club, ready to kick the party into high gear. River brought his guitar and waited in anticipation of taking the stage. He was like a little boy at a school play. Flea and River had met on the set of *My Own Private Idaho*, and there was an instant rapport. Flea was a hip musician who wanted to dabble in acting, and River was hip actor who really wanted to be a rock star. They became inseparable. By all accounts, River had not taken any drugs yet. He was so excited, and wanted to be 100% when he went on stage to play beside his best friend. Unfortunately, the stage was already overflowing with musicians, and there was no room left for River. Disappointed and hurt, he began casing the crowd for a dealer. He found one.

Meanwhile, back at the ranch, Joaquin, Rain and Samantha were enjoying the evening in a booth toward the back of the room. They all assumed River was about to take the stage. He had actually gone into the bathroom with a drug dealer, and snorted a massive speed ball: a combination of heroin and cocaine. The same concoction killed John Belushi ten years earlier. Right away, he became violently ill, and began puking his guts up. He screamed at the dealer "What the fuck did you just give me?" between pukes. He began shaking, his heart heart racing, breaking out in a cold sweat. As if he hadn't had enough drugs, some rocket scientist thought this an opportune moment to give him a Valium. By the time he stumbled out of the bathroom, and back to the booth, he had less than an hour to live. He complained that it was hard to breathe, then passed out at the feet of his friends. When he regained consciousness, he asked Samantha and Joaquin to help him outside for some air. While being helped out, one of the bouncers asked what was happening, and River reportedly replied, "I'm dying, man."

Once outside, he collapsed on the sidewalk, and the violent seizures began while his head thumped on the concrete for eight minutes. Rain threw herself on top of his body to stop him from shaking, while everyone else just stood around, not believing their eyes. Some people even laughed. When you're stoned out of you're mind, you don't make the best choices. A witness said he looked like a fish out of water flopping and flailing helplessly on the hard cement. Finally, Joaquin ran to the nearby phone booth and dialed 911. Where's a cell phone when you need it? By the time the paramedics got there, he was already gone. River Jude Phoenix was dead at the age of twenty-three on a public sidewalk in front of snickering strangers dressed in Halloween costumes.

To see what River could have been, look at his brother Joaquin and what he's done. That's what River cheated us out of. Look at Leonardo

DeCaprio. He and River were contemporaries. Both started out as gifted child actors, and both saw that it wasn't about fame or money, or even beauty. It was about art. DeCaprio became one of the finest actors of his generation. That's what River cheated us out of. His mom said, "When the wind blows I see River, when the sun shines I see River, when I look in someone's eyes and make a connection, I see River. To have death transformed into another way to view life is his huge gift."

River himself had said of his career, "I'd rather quit while I'm still ahead. There's no use overstaying your welcome." Ah, River...as if that would ever have happened.

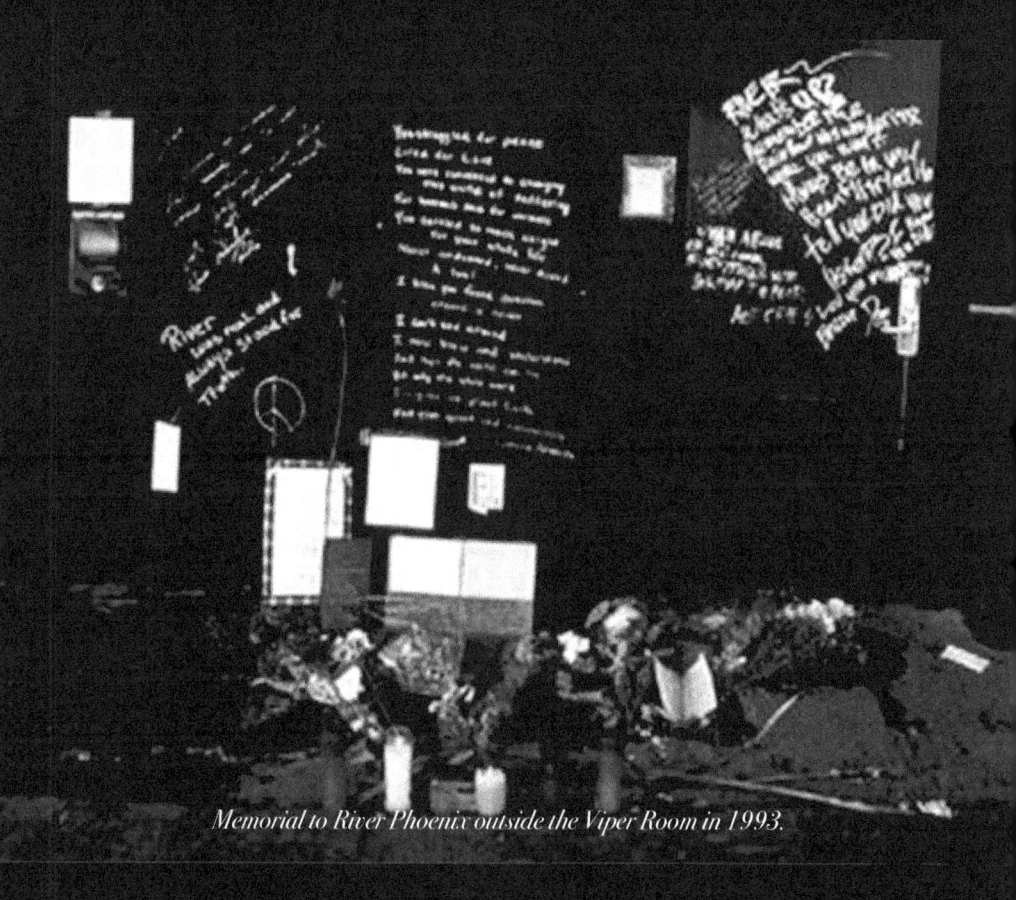

*Memorial to River Phoenix outside the Viper Room in 1993.*

# Errol Flynn

T he youngish man with the debonair, movie star mustache, lying prone on the metal table, looked better dead than most men did while living. His skin showed the signs of fast living and alcohol abuse (lots of alcohol abuse), but his body was still chiseled, and his features still perfect. He was only fifty, but he had crammed dozens of lifetimes into his half-century share of this world. It all played out in front of millions of adoring fans, who loved him because of, and perhaps in spite of, his quite literal and unabashed lust for life.

Errol Flynn was the kind of guy your mom warned you about right after she slept with him. He was the kind of guy your dad might have followed around in high school just to bask in his coolness and borrow his letterman's jacket. He was that rare breed of human that women forgot how to be ladies around, and men simply worshipped. He was born in Tasmania (the little devil) to Australian parents, and started things off on the right foot straight away by getting expelled from school for having sex with the laundress.

*Flynn as Robin Hood*

He had a successful career both on the stage and on the screen in Australia and England, prior to crossing the pond to the 'States and becoming an overnight sensation in the 1935 big-budget adventure film, *Captain Blood*. His stunning looks were all Hollywood needed to declare him a star, and typecast him in one swashbuckling feature after another. He made eight films with actress Olivia de Havilland, with whom he was rumored to be truly enamored. For her part, Ms. de Havilland denied that any serious hanky-panky went on, but loved to recount the practical joke she played on Flynn during the filming of *Robin Hood*. In a particularly erotic kissing scene, de Havilland purposely kept flubbing her lines so that they had to do one take after another, coaxing nature to finally bulge through under Flynn's green tights. If Flynn didn't sleep with de Havilland, she must have been one of only two women in Hollywood (the other being Bette Davis). Still, is there a more wonderful sight in all of classic Hollywood than Robin Hood, young and ridiculously beautiful, gazing into Maid Marion's eyes before planting a kiss that went on into eternity?

Flynn didn't seem to mind that he was just a pretty boy in pretty pictures. The money rained down, and along with it the drugs, the alcohol and the women. He developed a reputation almost immediately for debauchery, and his antics became legendary. He and fellow partner in lewdness, David Niven, threw wild parties at Marion Davies' "beach house" (actually a palatial estate sprawled across the sands of Santa Monica that would have impressed a Tsar) which they sublet from Davies in the late '30s. Nicknamed "Cirrhosis by the sea" by Carol Lombard, it was the orgy-house to end all orgy-houses, and a place where Errol could pretend he was a carefree bachelor, when he actually wasn't. He had been married to Lili Damita for years, but this inconvenient reality did not seem to slow him down. These beach parties were awash in booze, cocaine, and all sorts of other illicit activities, and they went on for days. Take that Hugh Hefner!

Flynn's impressive residence on Mulholland Drive was also party central. It contained some interesting architectural novelties, as Ron Wood, of the Rolling Stones, found out after he purchased the property in the '70s. "Errol had a two-way mirror, and a speaker in the ladies room," he said. He also had a black leather padded bar, with a secret compartment that opened into a cramped viewing room that had a two-way mirror looking into the restroom. Perve! In addition, he had a two-way mirror installed in the guest bedroom and a crawl space in the attic above, which served as the viewing room for his voyeurism. Robert Douglas, his costar in *Don Juan*, claimed Flynn showed him the room, and they proceeded to have some fun with the young, naked couple sleeping there at the time. Flynn pushed a button, and up popped a screen, which woke them up. Flynn pushed another button, and a porn movie began playing. They were so shocked they just sat there, watching. We got bored and went down to get a drink." Tsk tsk, Errol.

As if two mansions overflowing with lewdness weren't enough, Errol took this act to the sea as well. He owned a 118' gaff-rigged schooner, christened Zaca, in which he offered deviant celebrity "sailors" a selection of free love and free booze to go with their free harbor cruise. After all, we're talking international waters here. No pesky moral laws to spoil the fun. "I like my whisky old and my women young!" he often declared.

Eventually, in 1942, all this nonsense caught up with Flynn in the form of a trial for statutory rape, brought by two fifteen-year-old girls who swore in court that he had seduced them into giving up their virginity. This was a man who could have nailed just about any actress in Hollywood, and did, yet stood accused of chasing after two street urchins, and forcing himself on them. It sounded far-fetched to the public, as well as Flynn's friends, some of whom formed a group known as "The American Boys Club for the Defense of Errol Flynn". Peggy Satterlee testified that Flynn had taken her aboard his yacht, and while gazing at the evening sky, whispered seductively into her ear, "That moon would look more beautiful through a porthole." Pandemonium ensued in the courtroom. Flynn just grinned, like a cheshire cat, through the whole thing. He was acquitted of all charges. A phrase was invented to describe his uncanny ability to escape consequence. He was "in like Flynn."

*Flynn and wife, Nora Eddington Flynn, on boat in Santa Monica, CA, 1946*

Far from ending Flynn's career, the publicity only enhanced his image as an unimaginable hunk. Things might have turned out differently for him if he had been reined in a little. But Flynn felt vindicated in his lifestyle, and he picked up right where he left off. One of the most famous stories describes the night the body of fellow drinking comrade, John Barrymore, was stolen from the morgue. Legend has it that Raoul Walsh and Flynn were sloshed at a local bar, The Cock and Bull, lamenting that they could not have one last drink with their dead friend. Raoul got an idea (cue light bulb above head). He excused himself and left Flynn to continue drowning his sorrows alone. Several hours later, Flynn staggered into his living room, flicked the lights on, and sauntered over to his bar to pour himself a drink, because he wasn't drunk enough, apparently. He walked past John Barrymore, stiff as a board, propped up in an easy chair near the bar, a drink jammed into his cold, dead hand. Flynn nodded to the corpse, and proceeded to grab a bottle of whisky. He stopped, whipped around, cried out, and let the whisky bottle fall from his hand. Raoul and two accomplices howled with laugher from the next room, where they had been hiding. This story has become an urban legend, and has been retold many times. Flynn himself recounted it in his autobiography, *My Wicked, Wicked Ways*, but then, he said a lot of things. Whether or not it actually happened seems to be irrelevant at this point. It's too good a story to die.

Flynn liked to drink. Seriously. He liked to drink a lot. He used to carry two fifths of vodka on the set with him, and get himself plastered between takes. When the studio banned him from bringing booze to the set, he injected oranges with alcohol, and ate his way to intoxication instead. Today we call this alcoholism. Back then, when Flynn did it, it was called interesting. More interesting were the rumors of his taking male lovers as well as female, a charge that has been hotly denied by those who knew Flynn. Biographer David Bret, who wrote a poison pen book about Flynn, insisted that he swung both ways. Two of his supposed conquests were Ross Alexander and Tyrone Power. Bret wrote that Power fell passionately in love with Flynn, but for the cavalier Flynn, it was all physical. Well, of course it was.

By the 1950s, Errol's wicked, wicked ways began to catch up with him. He became bloated and old before his time. In 1952, he won critical acclaim for his portrayal of a suave drunk in *The Sun Also Rises* (I wonder why), and he gave a truly magnificent performance as John Barrymore in 1957's *Too Much Too Soon*. He grew a bit more serious in his middle years, traveling to Cuba, and taking up Castro's cause, who was then just a freedom fighter, rather than the evil communist scourge that he would later be painted. By the time he penned *My Wicked, Wicked Ways*, Flynn was depressed, and suffering from numerous physical ailments, including malaria, chronic back pain (hence the morphine and heroin use), lingering tuberculosis, and STDs. The autobiography was a bestseller, and is still considered one of the most entertaining works of its genre.

He was married to Patricia Wymore when, in 1959, he met a fifteen-year-old ingénue named Beverly Aadland. The two were in talks with director Stanley Kubrick to star together in his film version of Vladimir Nabokov's controversial novel about man/child love, *Lolita* (how appropriate). He suffered a massive heart attack while visiting Vancouver. He was too ill for the flight back to America, and was taken to a friend's apartment, where in true Flynn style, he threw a party. A good time was had by all, and he died before the ice had melted in the drinks, in a bedroom where he had gone to rest. No one would have expected anything less.

Strange stories seemed to follow Errol, even after death. Glen McDonald, the coroner present for Flynn's autopsy, told a tale that has to be

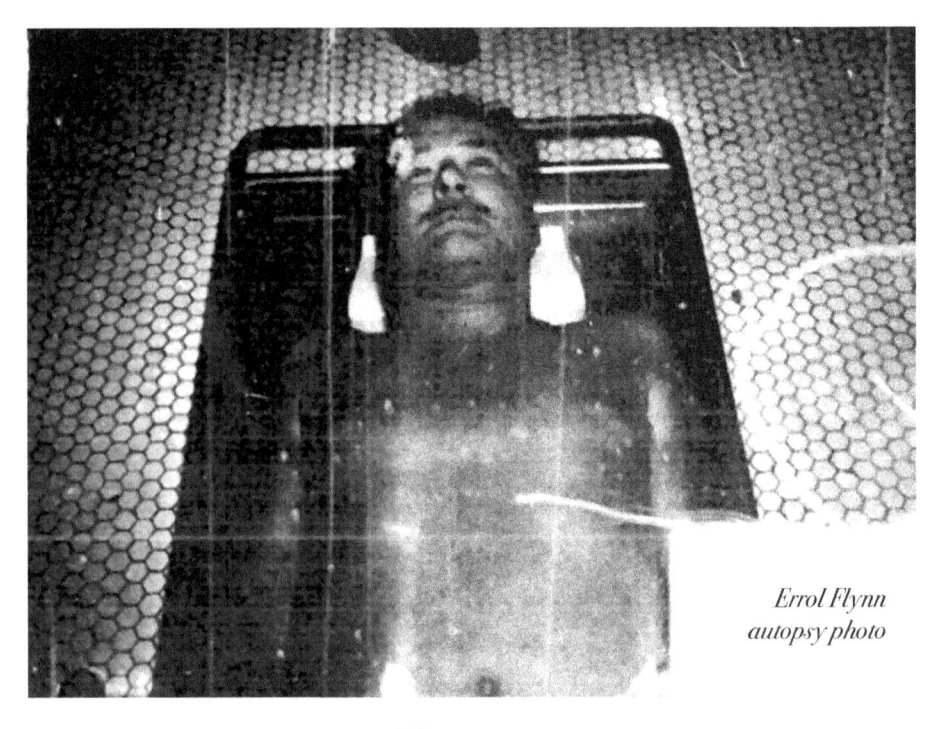

*Errol Flynn autopsy photo*

the most bizarre urban legend yet. According to Glen, the official cause of death was (deep breath): myocardial infarction, coronary thrombosis, fatty degeneration of the liver (surprise), portal cirrhosis of the liver, and diverticulosis of the colon. The pathologist noticed several warts at the tip of Flynn's member, from years of venereal disease, and in some twisted kind of penis envy, insisted he needed them as a teaching aid, or something. Glen said absolutely not, but while he was out of the room, said pathologist went snip-snip, and when Glen returned, Flynn's penis was bare, and the warts stewed in a jar of formaldehyde. Furious, Glen told the pathologist to "PUT THEM BACK!" and so he did....with scotch tape...I kid you not. Errol would have laughed his ass off.

In his autobiography, there is a hint that betrays a touch of annoyance with his sex-crazed, party boy image. "What makes any one think I am less concerned with the verities of life than anyone else? Was it all a prank that I went to loyalist Spain, that I sided with Castro, that I have plumbed the sea depths and traveled the world? Who could live with himself believing he was a symbol of sex and nothing more?"

It's ok, Errol. We loved you just the way you were...penis warts and all.

*Flynn's coffin on Los Angeles Union Station train platform, 1959*

# Chris Farley

A huge man—grossly overweight—hams up an exaggerated display of hitching up his pants, as he crouches in front of two teenagers sitting on a couch. He wears thick glasses, a green tie, checkered sports jacket, and the mannerisms of a man teetering on the edge. "My name is Matt Foley, and I am a motivational speaker. I am 35 years old, I am divorced and I live in a van down by the river!" Such were the immortal words, spoken on *Saturday Night Live*, by one of the most gifted comedians of recent times, Chris Farley.

Farley was an unlikely celebrity. He was more like that overweight kid at school, who was never picked for basketball, so he turned to comedy to compensate. He also turned to other things. He was born into an Irish Catholic family in Madison, Wisconsin. He attended the private Catholic high school, Edgewood High School Of The Sacred Heart, where he used binge drinking as a way to overcome his shyness, and to fit in. His best friend was a football jock—tall, athletic, handsome—everything Chris wanted to be but wasn't. In his own words, "I got blind drunk every weekend." This tactic worked, for a while. He found that people responded to his silly antics and clownish behavior while drunk, and he became well-liked by the "in" crowd, if not actually a part of them. One friend remembered sitting in the library with Chris and some other kids. Chris had spent the hour cracking everyone up, and then he got up and left for class. One kid watched him go, then said, "He's going to be on *Saturday Night Live*." Everyone nodded. Definitely.

When he went away to college at Marquette University, he was away from his parents and any type of restraints, and his weekend partying became his nightly partying. He added marijuana to his routine, and got stoned every chance he could. After graduating from college, he worked briefly with his father, a VP at the Scotch Oil Company in Madison. He was the boss's screwup kid, showing up late, or not at all, and often coming to work high.

Chris was aimless and insecure about his future, but he knew that he had a gift for making people laugh. He left Madison for Chicago, and joined the famous improv theater group, Second City. He just walked up onto the stage, auditioned, and was hired. That's how good he was. Second City was legendary in the comedy world, having spawned most of the original cast of *Saturday Night Live*, including Chris's idol, John Belushi. Chris more than looked up to Belushi, he wanted to be Belushi. During a motivational speech, just before he died, he said of his obsession with John, "I read an article about him in *Wired* magazine. A lot of people read *Wired* and thought, "Man, that poor guy. I never wanna do drugs again!" But I was like Yeah! If that's what it takes, I'll do it 'cause I wanted to be like him in every way, like all those guys from the show. I thought that's what you had to do."

Chris might have been a junkie, but it never seemed to hurt his work. He quickly became one of the most popular Second City acts, which is why Lorne Michaels picked him to join *SNL* as a permanent cast member in 1990. For a comedian, this was the equivalent of God picking Moses to be a prophet. Chris was thrilled. He was following in the footsteps of his idol. He must have thought he was living a dream. He quickly took his place among the "not ready for prime time players," and set about delighting audiences for the next four seasons in a style that had not existed since Belushi's physical comedy of the '70s. His legendary skits included an obese Chippendale dancer, strutting his blubber along side the chiseled physique of Patrick Swayze; the aforementioned Matt Foley, homeless motivational speaker; a cafeteria lunch lady; and Bennett Brauer, crude Weekend Update commentator, who often got side tracked from the subject at hand by stories of his own personal hygiene. Self-effacing as always, Chris quipped, "They'll come to see the fat boy fall down."

Chris became good friends with fellow cast members David Spade and Adam Sandler. Sandler was like the skinny, smart-aleck little punk to Farley's drunk best friend. The two were well-known for their offscreen antics, which included prank random phone calls from the *SNL* offices, wherein Farley would fart into the receiver, while Sandler spoke in an old lady voice. They would also ride around in a limo together, mooning traffic as the whim struck them. Ah, to be young, wasted, and famous in New York.

Farley's substance abuse was so out of control that first year on *SNL* that the producers forced him to go to rehab. For a while, it looked like this might actually have worked. Chris stayed sober for the next three years. Then things got rough on *SNL*, and he slid back into his old ways.

Chris's addictions and self-esteem demons began to take control of his life. This was the chubby, awkward kid who always kept a rosary nearby, went to mass every Sunday, and just wanted to be loved. If he had to act ridiculous or make fun of himself to do it, that's what he did. If he had to get high to get his courage up, that's what he did. In the beginning, he was able to keep it together, but as the years wore on, and the pressure began to build along with his *SNL* fame, he began to lose it.

Finally, in 1995, he and Sandler were fired from *SNL*. In addition to the pranks and frat-boy behavior, management had grown tired of Chris's increasingly erratic behavior. Chris was in good company, however, as nearly the entire cast from that season either left or was fired.

Chris decided to branch out into films, now that he had lots of time on his hands. He and David Spade starred in two successful films together, the hilarious *Tommy Boy* and *Black Sheep*. He also made *Beverly Hills Ninja* and *Almost Heroes*, his last (and worst) film. By *Almost Heroes*, in 1997, he was having a hard time keeping his addictions from impacting his work, causing numerous shooting delays and cost overruns.

Chris spent the last two years of his life in and out of rehab—seventeen times. He and Amy Winehouse would have hit it off nicely. Periods of sobriety came and went, and he would be right back in it again, funny fat wasted guy everyone invites to parties. He longed for a deep, personal connection with a woman, but didn't think any would have him, so he hired prostitutes instead. He took them out to eat, dance, enjoy shows, and referred to them as girlfriends. Chris called the outpatient rehab programs a joke, and said he beat drug tests by carrying around someone else's urine all the time. "I was crying all the time because I could not stop. I could not imagine a life of sobriety because drugs and alcohol were the only thing that was my friend. I knew I was in trouble."

In March of '97, while at an *SNL* cast reunion in Aspen, his profuse sweating, strange behavior, and obvious weight gain (he topped the scales at nearly 300 lbs) got everyone's attention. Chevy Chase, in a helpful, fatherly fashion, took Farley aside and told him, "Look, you're not John Belushi. And when you overdose, or kill yourself, you're not going to have the same acclaim that John did. You'll be a blip in *The New York Times* obituary page and that will be it. Is that what you want?" Well, no, of course that's not what he wanted, but he was an addict, and simply unable to muster the kind of inner strength it takes to overcome that. In July, after appearing completely blitzed at a Planet Hollywood opening in Indianapolis, he told a fellow actor who tried to calm him down that he intended to "Live fast and die young." Did he really mean that?

The last week of Chris's life would have put Nero to shame. He'd moved to Chicago, and was living in the prestigious Hancock Building. In December of '97, he decided to tear through nearly every single bar and holiday drug party he could find. He began this quest on December 14, with a round of binge eating, binge drinking, and binge everything else at his favorite club, Karma. He engaged in a post-Second City reunion pub crawl on December 15. On December 16, he spent the day with a prostitute named Autumn, drinking vodka, smoking pot and trying to score drugs. In the early morning hours of December 17, he hit a local upscale bar with his brother and assistant, and left with two prostitutes. He hit another party in Lincoln Park at 6 AM that same morning, where he met a stripper named Heidi. According to Heidi, he spent hours ingesting massive quantities of coke, heroin and booze before he came back to her apartment, where more drugs were consumed.

At 11 PM, they moved their two-person party to his apartment. Chris was so far gone at that point that he couldn't even get it up. Heidi was growing impatient, and asked to be paid, not only for her time, but for all the drugs she fronted him. Chris, possibly in a pathetic attempt to keep her there so that he wouldn't have to be alone, claimed his friend had actually hired her, and that it was he who was suppose to pay her. Fed up, she decided to leave. Chris tried to follow her, but collapsed about ten feet from the door. "Don't leave," he pleaded. So, not exactly being the hooker with the heart of gold, she left Chris there, struggling for breath, but not before the enterprising young businesswoman decided to snap a photo. For her scrapbook, no doubt. This was at around 3 AM on December 18.

Chris was found at 2 PM that afternoon by his brother, who had been unable to reach him by phone. Chris had not slept in four days. He was on his back, pretty much where Heidi left him, stiff and blue. He died alone, hours earlier. He was thirty-three, just like John Belushi. Toxicology reports gave the cause of death as acute cocaine and morphine intoxication, just like John Belushi. He wanted to be like John so badly, and he succeeded in the worst way.

When fellow cast member Phil Hartman bid farewell to *SNL* on his final show in 1994, the entire cast lined up like the Von Trapp children, and sang the song from *The Sound of Music*. Chris was the last one to add his goodbye. Instead of doing his bit and leaving the stage like the rest, Chris started out as the irrepressible Matt Foley, but transitions into a little boy who pretends he's sleepy, and sits down on the steps, yawning and rubbing his eyes. Phil sits down next to him and puts his arm around him. "You know, I can't think of a better way to end my eight years on this show than this," he says, as Chris snuggles his head tenderly into Phil's shirt. Together they sing the final line in the song, waving goodbye, as the lights dim in the studio, until only a single circular spotlight remains on their faces. "Goodbye. Goodbye. Goodbye." The camera slowly pans closer, and the spotlight goes out.

Both would be dead within three years. Phil would be murdered by his wife, and Chris would burn out. Fate has a strange way of pointing to itself sometimes.

Barbara La Marr

The striking fourteen-year-old girl stood before the judge, trembling a little. He took one long look at the stunning beauty, who looked five years more matured than she actually was, and declared her "much too beautiful and young to be on her own in Los Angeles." Found dancing in a burlesque show, Reatha was given the choice between a court-appointed guardian, or going home to her parents. Writer and actress Adela Rogers St. Johns just happened to be in the room that day, witnessing the start of a byline that would forever precede the girl. She brought Reatha Watson back to her office at the *LA Examiner*, introducing her to the editor, Jack Campbell. A seasoned newspaperman, Jack knew a great byline when he saw one, and published a two-page spread on Reatha the following day, introducing her as "The girl too beautiful". It was not the first dance for the press and Reatha, but from then on, she'd have her pick of partners and music.

In 1896, Reatha Dale Watson was born in Yakima, Washington, to a newspaper editor and his wife. Reatha's intelligence, wit, and creativity lent themselves from the start to artistic pursuits, as did her ardor for anything exotic. It would be this inner wellspring, bursting her every seam to get out, that would later lead her to claim that her 'real' parents were French and Italian nobles descended from Napoleon, and that she was really born in Richmond, Virginia. Her two half-siblings, two full-siblings, and the Census, among other things, reveal these stories as merely her way of reclaiming her mundane existence in a way that better suited her tastes. Then, however, the press loved a good story, and she dangled fresh intrigue above their hungry mouths like a killer whale trainer at SeaWorld. One such morsel, dropped casually in an interview later in life, held that she was abandoned by her parents in Los Angeles at the age of four, left alone to roam the streets as a waif, and from there, clawed her way to fame. The Census and a newspaper article or two say different, but with a creativity switch stuck in the "on" position literally all the time, she probably could not help herself. She was never abandoned by anyone, least of all her parents. They christened her "Reatha". How exotic is that? She asked to be called "Beth", and "Beth" it was, at least while she was home.

The family moved to Portland, Oregon in 1900. In January of 1904, her parents brought seven-year-old Beth to a lot sale, which was covered in the local paper. She was chosen to take the tickets of those who won a free lot. Both ticket holders tipped her five dollars, and she declared, "Now I am going to buy a doll buggy." Both of her proud, natural parents beamed. They remained in the area for about a decade, and Beth attended a convent school. In 1910, they moved Fresno briefly, where Beth's mother had her privately tutored at home and then they moved again, to Los Angeles, within a year.

Now fourteen and in the city of angels, Beth took every opportunity to run off both on her own, and with her older half-sister, Violet, exploring the stores, and clubs, and people. She was in love with improvisational dance, as made popular by the exquisite Isadora Duncan, and began performing in clubs and cafes, and in burlesque shows. Beth usually lied about her age to get in the door. The sight of this ravishing child, moving to the beat of her own soul, must have made grown men wet their pants. She was spotted by authorities, brought in, banished from her new cultural mecca by the judge, for being too beautiful. This first banishment from the city was for her protection.

At sixteen, Violet and a male companion, C.C. Boxley, picked her up under the pretense of taking her up the coast to the beach. They heard Beth was entertaining men privately, as well as dancing, and planned to take her away away and cajole her into making them some money. Beth's mother had been uncomfortable when Violet arrived that day to retrieve a photo of hers, because they had not been getting along. Trying to keep the peace, she repressed her discomfort, while Violet slipped away with Beth. When she noticed Beth was gone, she called police, and a nationwide search began. The aspiring kidnappers had Beth write a note to her parents, and mailed it from San Francisco, hoping to cover their tracks, but Police knew that Violet's daughter was still in school in Tacoma, and aimed catch them there. The next day, with the story in every paper and all over the radio, they decided to take Beth back home and pretend they had no idea what all the fuss was about. Charges were brought, and Beth even testified against Violet in court, but the case was later dropped. Officials noted that they could not be certain that Beth had not been a party to the plan. Still, what could possibly come next in this young girl's life? How about an honest-to-goodness cowboy sweeping her (literally) off her feet that very same year?

Beth was driving though the area around Yuma, Arizona, not long after returning from her first kidnapping. The family has moved to El Centro, California, and Yuma was a closer target for her curiosities than Los Angeles. She would say later that she was performing in western films there, but as of yet no one has ever seen any of them. Out of the blue, she was scooped up out of a slow-moving convertible by a man on horseback, and carried off into the sunset. Who needs movies when things like this happen to you in real life? His name was Jack, and he owned a ranch nearby. Beth was still only sixteen, and must have been swept off her feet by the romance of it all, because she agreed to marry him on the spot, and soon became Mrs. Beth Lytell. Romance can only take one so far, especially for a such stunning little thing not meant for the isolation and lack of exotic culture on a windswept desert ranch. She began to pine for the attention and adoration she had enjoyed back in the big city, and this broke Jack's heart. He must have realized, after storming out on her for the hundredth time frustrated by her inability to see the rustic riches laid out before her, that he would eventually lose her forever. He rode his horse for hours in the pouring rain that day, sulking. When he finally came back, he was shaking with fever. He died two days later from a broken heart. Ok, he technically died from pneumonia.

The Girl Too Beautiful was heartbroken, and returned to LA to resume her infiltration of the entertainment business, hanging onto her married name for a while to accentuate and support the inevitable tale. When she wasn't busy being crowned Miss Too Beautiful by judges, and being kidnapped by cowboys, she wrote stories and poems. Damn, was there anything this girl didn't do? Her explorations of the culture of show business extended further into partying (AKA drinking). She gave a harrowing account of being kidnapped (not again!) by three people at a particularly wild affair, and being gang-raped for hours. What was it about this woman that made people think they could just spirit her away and do what they wanted with her, and never realize they were not the hunters, but the hunted? Obviously, being coveted beyond reason is one of downsides to possessing great beauty, and Beth experienced it all too often, but, like an alchemist, she could transform the lead of base attention into the gold of influence, notoriety and cold, hard cash. Nature would throw her in the path of a wild horse again and again, and each time, she would emerge riding it like a pony.

In 1914, plied by silky words and expensive gifts, she married wealthy, prominent attorney Max Lawrence. Not twenty-four hours into the marriage, the cops arrested her new husband, and threw him in jail for bigamy. He already had a wife and three kids, and his real name was Lawrence Converse. Converse was so distraught that he screamed as they were slamming his cell door, "I had to possess her magnificent beauty!" He banged his head on the wall for two days, later solving everyone's problems by dying of blood clots in the brain. Beth had been married and widowed twice, and she wasn't even eighteen. You go, girl! Her beauty was not only arresting, it was also, apparently, a deadly weapon. In court, police and social services officers actually discussed the need to protect all Los Angeles men from Beth. Later that month, the courts once again exiled her from the city, and sent her back to her parents. Beth somehow had the law building her legend for her. There was a cost, though. The film studios shut her out over the controversy.

In 1915, she formed a dance partnership with dancer Philip Carville, and they danced their way across the country, performing in some of the most elegant supper clubs. Another panting admirer, Phil Ainsworth, entered her life, following her from city to city, begging her to marry him. She eventually did, probably just to get him off her back. Ainsworth presented himself as a gentleman of means, but was not. The jig was up when he went to jail for check forgery. Apparently, he had been lavishing his bride with jewelry, clothing and extravagant trips, all with stolen money. He was sent to San Quentin to think about things, and Beth was again left alone. For the rest of his life, Ainsworth insisted that she was the most beautiful creature ever created.

Beth entered a period of wild abandon, having numerous affairs, one most notably with younger, unknown writer, Ernest Hemingway. Her drinking and cocaine use increased, and she often quipped, "I never sleep more than two hours a night! I have better things to do." She was also fond of saying "I like my men like I like my roses... by the dozen." She loved dance, art and literature, and was attracted to men who shared those interests. She thought she found a kindred spirit in Ben Deely. Ben was much older, an alcoholic, and a compulsive gambler, and like all the rest, worshipped the ground she walked on. They would do all-night, slam writing/drinking/drug sessions that would often stretch on beyond sunrise.

The movie business was in its infancy when she decided to write screenplays for films. This is a woman who had the face that launched a thousand ships, yet wanted to be behind the camera, rather than in front of it. That's how deep she was. Of course, everything fell into this woman's lap, and success, as a screenwriter was near instant. She ended up writing six scripts for Fox Studios, before pressure from directors and casting agents to appear in front of the camera finally caused her to drop writing for stardom. It's like Elizabeth Taylor hunched over in a writers meeting, pen in hand... as if that would ever last for very long. Stepping before the cameras at last, she became Barbara La Marr.

Barbara's perfect face flashed across the silver screen, in small roles and then in larger ones. Soon she was a sought after leading lady, starring in such blockbusters as *The Three Musketeers* (with Douglas Fairbanks), *The Prisoner of Zenda*, *Arabian Love*, *The Eternal City* and many more. The money rolled in. It was the 1920s, the jazz age, and The Girl Too Beautiful was billed as "the most beautiful woman in the world." She bought a mansion in the hills, dumped her drunken husband, and proceeded to live a life Fitzgerald could only write about. She threw lavish parties that people talked about for years afterwards. She was so stunning that her contemporary, Mary Philbin, recalled nearly fainting at the sight of her, shimmering in her dazzling designer gown, at a Hollywood premiere. In addition to her great beauty, she was known for her wit, her humor, her generosity and her intelligence. Talk about the whole package, Barbara was the whole package with the rest of the store thrown in for good measure. They don't make them like this anymore, folks.

Creatures so exquisite and extraordinary do not last long in this world. On the set of *Souls For Sale*, in 1923, she slipped and sprained her ankle. The studio doctor gave her morphine so that she could keep working. Really? What was wrong with aspirin? Now, in addition to booze, she became a morphine addict. The great decline had begun, but not before she threw the world a few more classic film gems. While filming *St. Elmo*, she and costar, John Gilbert, had a passionate affair. Both were achingly beautiful, sensitive souls, and of course, tragically doomed. What a sight they must have been, smoldering into each other on a giant, flickering screen. Around this time, Barbara spent some time in Texas, returning home with a baby. She claimed her bay was adopted, but many in the business believed she had the child out-of-wedlock, and pretended to adopt in order to maintain respectability. Hayes hadn't raised his ugly head yet, but an illegitimate birth would have destroyed her career. She named the baby Marvin Carville La Marr (Carville? Wasn't that the last name of her dance partner way back when?), and he became the one bright spot in what was soon to become a very dark period for Barbara.

Also in 1923, she met and married her fifth and final husband, cowboy actor Jack Dougherty, and by all accounts, the marriage was a happy one. But by then, Barbara was in trouble. She was struggling with her addictions, eating too much, sleeping too little, and it showed. She gained weight, looked tired on the set, and got sloshed and stoned during shoots. The weight gain upset her more than anything, and she went on a crash diet that consisted of morphine, highballs and fasting. There was even a rumor that she swallowed a tapeworm to speed up the process. She was still always the first in the door to the clubs and parties, and the last to leave. Wow. People think Lindsay Lohan is a party girl. All of this affected her work, and Metro canceled her contract.

Undaunted, she moved to First National, and continued her work at an insane pace. Did she know something no one else knew? Metro executive Paul Bern fell passionately in love with Barbara while she was in her free-falling years. Bern would later go on to marry Jean Harlow, then kill himself over her. How did this rather unattractive, sinister-looking little man manage to get two of the most gorgeous actresses in history to be with him? Was he that good? Anyway, he begged Barbara to take time off and try to get clean, but she either would not, or could not, stop. She was shooting up, sniffing coke, and swigging vodka on the set of her last film, *The Girl from Montmartre*, when she collapsed. This shooting star was about to flame out. She never finished *The Girl from Montmartre*. Her marriage was already crumbling and only Bern remained by her side. Her ugly secret was out, and the Hollywood community, predictably devoid of compassion, treated her like a leper. She slipped further into illness, falling into a coma, and finally dying on January 30, 1926. She was twenty-nine. Her official cause of death was tuberculosis and nephritis, but everyone knew it was life that killed Barbara. Oh yeah, and drugs. Forty thousand mourners attended her funeral. Suddenly, she wasn't a leper anymore, just a tragedy that no one saw coming, and everyone was sorry about. There really is nothing like the hypocrisy of Hollywood. She was ravishing, even in death, her coffin open for everyone to see what had been lost. Her lovely face draped with a sheer, white lace death-shroud. After all is said and done, we are left with one question. Is it really possible to be too beautiful for this world? For Barbara La Marr, it was.

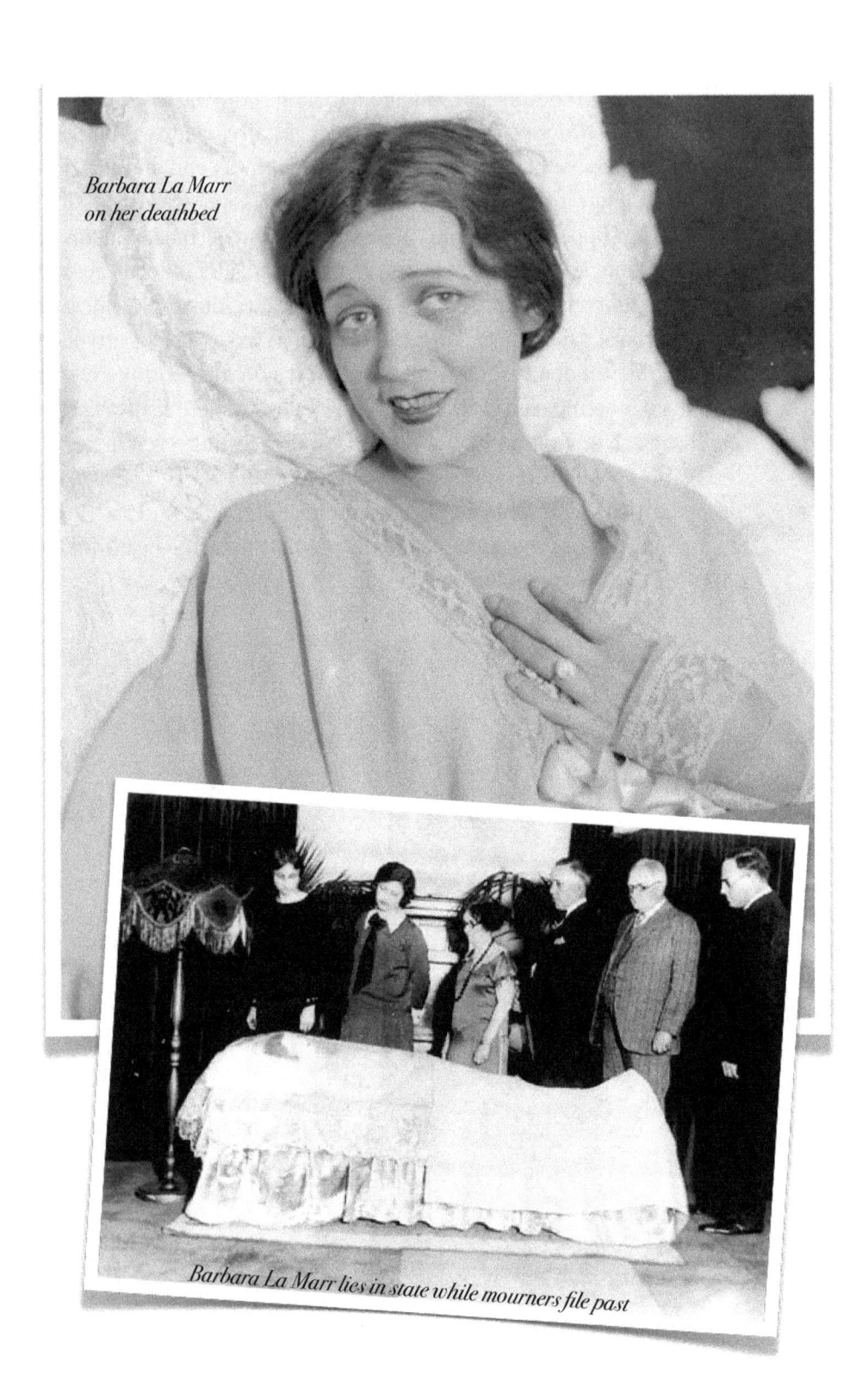

*Barbara La Marr on her deathbed*

*Barbara La Marr lies in state while mourners file past*

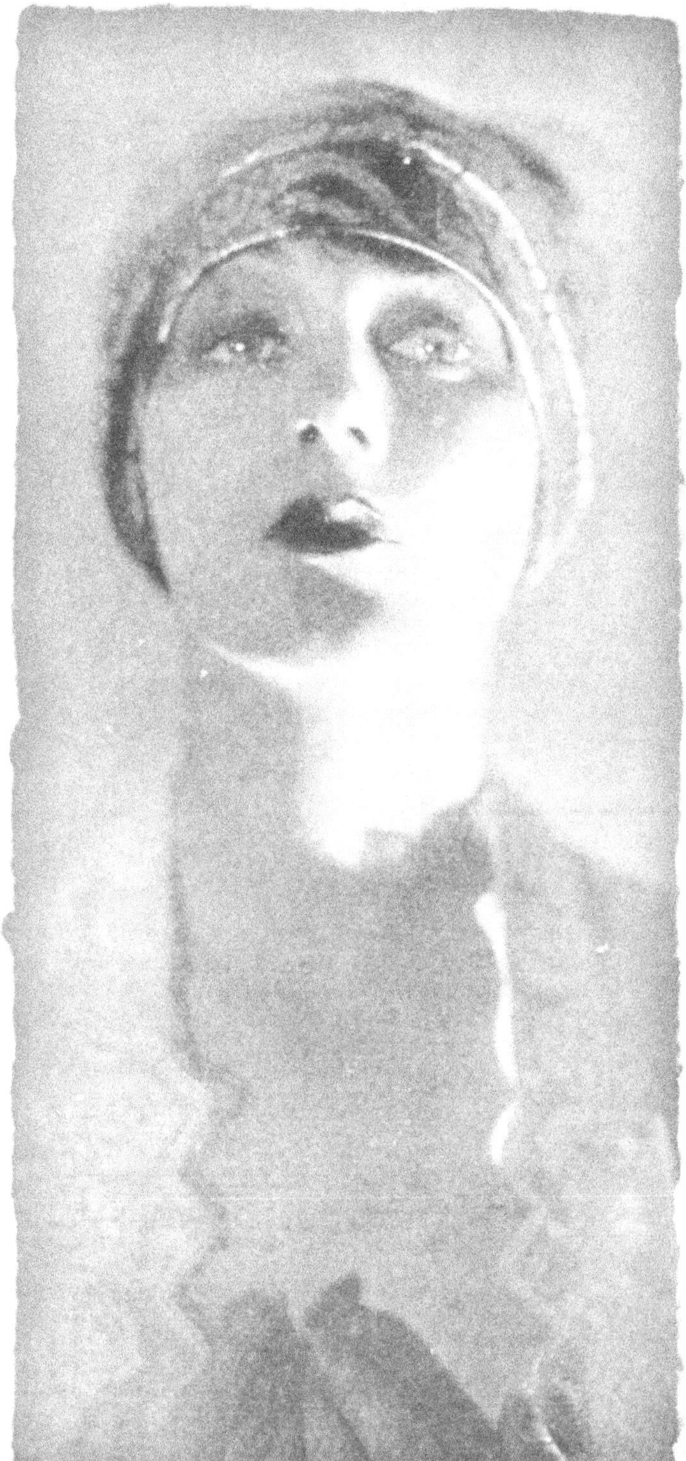

# By Their Own Hand

What is sadder than the death of a gifted, unique entertainer who is unable to see in themselves what the world seems to see so clearly? Few tragedies compare to the grief caused by the impetuous actions of a star who cannot see past their own abject misery to find redemption in the knowledge that things will get better. Depression is an ugly, ugly thing. It robs the world of the fragile, the beautiful and the delicate. In Hollywood, depression destroys those stars who are too honest to play the game, and too gentle to handle the consequences.

Freddie Prinze

*Freddie Prinze and Jack Albertson in Chico and the Man*

When *Chico and the Man* premiered in September of 1974, the young Puerto Rican comedian in the title role quickly became a major star. There was no long, drawn-out climb to the top for this man, no heavy-duty setbacks or paying of some significant dues. Freddie Prinze's rise to the top was a real example of a much overused hyperbole—he was literally an overnight sensation.

Not bad for a kid from Washington Heights in Manhattan. He was born Frederick Karl Pruetzel, to a Puerto Rican mother and a German father, in 1954. He was a chubby child, which made him unpopular in school. His mother introduced him to ballet, in the hope that he would trim down, and become more graceful. "I fit in nowhere," he said of his boyhood, "I was a miserable fat schmuck kid with glasses." The ballet worked like a charm, however, and soon Freddie developed a love of performing.

He enrolled in the prestigious Fiorello H. LaGuardia High School of Performing Arts, where he discovered his knack for comedy. But he was already showing signs of the restless spirit that would lead to his early downfall. Rather than stay at the school and further hone his craft while getting an education, he decided to try and make success happen faster. He dropped out at the age of sixteen, and found himself doing standup in New York at one of the most prestigious comedy clubs in the country, The Improv. He had a brilliant, intuitive grasp of comedic timing, and a particular talent for making audiences laugh at otherwise serious subjects. Much of his comedy revolved around the discrimination and harsh stereotyping that Latinos, and other ethnic groups, suffered in white society. Like Richard Pryor before him, he was able to make people laugh at very ugly realities, while pricking their conscience at the same time. He decided to change his last name to Prinze, dubbing himself "the Prinze of comedy," while often referring to his ethnicity as "Hungarican".

Freddie was so good that, in 1973, Johnny Carson invited him to be a guest on *The Tonight Show*, the highest honor a comedian in the '70s could hope to receive. Carson was known for discovering and encouraging new talent. He must have recognized how special Prinze was, because after Freddie's routine, Carson did something that was almost unheard of—he invited Freddie to come sit with him and chat. Seriously, people were shocked! Carson never did that. It was considered a high enough honor for a first time comedian just to be granted a five-minute stage appearance. A relationship was born, and Freddie became a regular on *The Tonight Show*, even guest-hosting on occasion. Not bad for a nineteen year old.

Freddie's high-profile debut on *The Tonight Show* led to an offer to play the title role in the new NBC sitcom, *Chico and the Man*. The show was about an elderly white mechanic who hires a cocky "chicano" kid, setting the stage for the comedic exploration of contemporary, interracial issues. It's almost as if they conceived the show for Freddy. The series was an immediate and huge success for the network, and soon Freddie was offered a five-year, six-million-dollar contract. In 1975, he recorded a successful comedy album, titled *Looking Good*, which was his catch phrase from the show.

Things were not all that they seemed, however. These were the 1970s, a time unparalleled in American history for its obsession with drugs and drug culture. The entertainment industry was particularly enamored with, and the comedy world was notorious for, its sanctioning of drug dependency amongst comedians who needed to be "on" and energetic late into the night. Who could forget Richard Pryor's flameout routine, setting himself on fire while freebasing cocaine in his home, or the brilliant Lenny Bruce and his heroin overdose at forty-one?

Freddie's youth, coupled with his astonishingly quick success, concocted a perfect storm, and he began taking drugs fairly early. Initially, it was coke to get him going and keep him going throughout the night. Then prescription Quaaludes, originally to help him battle clinical depression, but to which he quickly became addicted. Ah, the '70s, and Quaaludes, or "'ludes" as they were known on the street. They were prescribed by the dozens for everything from a toothache to anxiety, but all too often ended up as a common party drug. They earned the nickname "disco biscuits" because of their popularity in clubs. It lowered inhibitions, increased sensitivity, and was highly addictive.

Freddie had met Kathy Cochran, a Nevada cocktail waitress, and married her in the summer of 1976. Supposedly, she had been arrested twice for prostitution, but the charges were dropped both times. The marriage was spontaneous, and began to fizzle almost as soon as they said their vows. Freddie really didn't need a bad marriage to add to his already fragile mental state, but that's what he got. He also got a new baby, Freddie Prinze Jr., just a few months later. Eight months later, Kathy filed for divorce, and Freddie was forced to move out of their home and into a hotel. Kathy claimed she feared for the safety of herself and the child, saying Freddie—wasted on 'ludes—would sometimes fall asleep with a lit cigarette in his hand. He had also been arrested in November of 1976, for driving under the influence of drugs and alcohol. On his own, unrestrained by the home environment, Prinze's drug habits filled these spaces in his life like weeds taking over an empty lot.

He was missing his standup gigs in Vegas, and showing up late to the set of *Chico And The Man*. Tony Orlando, his best friend, said Freddie also began talking about suicide. They discussed it often at Orlando's home in the Hollywood Hills. Other friends said that they had begun receiving late night calls from Freddie, saying he needed peace, and he needed to go home. His last public appearance was at the presidential inaugural ball in January, 1977. He and his secretary, Carol Novak, were at his hotel on January 28, when he was served with a restraining order by Kathy. He would not be allowed to see his son. Distraught, he talked suicide yet again, and Carol told him to grow up. He went into the bedroom, and the next thing she heard was a gunshot, and something hitting the floor. She ran in to find Prinze looking up at her, grinning. "I fooled you!" he said. She called his psychiatrist, Dr. Kroger, who took away his gun and pills. Carol stayed with him that night, as she had done nearly every night that week.

The next day, Freddie showed up to the set whacked from the handful of Quaaludes he'd taken that morning. Guess he hadn't handed over all the pills? This was unusual, even for him, as he was usually enough of a professional to abstain while at work. Before he left the set that day, he phoned Dr. Kroger, demanding his guns and pills back. The ever-obliging psychiatrist left them with his secretary, and Prinze picked them up. Seriously, do you think maybe Dr. Kroger given this a wee bit more thought?

Back at the hotel, things went from bad to worse. Freddie was even more messed up on even more pills, waving the gun around, and threatening suicide again. The good doctor Kroger came over, at Carol's request, to try and reclaim the weapon, but Freddie was having none of it. Kroger did manage to remove the clip, slipping it into his pocket, but Freddie noticed, threatening to break his neck if he didn't give it back. Carol, exhausted, having spent days away from her own home and family while babysitting her unstable boss, left Freddie in the capable hands of Dr. Kroger, and went home. She called him as soon as she could, and when he answered, she asked if the doctor was still there. Freddie said, "No". Great.

Freddie made a series of farewell phone calls, including one to his business manager, Martin "Dusty" Snyder, at approximately 3 AM. Snyder rushed over, and found a completely irrational Prinze, sitting on the couch, and alternately placing the gun to his head, then taking it down to make more phone calls. Snyder tried to get him to give up the gun, but Freddie refused. He called his mother, then his ex-wife, telling them both, "I love you but I can't go on. I need peace." Snyder tried to reason with him, telling him he had so much to live for, and reminding him of his obligations to his mother, and his son, but it was like talking to wall. Freddie had made up his mind. He put the gun to his head one last time, and as Snyder lunged for the weapon, he fired a .32-caliber bullet into his brain. He was rushed to UCLA Medical Center, where he died thirty-three hours later. He was twenty-two years old.

People reacted to Freddie's death with the usual clichés: shock, disbelief, sadness. Everyone lamented the wasted life that once held such promise, blah blah blah. This guy had been crying out for help for months, yet only when it was too late did anyone pay attention. It's like that line in the song, "If I Die Young": "Funny when you're dead, how people start listening."

Freddie Prinze never blamed Hollywood for his problems. He said that Hollywood creates an environment where people can mess themselves up. That's an understatement. Freddie's son, Freddie Prinze Jr., went on to become a well-respected actor, and today, there is a whole generation that barely knows Freddie Sr. ever existed. His famous son knows. Of his father's legacy, Freddie Jr. said, "If people would only think of his gift instead of his death, I would love it. I have this album of his, *Looking Good*, and no matter how upset I was, anytime ever, the second I played it, he could make me laugh. I won't let people forget."

Freddie would have loved that.

# Peg Entwistle

Hollywood Boulevard: "the boulevard of broken dreams". There came to it a golden-haired girl, whose only dream was to be a movie star. But she was just one of hundreds. She was not striking or talented enough to set herself apart from the throng of other hopefuls, who regularly invaded the studios and talent agencies in search of a place in the spotlight. Yet, people still talk about her today. Her name was Peg Entwistle, and she did not live to enjoy her fame, as her only claim to it was in the method of her death.

She was born in Port Talbot, Wales, in 1908. Her parents divorced soon after, and her father was granted custody of Peg and her two younger brothers. The family decided to move to New York in 1913, so that her father, Robert, could pursue a stage career. She became enchanted with show business as she accompanied her father to his plays and watched his performances from the wings. Tragedy struck Peg early. In 1922, her father was killed in a hit-and-run accident in Manhattan. Sent to live with her uncle in Boston, she eventually joined a prestigious repertory company called the Henry Jewett Players. She got the attention of a little girl in the audience while she was performing in Ibsen's *The Wild Duck*, impressive enough in the role of Hedvig to inspire young Bette Davis, who cited Entwistle's performance years later as what inspired her to become an actress.

She joined the New York Theater Guild in 1926, and made her debut on Broadway that same year. She married an older man, Robert Keith, but it lasted only two years. Seems Keith had failed to mention his previous marriage to a crazy woman, and the ongoing custody dispute he was having over his six-year-old son, Brian (as in Brian Keith of *Family Affair* fame, who would go on to have a daughter who committed suicide, and who would commit suicide himself weeks after her). She would go on to appear in ten Broadway productions in six years. Her future as a respected Broadway actress was assured, and stardom a real possibility, but Peg had another kind of stardom in mind.

While on tour in the play, *The Mad Hopes*, in Los Angeles, she stayed with her uncle at his Beachwood Drive home in the Hollywood Hills. She was enchanted with the fairytale atmosphere of California, and its fledging entertainment industry. Three days after the play closed, she got a call from RKO Pictures, inviting her to screen test for a supporting role in the film, *Thirteen Women*, starring Myrna Loy and Irene Dunne. Peg was thrilled.

She got the part, and by all accounts, she did fine. However, after an initial screening, fourteen minutes of the film was cut due to poor audience reception, and most of Peg's part ended up on the cutting-room floor. It would be her only film role. RKO chose not to offer her a long-term contract. She spent the next six months auditioning, and being rejected, for every part she came across. Her finances dwindled until she could no longer afford to move back to New York, to rejoin the theater life she had so carelessly left behind. It was 1932, the edge of the depression, and the future looked grim.

Beachwood Drive is a narrow road that winds uphill towards the towering Mount Lee. In 1923, William S. Chandler, owner of the *Los Angeles Times*, was building houses in Beachwood Canyon, and decided to erected a massive set of letters at the top of Mount Lee spelling out the development's name: "Hollywoodland". Each letter was constructed of metal and scaffolding, and stood forty-three feet high. Four thousand light bulbs were used to spectacular effect, illuminating one group of letters at a time, "HOLLY", then "WOOD", then "LAND", before lighting the whole sign. It was very impressive. In the 1920s, the sign was not the iconic symbol of the film industry that it is today. It was just the remains of an old advertising campaign. As the popularity and influence of films and influence spread across the country, the term "Hollywood" took on new meaning, and the sign, new significance.

Peg lived in the shadow of that great sign at her uncle's home. Every time she left the house, its towering presence shone down on her. Its four thousand lights blazed, night after night, visible for miles in any direction. She must have felt almost mocked by the symbolism of the letters. Her clinical depression and seemingly failed career didn't help either. On the evening of Friday, September 16, Peg put on her hat, her high heels, her blazer and grabbed her purse, leaving her uncles house to visit friends, or so she said. Instead, she walked straight up Beachwood drive, to the sign.

The road runs about four miles up, and the rest of the trip crosses a steep incline of scrub brush and rocky terrain. This is not an easy climb in walking shoes during the day. Peg had on high heels, a skirt, and it was night. She must have been extremely motivated. The lights must have been blinding as she approached her destination, turning the night into day, at blinking intervals. A utility ladder still clung to the back of the letter H. She carefully removed her jacket, laying it on the ground

*The Hollywood Sign, 1940.*

beside her purse. Then she climbed up the utility ladder until she was standing at the very top of the sign, the lights burning into her eyes. The town that had coldly rejected her twinkled below as she threw herself off, slamming into the rocky ground five stories beneath the letter H. She was twenty-four.

Two days later, a woman was out walking her dog, and discovered the purse, jacket, and one shoe. She peered into the ravine, and saw Peg's broken body lying below. Inside the purse was a note that read, "I'm afraid I am a coward. I'm sorry for everything. If I had done this a long time ago, it would have saved a lot of pain. PE".

Peg Entwistle has received so much fame from her rash, desperate last act that it's a wonder no one else has followed in her tragic footsteps. She has become the embodiment of innocence crushed, dreams dashed, and lives cut short by the cruel reality of being one of hundreds, desperate for recognition in a business that gives no quarter, and no damn, for it's aspirants.

A persistent rumor has flittered down through the years, that an offer from the Beverly Hills Playhouse, for the lead role in a play about a woman driven to suicide, arrived in the mail for Peg the day after her body was discovered. That ending would be just too "Hollywood" to be true, wouldn't it?

# Marie McDonald

The truck driver could hardly believe his eyes. Was that…could it be…a woman wandering down the highway…in her bathrobe… in the middle of the night?! He pulled his mighty big rig over and climbed down. Approaching the middle-aged woman, silhouetted in his headlights, she seemed disoriented and a little banged up, so he offered her a ride into town. The next day, the papers exploded with the headlines "Wandering In Desert! Star Found Bruised, Beaten!" Thus began another bizarre chapter in the strange life of "The Body": Marie McDonald.

Marie was born in 1923, to a former *Ziegfeld Follies* dancer, and a prison warden, in Burgin, Kentucky. Yeah, don't ask. Her parents separated when she was seven, and her mother eagerly pushed Marie towards a future in entertainment as she developed into a beautiful teenager. She entered every small town beauty contest there was, including Miss Yonkers, Miss Loews Paradise, and Miss Coney Island. She won the Miss New York title for the Miss America competition, which brought her to the attention of George White, who cast her in his review, *George White's Scandals*.

She toured with the show, ending up in Hollywood after *Scandals* played the Biltmore Theater there. She posed for famous illustrator, Alex Raymond, who used her as the model for both Dale Arden and Princess Aura in the *Flash Gordon* series. She hastily married Richard Allord—a frat boy pal of Errol Flynn's—but had the marriage annulled three weeks later when she found out the diamond ring he gave her was fake.

While playing a chorus girl in the Busby Berkeley film, *Ziegfeld Girl*, she met Sir Charles Frederick Bernard, who helped her get into films. He got her set up with a standard contract for Universal Pictures in 1941, and she then got small roles in such films as *Melody Lane*, *It Started with Eve*, and *Pardon My Sarong*. A long career with Universal was not to be, however, and the studio dropped her contract after only one year. Signing with Paramount, she shined as a voluptuous secretary in the film, Lucky Jordan. She fell for high-powered Hollywood agent, Vic Orsatti, and married him in January of 1943. Her career was going nowhere though, with a string of small parts in less-than-A-class pictures that year. When her contract ran out, she let it go.

Signing with independent producer, Hunt Stromburg, she scored a few good roles, most notably in the drama, *Guest in the House*, which garnered her some of her best reviews ever. On the other hand, she was also tagged around then with the nickname, "The Body", by a genius publicity agent at United Artists; a title which followed her throughout her career. She became one of the most popular WWII pinup girls, appearing on the cover of Yank (at least they're honest), the Army weekly, twice in one month. After working in several other mediocre films, she broke her contract with Stromburg, suing him in court for failing to promote her career to the extent he had promised. She received nineteen dollars and sixty-seven cents compensation, for bus fair from San Francisco to LA. Where's the dream team at a time like that?

She starred in the *Heaven's Gate* of its day; an expensive, MGM-backed, musical flop titled *Living In A Big Way*, costarring Gene Kelley. Let's see, 1947, MGM, musical, Gene Kelley...how was this not a huge hit? Marie blamed it on the hatchet job that went down in the editing room: "No one saw that picture except my husband and my mother. It was a great script we had. Then it was torn in half and thrown out a window by a genius at Metro." Marie decided to wash this down with a trip to Reno, expressly to divorce Vic. While in Reno, Marie had a brief but tumultuous affair with mobster, Ben "Bugsy" Siegel. Bugsy also hired her to ride atop his float as "Queen Of The Flamingo" in the Heldorado Days parade.

Marie returned home, marrying millionaire shoe tycoon, Harry Karl, while swearing that "This is forever." She then toured across the country as a nightclub act. When she got back, she was cast in *Tell It To The Judge*, followed by *Hit Parade* in 1950. Neither film helped her floundering career, but she did score the juicy role of Billie Dove, in the stage production of *Born Yesterday*, at The El Capitan Theatre. She shone in that part, winning praise from critics and peers alike. It's too bad she hadn't done the play before George Kaufman cast the film role, or things might have turned out differently for Marie.

Meanwhile, her marriage to Karl had not gone very well. She was often ill, and her new millionaire husband dropped a quarter-million dollars on medical bills in an effort to determine why. She had many miscarriages (possibly due to her serious Percodan habit), and was arrested for a hit-and-run accident, and for driving under the influence of drugs. Karl, for his part, was charged with assault with a deadly weapon, and for trying to run down two reporters outside the courthouse. He felt throwing money at his marriage might fix it, so he gifted Marie a custom Cadillac Le Mans roadster. The car was equipped with a television set (in 1954!), a radio telephone, and a chrome and gold cocktail bar (not sure how they managed to fit all of that into a roadster). The paint job alone cost a fortune, as it was platinum dust-based paint. He was wrong. Even though Karl made Marie probably the first woman in the world to chat while driving, she divorced him right after that, saying the reason she was sick all the time was because she was, in fact, allergic to him.

Feeling that she may have been a bit too hasty, Marie set sail with Karl to Europe, attempting to re-marry him in four distinct countries, before finally returning to the 'States to have the happy nuptials in Yuma, Arizona. The marriage lasted all of a few months before they separated again. A third reconciliation also proved short-lived...and that's about when Marie was found wandering in the desert near Indio, California, cloaked in her bathrobe and visibly worse for wear, in the middle of the night.

Marie claimed that two men broke into her home, robbed and beat her, then forced her into their car, to release her in the desert several hours later. She was bruised, sporting a black eye, and two missing

*Marie spins her kidnapping tale to the press.*

teeth. Police were suspicious, however, when they found a ransom note in her fireplace that had been pieced together with letters from a newspaper found in Marie's house. They also found the novel, *The Fuzzy Pink Nightgown*, about a movie star who is kidnapped from her home and held for ransom. Hmm. To distract from these discoveries, Marie loudly opined that ex-husband, Harry Karl, must have been behind the kidnapping. She so obliging to the nice policemen, and put on her best house robe, as her living room and front yard filled with reporters eager to watch her reenact the crime. For once, she was the star of the show, and she basked in the attention. Eventually, Marie confessed that it was all a hoax; a desperate attempt to save her sagging career.

It worked…for a while. Marie put out an album that year, *The Body Sings*, which sold well. She divorced Karl again for the last time, and a million-dollar settlement. In 1958, she played in the Jerry Lewis comedy, *The Geisha Boy*, wonderful as a temperamental movie star (not exactly against type). She returned to the Moulin Rouge Theater—formerly the Earl Carroll Theater—where she was fired while still a chorus girl. This time, she was the headliner, and felt well-earned triumph as the curtains rose to a roaring crowd. Harry Karl was in the house, with an agenda. He paid minions to shower her with eleven bouquets of red roses as she took her final bows on stage, and when she returned to her dressing room, there was a $10,000 mink coat and a Cartier watch waiting for her. Seriously? Didn't she accuse him of kidnapping her the year before? Why did she divorce this guy again?

Marie could have had a long, enviable nightclub career, but she let go of the movie star dream, despite the profound frustration of it. She married two more men, Louis Bass and Edward Callahan, and if you've not kept count, that makes six marriages to five men in twenty years. That beats Liz Taylor's record. Speaking of Liz, Marie dated Michael

Wilding, who was married to Taylor at the time, but he would not leave her for Marie. Taylor dumped him for Mike Todd anyway, and the beat goes on.

In 1963, Marie did one last film, with another over-the-top, blonde dynamo—Jayne Mansfield. *Promises, Promises* was bad all-around, from the horrible set, to the tasteless, semi-pornographic end product. Jayne disliked Marie right away, probably out of jealousy (no one ever called her "the body"). Both stars were in their twilight years. Neither had been an A-lister, and both were reduced to doing semi-nude scenes while mugging outrageously for the cameras in an "independent" film that would be banned in several states upon release. Jayne thought Marie was getting special concessions and trying to upstage her (I'm sure she thought this about every actress she ever worked with), so she made Marie's life a living hell on set. Marie couldn't wait for the whole thing to be over.

Soon, it would be over for Marie. She had already tried suicide once, shortly after her second divorce from Karl. She was hooked on Percodan, and suffering from chronic insomnia. She had a nervous collapse while on a nightclub tour in Australia, and was committed to a psychiatric institution, from which she made a daring escape, claiming they were trying to brainwash her. Back in the 'States, she was arrested for trying to forge Percodan prescriptions, and placed on probation. She had bleeding ulcers, and her heart stopped during an operation to remove part of her stomach in an attempt to stop the bleeding. Unbelievably, she married for a seventh time, in 1964, to the co-producer of *Promises, Promises* (hmm, maybe she was receiving special treatment), Donald Taylor.

It was Taylor who found her slumped over her dressing table, dead from a overdose of either Seconal or Percodan, no one seems to know. She was forty-two. Her death was ruled an accidental suicide, but maybe Marie just got tired of it all. Taylor walked into that same room, and took a fatal overdose himself, two years later.

Marie desperately wanted to be a movie star, not just a novelty act. Too bad the drama in her real life far outweighed any performance she ever gave on film. The sad footnote to her legacy is that she is still remembered as "The Body," and not as the pretty, talented and versatile human being who gave Judy Holiday a run for her money in *Born Yesterday*.

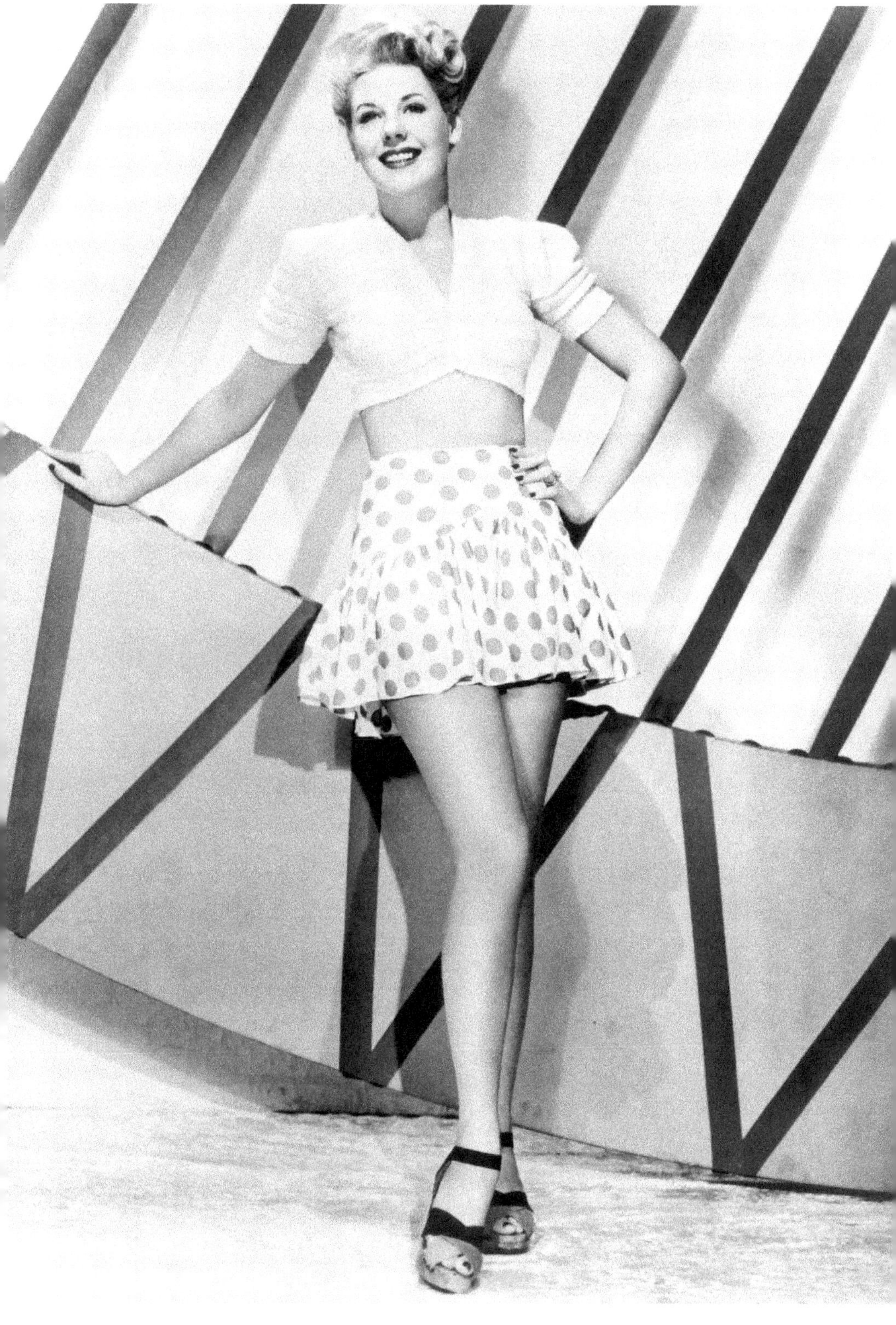

Margaux Hemingway

T he camera soft-focuses on a beautiful woman, her silk scarf blowing in the wind, the hint of a seductive smile playing on her lips, as she dabs perfume from a large bottle to place behind her ears. Her face is arresting, her cheekbones chiseled and high on her face, her mouth seductive and her thick eyebrows lend an almost scholarly impression. Cut to the same girl, floating down a river in an evening gown, drinking champagne and laughing, beside a gentleman in a tuxedo. The message is clear. You too can feel beautiful and live a glamorous life. Just buy this perfume, and the world is your oyster. But for the girl in the ad herself, it was an illusion; a cruel lie that she would be unable or unwilling to overcome; a sentiment that would eventually destroy her.

Photos and videos of Margaux betray the striking similarity between her and her famous grandfather, Ernest Hemingway. She had the same intense eyes, the same thick, dark brown eyebrows, and the same thoughtful expression. With those, she also inherited his restless spirit, his love of alcohol and his clinical depression.

Born Margot Louise Hemingway in Portland, Oregon, she changed her first name to Margaux after learning that her parents, Puck and Jack, conceived her after downing a bottle of Chateau Margaux wine. She grew rapidly from her awkward stage adolescence, and into a statuesque, six-foot stunner by age fourteen. Her family, including baby sister Mariel and elder sister Joan, moved back to the Hemingway family farm in Ketchum, Idaho; where her grandfather shot himself in 1961. Her father, Jack, was as fanatical an outdoorsman as his father was, and life on the farm was paradise.

*Margaux, and her sister, Mariel.*

Her beauty got her discovered. During a trip to New York, while lounging in the famed Palm Court at the Plaza Hotel, she was seen by promoter Errol Weston. He saw her potential on the spot. Almost overnight, she had a million-dollar contract as the spokesperson for Faberge's new perfume, Babe. It was the first million-dollar contract ever awarded to a model.

She moved in with, then married Weston, and hit the '70s disco party circuit. Studio 54 was a drug and celebrity infused, glittering den of iniquity that would spin anyone's head, but Margaux had been a regular there since she was a kid, sailing right past the velvet ropes, mingling with the likes of Liza Minnelli, Bianca Jagger and Andy Warhol. She appeared on the covers of *Vogue* and *Time*, and amassed a vast collection of designer clothes—mostly gifts from her modeling gigs. She was one of the first supermodels to be known by her name, and not just her face.

With the fame and attention also came the drugs and alcohol. Because she was famous, her age was no problem when she wanted a drink. She used to say "I don't need my ID. I have my eyebrows!" Studio 54 was well-known for its drug-friendly environment. It was the '70s! Literally everyone around her was doing them, including the rich and famous; her new "friends," whom she desperately wanted to impress.

What she had working for her in this was her relation to one of the greatest American writers of the 20th century. Celebrities are drawn to other celebrities, especially those whose mythos dwarfs their own. Her grandfather's larger-than-life legend went beyond his exquisite books and short stories. He was a towering figure: sportsman, adventurer, and an epic hellraiser. He was also an alcoholic, and to Margaux, living up to the name meant being able to drink herself into a stupor without it showing—partying all night at Studio 54, then ready and able the next day for those 6 AM photo shoots. A lot of substances are needed to accomplish that, even for the young. Margaux had a secret that made this lifestyle particularly risky. She was an epileptic, and had to take phenobarbital—a very powerful drug—to control her seizures. Alcohol and phenobarbital are a dangerous combination. Soon, she was also a coke fiend, and her marriage crumbled.

In 1976, she made her film debut in *Lipstick*, a slick mystery about a model who is stalked and raped by a psychopath. It also featured her baby sister, Mariel. The movie was terrible. The script, the direction, and the acting were all brutally panned by critics, and audiences stayed away. Mariel's performance was the one bright spot in the film. Critics raved about the fourteen-year-old, predicting a successful career ahead for her. Margaux felt the public had tired of her, and now sought the next Hemingway to fetishize. "It was as if people were tired of me and gave her all the attention," she said years later. The critics were right about Mariel. Her career took off, and she spent the next decade as an A-lister in Hollywood, while her sister spiraled into oblivion.

In 1979, Margaux married Venezuelan filmmaker, Bernard Foucher, and moved to Paris. Does it get more glamorous than that? A supermodel, a South American filmmaker, and Paris. Should have been bliss. It wasn't. They attempted a film project together, a documentary about her grandfather, which took four years of Margaux's life, going absolutely nowhere. Frustrated and depressed, she divorced for the second time in 1985, and turned down a darker road towards dysfunctional alcoholism. She gained seventy-five pounds, often contemplated suicide, and wondered what she was going to do with the rest of her life. She might have died back then, if she hadn't checked herself into the Betty Ford Clinic. She emerged from her twenty-eight-day stay confident that her life was back on track.

But the world had moved on. She was in her thirties, still ravishing, but in a town where youth is everything, she was over the hill. She had made one film since *Lipstick*, a French movie called *Love in C Minor*, which did nothing to further her career in America. Her options were limited, she owed money to the IRS, and she was in debt, so she decided to take Hugh Hefner's offer, and pose nude in *Playboy*.

OK, so now that's out of the way, where does an out-of-work actress go from there? Margaux couldn't answer that. There were no offers, either for modeling or films, so she embarked on a spiritual journey that would take her from a shaman's tent in the northwest, all the way to the shores of India. Things went badly in India, however, where her behavior became erratic in a culture with strict social guidelines. She spent time in an Indian jail before friends and family were able to bring her back to the 'States and hospitalize her. She was losing her grip on reality.

By the mid-'90s, she had alienated most of her family, and was living alone in a rented bungalow in Santa Monica. She had only been living there for three weeks when it all came to an end. On July 1, having not heard from Margaux for three days, her friend, Judy Stabile, went to the apartment to check on her. She got no response when she knocked, so she peeked in through the bedroom window, and saw a horrific scene.

Judy enlisted the aid of a nearby construction worker to break into the house. He took two steps in, then quickly stepped back out, saying the smell was overwhelming. They called police. The scene was more than a little strange. Margaux's nightstand had been set up like a pagan altar, with human- shaped candles, pendants encircled by a white satin ribbon, and pieces of paper that had been crumpled into the shape of hearts. On the pieces of paper were written "love, healing, protection for Margaux forever." Margaux's body was badly decomposed, severely bloated, and her skin blackened and slipping. She had been lying in there with no air conditioning, in the Southern California early-summer heat, for three days. She was found thirty-five years—almost to the day—from her grandfather's death. She was forty-one. The long goodbye was over.

The odds were stacked against Margaux. Her great grandfather, grandfather and uncle had all committed suicide. Mental illness and alcoholism were family traditions, never addressed, always swept under the great, all-encompassing fabric of the Hemingway legacy. Margaux based her self-esteem on her appearance, and when her looks began to fade, she had nothing else to hold onto, so she just fell. She kept on falling until she hit the bottom, and checked out with an overdose of phenobarbital.

The sad truth is, Margaux had really checked out years before. The woman found dead in Santa Monica barely resembled that girl who sold millions of bottles of perfume, and floated down a river in an evening gown, all those years ago.

Maybe she never really was that girl at all.

# Lupe Vélez

*Jimmy Durante, Lupe Velez, and the Mills Brothers in Strictly Dynamite (1934)*

The elaborate bedroom was straight out of a Hollywood movie set. The floor covered in a thick, plush white rug; floor-to-ceiling mirrors on the walls; candles and flowers positioned to confer the hushed effect of a chapel. Two huge portraits of a beautiful woman hung across from each other, while a huge ten-foot wide bed, with massive black, silver and gold headboard, dominated the space. Above the headboard, a giant gilt crucifix. Lying in the bed, swathed in white satin sheets, full stage makeup, and a lovely formal gown, was the "Mexican Spitfire" of movies, Lupe Vélez. She looked ready for her close-up, Mr. DeMille—her last one. Decades later, a vile little Hollywood hanger-on would tarnish this image, with allegations of a vomit-laden trail leading from the bed to the bathroom, and a woman whose head was jammed down a toilet in a decidedly grotesque and unglamorous pose, drowned. It's time to set the record straight.

Lupe was born in San Luis Potosi, Mexico in 1908. A gifted dancer, she adored performing from an early age. As a child, she sold kisses to men, in exchange for portraits of her favorite movie stars. In 1927, she moved to Los Angeles, and caught the eye of producer Hal Roach, who cast her in her first film, *Sailors Beware*. She followed this up with a breakout role in the Douglas Fairbanks adventure film, *The Gaucho*. At first, Douglas Fairbanks didn't think she exuded enough spunk for the character, but when a stagehand stole her dog as a prank, the barely five-foot-tall actress severely beat him, and seeing this, Fairbanks he hired her on the spot. *Gaucho* made her a star.

Lupe wasted no time in living up to her various nicknames, which included The Mexican Spitfire, The Tornado, The Hot Tamale (racist, I know), The Hot Pepper, and the not-so-subtle Whoopee Lupe. Her temper itself was famous, as were her numerous and highly publicized love affairs. Her lovers included Charlie Chaplin, Douglas Fairbanks, Clark Gable, Tom Mix, John Gilbert (must have been on the rebound from Garbo), and many others. She had a reputation for outrageous public behavior, including violent public brawls with her love interests, and crude, cockfight-and-pornography punctuated private parties. She left scars on her lovers, both physical and mental, and crammed several lifetimes of baggage into her brief tenure on this earth. She said "I do not like to see any one man too often. The same face over and over. Pretty soon his nose begins to look like the nose of a dog to Lupe.", and "People want to talk and I like to give them something to talk about." Often compared to the other Latina Hollywood star, stoic Delores Del Rio, Del Rio's classier image was a stark contrast to Vélez's childish shenanigans and publicity stunts.

She went on to play exotic leads in several well-received films, including *Resurrection*, *West of Zanzibar*, *The Half-Naked Truth*, and (what else) *Hot Pepper*. She got involved with a very young Gary Cooper in the late '20s, and their public brawls made the headlines for three tumultuous years. Lupe proclaimed that Cooper had the biggest organ in Hollywood (and who would know this better?), but not the ass to push it in well." This is blush-inducing stuff, people. Vélez was notoriously jealous, reportedly tailing Cooper wherever he went, and insisting on being on the set whenever he made a movie. In an act that gives *Scent of a Woman* a whole new meaning, she once unzipped his pants in public, went down on her knees and smelled his crotch, proclaiming she could smell another woman's perfume. Cooper wanted to marry her, believe it or not, and all good Catholic girls want to get married (don't they?), but his mother did not approve. Wonder why. When he finally married someone else, Lupe didn't take it so well. She followed him to the train station, pulled out a pistol and shot at him, narrowly missing as he dove into to a car. Wow, spitfire indeed.

In 1934, Lupe licked her wounds by marrying male physical perfection personified, Olympic champion and *Tarzan* star, Johnny Weissmuller. She left her mark on this man as well, or should I say marks, as in scratches, bruises and bites. This girl needed to learn that passion is one thing; violent rage another thing entirely. Her appetite for sex was insatiable, and it has been said that she loved like a wild animal. Her sexual aggression knew no restraint, and she flirted with the description "nymphomaniac". The marriage lasted five years, which is shocking in and of itself.

She began making a series of pictures called *The Mexican Spitfire*, which became the work for which she was best known. The series exploited her race and her reputation so overtly that it seems unlikely she would ever have been able to overcome the typecasting fallout, and be allowed to play different, more serious roles. As the popularity of the theme waned, she found herself on the far side of her thirties, no longer young by Hollywood standards, and dating a smalltime Austrian actor who worked part-time dubbing French dialogue in films for Warner Brothers—quite a comedown from Gary Cooper and Johnny Weissmuller. His name was Harald Ramond, and she soon found herself pregnant with his child.

According to most written accounts, when Lupe informed Ramond about the pregnancy, he was cavalier and aloof, refusing to marry her. Lupe's own suicide note served to skewer his reputation by leaving the world with the impression that he was a heartless cad, who abandoned her, and their child, to their fate. "To Harald. May God forgive you and forgive me to take my life and our baby's, before I bring him up with shame, or killing him. Lupe". However, Ramond told a newspaper years later, that Lupe had been the love of his life, and that he intended to marry her, but they had yet to set a date. Really?

I guess no one told Lupe. Despondent, and acutely aware that news of an illegitimate child would destroy what little remained of her career, she bid farewell to a few friends on the evening of December 14, 1944, then climbed the stairs to her lavish master bedroom suite. She lit candles, arranged flowers, dimmed the lights, dressed herself with great care, then descended into her massive bed, took seventy-five Seconal tablets, and died. She was thirty-six. Here's where fact and myth diverges. In Kenneth Anger's infamous slash-and burn, tell-all mess *Hollywood Babylon*, Lupe doesn't actually die in her bed, but is suddenly awakened with violent nausea, and crawls, puking all the way, to her bathroom toilet, where she passes out with her head still inside the toilet bowl. Her housemaid discovers her the following morning, still as she passed out, with her head stuck in the toilet. Since the only accounting of this ever happening comes from Anger, and is not backed up by any official reports or eyewitness accounts, the only conclusion to be drawn is that Anger was mistaken (I'm being polite).

In the recent biography about Lupe, *Lupe Vélez: The life and Career Of Hollywood's Mexican Spitfire*, author Michelle Vogel dug up a little-known memoir published by former Beverly Hills chief of police Clinton H. Anderson. Anderson was the first man on the scene of Lupe's suicide. He states in his memoir, *Beverly Hills Is My Beat*, published in 1960, that Lupe was found dead in her bed. As Michelle reminds her readers, seventy-five Seconals is a debilitating, lethal dose that would have knocked the petite Vélez comatose in minutes. Michelle also puts forth the theory that Lupe was actually pregnant by Gary Cooper, who was married to someone else, and in any case, done with Lupe, so she knew her options were limited. Its hard to believe her last act on this earth would be to destroy the reputation and career of an innocent man in order to protect Coopers' reputation, but then who really knows what she was thinking? Abortion is a sin, but suicide is a...lesser one? She doesn't want to "kill" her baby, but she's okay with taking both thier lives instead of just the one? Sounds like she wasn't really thinking at all.

It's sad that Lupe Vélez has now slipped into the shadows of obscurity, remembered for her horrific death, when she is remembered at all. It's safe to assume that if Anger had not mentioned her in *Hollywood Babylon*, her name would have passed even further into oblivion. Lupe Vélez is a good example of how fame, or infamy, is truly a mixed blessing.

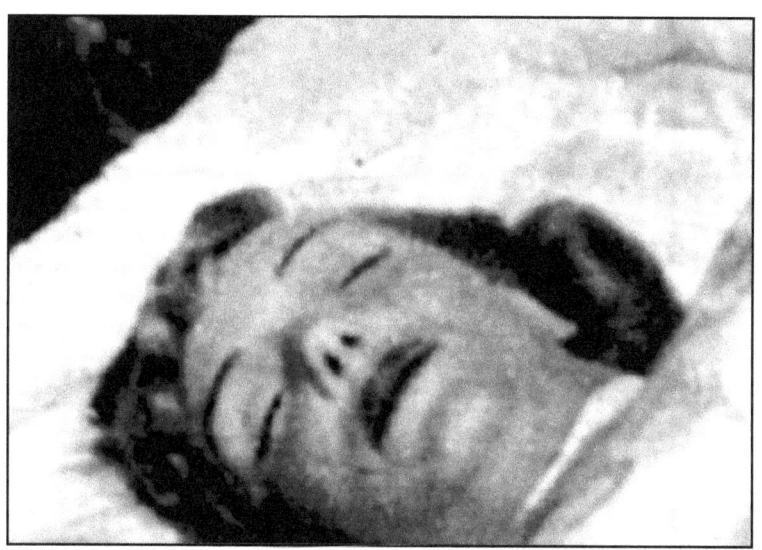

*Lupe Vélez at her funeral.*

Jean Seberg

The beautiful teenager with the ponytail and the tight-fitting, yet professional suit demurely resisted looking directly at the man standing behind the camera questioning her. Smiling nervously, she answered: "My name is Jean Seberg." "Where are you from?" he asked. "From Marshalltown, Iowa." "When were you born?" "November 13, 1938." "That makes you what age?" At this, the girl's eyes search upwards as she leans forward. "Seventeen...and eleven months." She is breathtakingly beautiful and charming, both in her innocence, and in her freshman attempt at sophistication. She would later become an overnight sensation, and sadly, the target of a vile character assassination campaign by an arm of the US government. This is the story of Jean Seberg, and what the FBI did to clean-cut, all-American Midwestern girls in its frenzy to keep America "safe from dangerous leftist influences."

Jean was like something sent from central casting; a corn-fed beauty straight from the heartland of the country who wanted to be an actress. She was almost too pretty to be "the girl next door", and that wasn't just publicist hype. Her father was a pharmacist, and her mother, a school teacher. It doesn't get much more Americana than that. She grew up in a Lutheran family, wore white gloves with pearl buttons, attended church every Sunday, and appeared in school plays. Like a million other pretty girls, she dreamed of being discovered, being plucked from the masses and set aside for stardom. Unlike a million other girls, Jean's dreams came true.

Her drama teacher, Carol Dodd Hollingsworth, along with a wealthy entrepreneur named J. William Fisher, realized her talent and potential. They wrote to director Otto Preminger about Jean. He was conducting a nationwide search for an unknown actress to star in his new film, *Saint Joan*, based on the stage play by George Bernard Shaw. Apparently, her small town connections won her a coveted reading in front of Preminger, and off Jean went to Chicago. Preminger was enchanted by Seberg's innocence and natural, spontaneous acting style. He brought her out to Los Angeles for a screen test, and cast her as the martyred French heroine shortly thereafter.

This girl was just seventeen, had only acted in high school plays and now was the star of a major Hollywood film. Otto, a notorious taskmaster, put the entire responsibility of the film's success on her young shoulders. Plus, it was fucking Joan of Arc, a role that laid waste to far more established actresses. He was very cruel to her on set, yelling at her in front of the crew, and she often broke into tears. In the climactic burn-at-the-stake scene, Jean's costume really caught fire, giving her mild burns and a fear of redoing the scene. The cameras captured that genuine trepidation, and that fear made it into the final cut. In his biography of Jean, David Richards wrote that Otto took Jean's sincerity and "stomped it into the ground", often requiring her to perform twenty takes or more for the most trivial of scenes.

Unsurprisingly, the picture bombed. It didn't just bomb; it really bombed, as in a *Heaven's Gate*-style disastrous fail. Critics panned Jean's performance as woefully amateurish and uneven. *The New York Times* wrote: "Miss Seberg, who emerged the winner in a well-publicized international search to play the soldier/saint, is, for all her evident sincerity, callow and unconvincing in a long, difficult and complex part." Otto got his share as well, with critics calling his directorial style of distant camera angles and impossibly long, uncut scenes indulgent and lacking intimacy.

Even so, Otto cast Jean again in his next film, *Bonjour Tristesse*, based on the novel by Francoise Sagan. Some say he was obsessed with making Jean a star and controlling the trajectory of her career. Gee, were he and Alfred Hitchcock comparing notes? Once again, Otto was abusive during filming, often threatening to replace her with Audrey Hepburn. Despite stellar costars, David Niven and Debra Kerr, this film flopped as well, with critics again dissing Jean's performance. *The New York Times* suggested she be sent back to that small town high school stage, and the *New York Herald Tribune* said she was horribly miscast as a French nymphet. This last failure virtually ended her mainstream Hollywood career. Too bad the same could not be said of Preminger. When she commented on Otto years later, Jean said, "He was the most charming dinner guest, and the most sadistic director."

She married millionaire, Francois Moreuil, while filming *Bonjour Tristesse*. The relationship was not a happy one. She chose to marry in Marshalltown, and the hometown crowd sensed a distinct pretentious hardness in the demeanor of their golden girl, a quality that had not been there when she left them, two years prior. Meanwhile, Otto hastily sold her contract to Paramount. "Preminger got rid of me like a used Kleenex." Jean remarked. Paramount cast her in *The Mouse That Roared*, which did fairly well with the artsy set. She sought to hone her acting chops, and applied to the Actors Studio, but they didn't even bother saying no.

Things started looking up for Jean when her husband introduced her to avant-garde French director, Jean-Luc Godard, who then had Paramount loan her to him for his film: *Breathless*. *Breathless* was not a mainstream, Hollywood cookie-cutter movie, but it brought Jean worldwide acclaim for her largely improvised performance. It was one of the first of a film movement known as French New Wave cinema, a style that was lampooned often, usually filmed in sharp black and white, featuring emotive characters talking in metaphors, angst-ridden and depressed, against stark backgrounds. Jean wore her hair in her now-famous pixie style, which became all the rage, even turning up on Audrey Hepburn.

Riding the wave, Jean returned to Hollywood, making *Let No Man Write My Epitaph*. It bombed, and Jean returned to France. In 1963, she married novelist, Romain Gary and had a son with him: Alexander Diego Gary. After making several French art films, Jean returned to the States to make *Lilith*, opposite Warren Beatty. This one was way ahead of its time. Think *Girl, Interrupted*, only more shocking. A female mental patient with nymphomania and schizophrenia becomes the obsession of an occupational therapist, who goes mad over her. *Lilith* was too artsy and non-conformist to win at the box office but Jean garnered the best reviews of her career. *The Washington Post* commended her for her "beautiful grasp and projection of the role." Today, the movie is considered director Robert Rossen's masterpiece, and it remained Jean's favorite, as well as the one she was most proud of.

Jean set about making herself a star of international appeal and renown, starring in a series of foreign films as the hapless wife, nymphomaniac, jewel thief, and spy. She did a mundane film for Universal called *Moment to Moment*, which failed at the box office, due mostly to bad direction and script. *Pendulum*, with George Peppard—did better—explored abuse of government power, a subject that keenly interested Jean. How ironic that she, herself, would fall victim to such abuse in just a few short years. She costarred in big-budget, musical-western, *Paint Your Wagon*, which was panned by critics, but did okay in theaters.

Rumors of a passionate affair with Clint Eastwood on set circulated. In 1970, she costarred in *Airport*, winning praise for her lovesick airline agent who pined for Burt Lancaster.

By *Airport*, her marriage to Gary had disintegrated. They divorced that year, but not before a rumor hit the press that Jean was pregnant by a well-known, Black Panther activist. Years later, it came out that this rumor was concocted by order of J. Edgar Hoover himself, to punish Jean for her financial contributions to the Black Panther Party and other "leftist" organizations. Under the Freedom Of Information Act, the shameful and sinister machinations of the FBI against Jean Seberg and others was laid bare for all to see. The FBI, using the Counter Intelligence Program, or COINTELPRO, conducted a vile smear campaign against Seberg based solely on Hoover's assumption that she must be sleeping with one of the Black Panthers, why else would she be donating to their organization. What? That's right. Hoover, in his twisted, dirty mind, could not wrap his brain around the fact that a beautiful, blonde Midwestern girl from Iowa could possibly support civil rights simply because she...supported civil rights! According to him, she must surely be somehow corrupted and compromised by a godless, biracial relationship that tainted her judgment, like a sexy black anti-American Satan. I did not just make that up. The stated goal of this operation was the "neutralization of Seberg" and "to cause her embarrassment and harm her image with the public, all while taking the usual precautions to avoid identification of the Bureau."

*Los Angeles Times* gossipist Joyce Haber published a piece about Jean on May 19, 1970, after receiving a "tip from a reliable source": "Let us call her Miss A...She is beautiful and she is blonde...Recently she burst forth as the star of a multimillion-dollar musical. Topic A is the baby Miss A is expecting. Papa's said to be a rather prominent Black Panther." *Newsweek* immediately reprinted it the following week with the added bonus of identifying "Miss A" as Jean Seberg, and the national distribution of this lie was assured. One part of the story was true. Jean was six months pregnant, but with her husband's child. Distraught, she took a massive overdose of pills, and was found unconscious on a beach on the island of Majorca, where she lived with Gary. He committed her to a Swiss mental hospital, where she miscarried two months later. The child, a girl they named Nina Hart Gary, weighed only four pounds, and was clearly white. Jean put the fetus in a glass coffin, and took it home to Marshalltown. She wanted everyone to see that it had all been a dirty lie, and it killed her baby girl. Gary claimed that Jean attempted suicide every year on the anniversary of the miscarriage. She would succeed, eventually.

The FBI's bag of dirty tricks didn't begin or end with mere bad publicity. Files released after Jean's death prove that they had her under surveillance—both in Switzerland and France—for years, and tapped her phone often. Jean was aware she was being stalked and monitored, and the stress weighed on her emotionally and psychologically, eventually driving her over the edge.

She and Gary sued *Newsweek*, as well as other publications, finally receiving a little over $10,000. They clearly didn't have the right lawyers. They went their separate ways, and Jean began a free fall from sober reality and into the dark realm of depression, barbiturates and alcohol. She had an affair with a Mexican gaucho while filming *Macho Callahan*. In *Kill*, the director was her ex-husband, Romain Gary, who remained in her life. Critics hated both films, and noted Jean's less than stellar appearance; how ill and tired she looked. In 1972, she married director Dennis Berry. Jean spent the rest of the '70s acting in French and Italian films, appearing only once in an American production, *Mousy*, with Kirk Douglas.

In her last years, Jean's social drinking became chronic alcoholism. Her marriage to Berry fell apart, and she went into steep decline. She bounced aimlessly from affair to affair, while Romain Gary watched helplessly, unable to stop the love of his life from destroying herself. At the time of her death, she was living in Paris with an Algerian boyfriend. She left the apartment on August 30, 1979, and was not seen alive again. It was the anniversary of her daughter's death. Jean took two bottles with her; one filled with water, the other with barbiturates. She was found ten days later, naked and decomposing beneath a blanket in the back seat of her Renault. She clutched a note, addressed to her sixteen-year-old son, Diego, which read: "Forgive me. I can no longer live in a world that beats the weak, puts down the blacks and women and massacres the infants. Understand me. I know that you can and you know that I love you. Be Strong. Your mother who loves you, Jean."

Days after Jean's body was discovered, FBI bureau chief William Webster held a news conference in which he confessed the FBI's crimes against an innocent, fragile woman, which contributed substantially to

[Newspaper clipping: Los Angeles Times, Friday, September 14, 1979 — headline "FBI Admits Spreading Lies About Jean Seberg / Circulated Story About Black Baby"]

her eventual demise. "The days when the FBI used derogatory information to combat advocates of unpopular causes have long since passed. Those days are gone forever." Thank Gawd Almighty for that, however this was no consolation for those who loved Jean, or Jean herself. Romain Gary tried to carry on, but the specter of his tragic love, a woman he could never truly let go of, haunted him until his own suicide, in 1980. Jean's son, Diego, was left an orphan under the shadow of both his parents' tragic fates. He eventually married, and lives an ordinary life, working in a bookstore in Spain. God bless him. Jean would have appreciated that. She is barely remembered today, other than for her failed first attempt at pleasing the world, in *Saint Joan*. Oh, and also for being one of the more famous people that the US government managed to unjustly kill in the name of patriotism. It's really a toss up, who had the more tragic life, *Saint Joan*, or the sad little girl who portrayed her.

At least Joan of Arc was canonized.

*Jean Seberg's grave in Montparnasse Cemetery, Paris.*

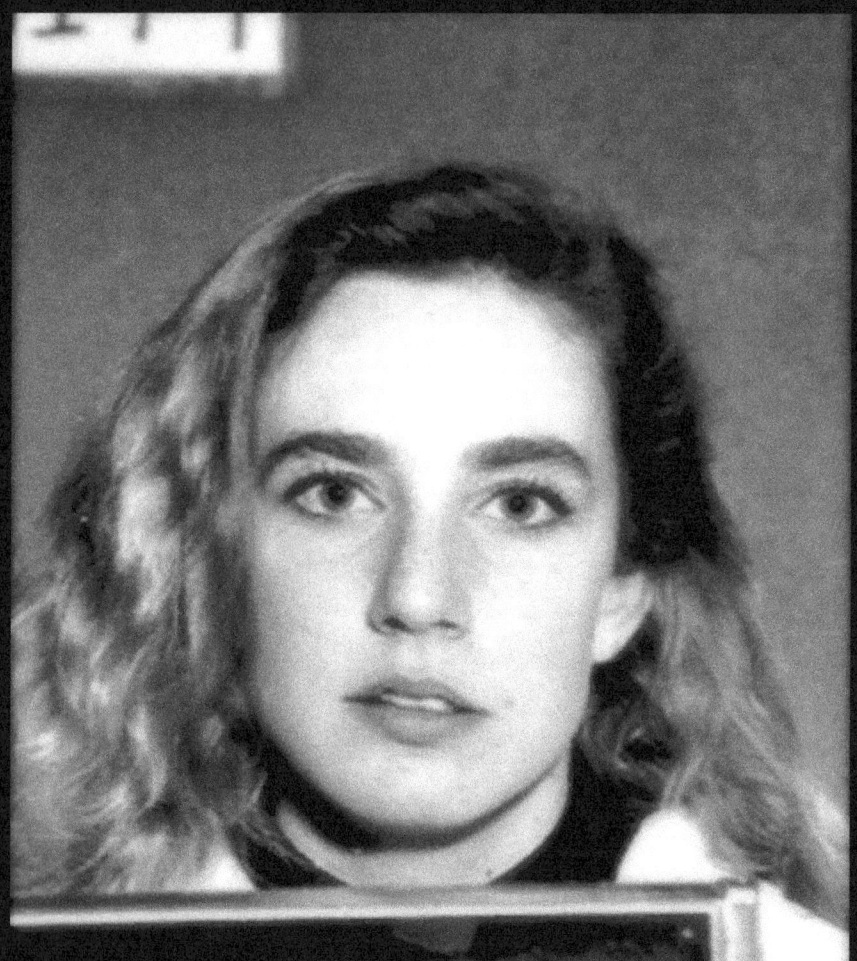

# Dana Plato

"**G**et this girl out of here! She's a has-been and a druggie!" the man with the thick Brooklyn accent hissed into the phone. "She just needs to admit that she's a ex-druggie, ex-con lesbian with mental health problems!" The girl at whom those comments were directed responded with polite restraint. "How do you know this, sir?" There was no answer. The host of the radio show chimed in, "That's a little rough, don't you think?"

It was *The Howard Stern* show. Stern had built a career out of humiliating semi-celebrities on the air for laughs. On this day, his guest was Dana Plato, the freckle-faced girl from *Diff'rent Strokes*, who had suffered a spectacular and very public fall from grace after she outgrew her childish appeal.

A few minutes later, another caller chimed in with more hurtful things to say. "You're loaded! You're lying! Why don't you get a urine sample from her?!" The drum beat for getting a urine sample from Dana began in the studio, with Howard leading the charge. They even plucked a strand of hair from her head, for testing later. Dana struggled to tolerate all of these indignities with good humor, but underneath her forced indifference there was a rising tide of darker emotion. She did not break down when caller after caller hurled unnecessarily cruel judgments at her, but she wept openly when two listeners offered kind reassurance and words of understanding. "I just want to tell you that I'm recovering and I believe everything you're saying. I understand," the young male caller told her. "Thank you sir." She said quietly, as she cried.

"Wow, you're really hurting, aren't you?" said Stern, as if this notion had just occurred to him. "I'm just tired." Dana said, choking back tears. "You're tired of it all?" he asked. "I'm just tired of it all. I'm tired of having to defend my character over and over and over again." She said, her voice cracking. "Did you ever consider suicide?" Stern asked. "Oh hell no!" she immediately answered. "I have a beautiful boy, so no. I'm okay in my skin. I'm okay with who I am, you know?" Earlier in the interview she had asserted, "My life is good. I've never been happier."

The next day, she was dead of a drug overdose. She was thirty-four.

It's easy to dismiss Dana Plato as yet another child star who couldn't adjust to the loss of stardom that came with adulthood, and self-destructed. It's less easy to look seriously at the issues of teenage addiction, and how the entertainment industry casually disregards child stars, then acts surprised when they become dysfunctional adults. Dana's fate was due in part to her own choices, but the culpability of the industry—which has a nasty habit of creating self-destructive, shattered people then walking away—is under-explored.

Dana was born to an unwed teenage mother on November 7, 1964. She was adopted by Dean and Kay Plato the following August. Kay had big plans for her new daughter and as soon as Dana could walk and talk, Kay took her to audition for commercials and television shows. By the age of seven, she had been in over a hundred commercials for brands such as KFC and Dole. She also showed promise as figure skater, and spent long hours practicing at the skating rink. She had bit parts in films such as *Return to Boggy Creek* and *Beyond the Bermuda Triangle*. Dana said Kay forced her to turn down the role of Regan in *The Exorcist*, as well as that of the child prostitute in *Pretty Baby*, because the two roles were not suited to her clean-cut image. She was training to try out for the U.S Olympic figure skating team and tried out for *The Gong Show*, where she was spotted by Al Burton, and offered a costarring role on his new sitcom, *Diff'rent Strokes*.

The show was a study in contrasts. A wealthy, white, middle-aged widower with a daughter adopts the two sons of his late black housekeeper, resulting in an evenly mixed yet unrealistically happy family. The set was tense almost from the start. Gary Coleman, who played the youngest boy, immediately stole the show. He was precocious and impossibly cute, owing much of his appeal to a genetic kidney ailment that stunted his growth, keeping him perpetually childlike. Dana and Todd Bridges (who played the elder boy) soon had reputations for wild behavior, on the set and off. The first three years were relatively smooth. Gradually, Bridges and Plato grew resentful of Coleman's spotlight. Coleman seemed to not age at all, while Bridges and Dana grew further every year from childhood cuteness into teenage awkwardness. The show soon revolved around Coleman, who became a huge star and cultural icon with his catch phrase "Whachu talken 'bout, Willis?", while Bridges and Dana saw their importance steadily diminish.

Dana was struggling with another crisis in her life. Kay was diagnosed with scleroderma, a truly awful disease that causes the slow hardening of the body's soft tissues—both inside and out—essentially mummifying the body, and resulting in a slow death. Kay was all Dana had, her adopted father having left them when Dana was a baby. The only contact she had with him was after she became famous, when he sued her for support, and lost. Kay spent long periods in the hospital, while Dana turned to alcohol and drugs to help her cope. When she was fourteen, she OD'd on Valium in her first suicide attempt.

In 1983, five years after she was cast on *Diff'rent Strokes*, Dana was fired. She had told the producers that she was pregnant by her rockstar boyfriend, Lenny Lambert. An unwed teenage mother had no place on the squeaky clean series, and she was let go. It was the last straw for the producers, who had put up with a lot from Dana, including coming in drunk and smoking pot on the set, and just not coming in at all. She was no longer the cute little girl they had originally cast, so it wasn't a hard call to make. It would be all down hill for Dana from there.

She married Lambert in April,1984. Wedding photos show a beaming Dana, looking like a little girl playing dress-up, with the lights of Las Vegas behind her. In July, she gave birth to a baby boy named Tyler. The marriage crumbled almost immediately, due mainly to Dana's inability to adjust to life outside the limelight. She and costar Todd Bridges would stay out all night together, clubbing and getting high, while Lambert was left at home to take care of their son. When she was home, they had terrible fights, and Lambert claims Dana was often reckless and irrational. She once threw herself into a plate glass window. Finally, Lambert had enough, and walked out on Dana, taking Tyler with him. Alone, addicted and angry, Dana walked into the hospital room of her gravely ill mother, and screamed at her to hurry up and die. Kay obliged, passing away the same week Dana's husband walked out.

Broke, feeling abandoned and without options, her addictions grew. She did what many desperate actresses do when trying to boost their career; she got breast implants and posed nude for *Playboy* in 1989. How many hopeless actresses have littered the glossy pages of *Playboy*? This only backfired on her. The public was aghast that little Kimberly Drummond would bare all in a nudie magazine after they had grown to love her as the spunky girl-next-door.

Dana received no acting offers after *Playboy*, and by the following year—having spent her centerfold money— she was forced to work for minimum wage at a dry cleaning store in Las Vegas. The press lapped this up, publishing videos and photos of her at work, with salacious headlines blaring how far the *Diff'rent Strokes* girl had fallen. It got her fired too.

In 1991, she held up a video store with a pellet gun, absconding with less than $200. The cashier recognized her, and told 911 she had been held-up by Kimberly from *Diff'rent Strokes*. Dana must have thought better of it, as she returned to the store with the money, only to be promptly arrested. So began her troubles with the law. When singer, Wayne Newton, heard about her arrest, he put up the $13,000 to bail her out, even though they had never met. Again, the press had a field day. She was given six years in prison, but the judge took pity on the freckle-faced defendant, and commuted her sentence to five years probation with four hundred hours of community service. She was also appointed a psychiatrist, whom Dana claimed got her hooked on Valium. She was brought before the court again, for forging Valium prescriptions, and again placed on probation. She behaved herself,and all seemed well when she her legal scrutiny ended in 1995.

Her legal problems might have been behind her, but her financial ones were not. She worked in soft porn films to pay her bills, the most notorious of which was *Different Strokes...The Story of Jack and Jill... and Jill*, which exploited Dana's previous role as an innocent girl on a family sitcom, showing her completely naked and making love to a woman. The contrast between these themes was enough to garner serious publicity for the movie and Dana, though not the kind she wanted. She opted to come out as a full-fledged lesbian, even appearing on the cover of *Girlfriends* magazine. In an interview conducted by respected lesbian journalist, Diana Anderson-Minshall, she announced to the world that she was a lesbian. Later, when Howard Stern and others interviewed her, she passionately denied it. This girl was seriously confused. Then, there was the video game. The less said about this truly degrading episode, the better. The game was called *Night Trap*, and was one of the first games to overlay live actors with CGI to create one of the slimiest, most violent pieces of crap ever sold to the public. Was there anything that Dana considered beneath her?

She cleaned up her act briefly, when she moved out to Oklahoma to get back with her ex-husband, and thier beloved son, Tyler. Managing to play the perfect mom for one year, she then fell off the wagon, gave up the pretense, and was using again, even in front of her twelve-year-old son, who found her drug paraphernalia strewn about the house when he came home from school. Lambert asked her to leave. She went to a bar, met a man, struck up a conversation, and was engaged to him a few days later. She scraped together enough money to buy a used motor home, and the two set up house in the camper, parking the vehicle in front of his mom's house. House warming gifts to themselves included lots of drugs.

Howard Stern to the rescue. Or not. Dana decided to do the infamous *Howard Stern* show to clear her name, as an acquaintance had gone on days prior, claiming she and Dana were hot lovers and that Dana was living on the streets. Howard had the most successful radio show of its kind in the country at the time, with three million daily listeners. Dana needed the exposure like she needed another drink, but she must have bought into the old adage, "There's no such thing as bad publicity." It was a disaster. Dana came off sounding pathetic, desperate, and less than honest about her current life and her substance abuse. In the high-camp fashion that he was known for, Stern waffled between feigned sympathy for her feelings, and tasteless gestures, such as forcing her to give a hair sample to prove she was clean. He made lewd offers to comfort her when she broke into tears at the sympathetic comments of one listener, and asked if she wanted to sit on his lap. Most of the callers were brutal, spewing cruel, senseless vitriol at Dana who tried to fend them off with insincere indifference. It was great stuff for the ratings, and everyone seemed to be having a good time, until Dana went home to her camper, and killed herself the next day.

Dana died of a drug overdose at the age of thirty-four. The coroner listed her death as suicide. It was mother's day. Her son, Tyler, was at home, clutching the gift he had picked to give him mom for mother's day, waiting for a call that would never come, and he never got over it. At his mother's memorial service, he wept openly, a little boy in a big man's suit, trying so hard to be brave. He followed in his mother's footsteps, becoming an addict like her. In 2010, at the age of twenty-five, on the eleventh anniversary of Dana's death, he blew his brains out, three days before mother's day.

There is a video of this beautiful girl, her face sprinkled with sun kisses, doe-eyed and innocent, patiently explaining to a reporter that people who have addictions do things they are not proud of, and that those people need help. She looks like a child, but her words betray her. She possesses the essence of innocence, but her eyes are full of a pain that innocence does not know. She is alone, even with a camera shoved in her face. She was everyone's little girl, and then she was just a little girl lost: lost to herself, lost to her dreams, lost to her son, and lost to us.

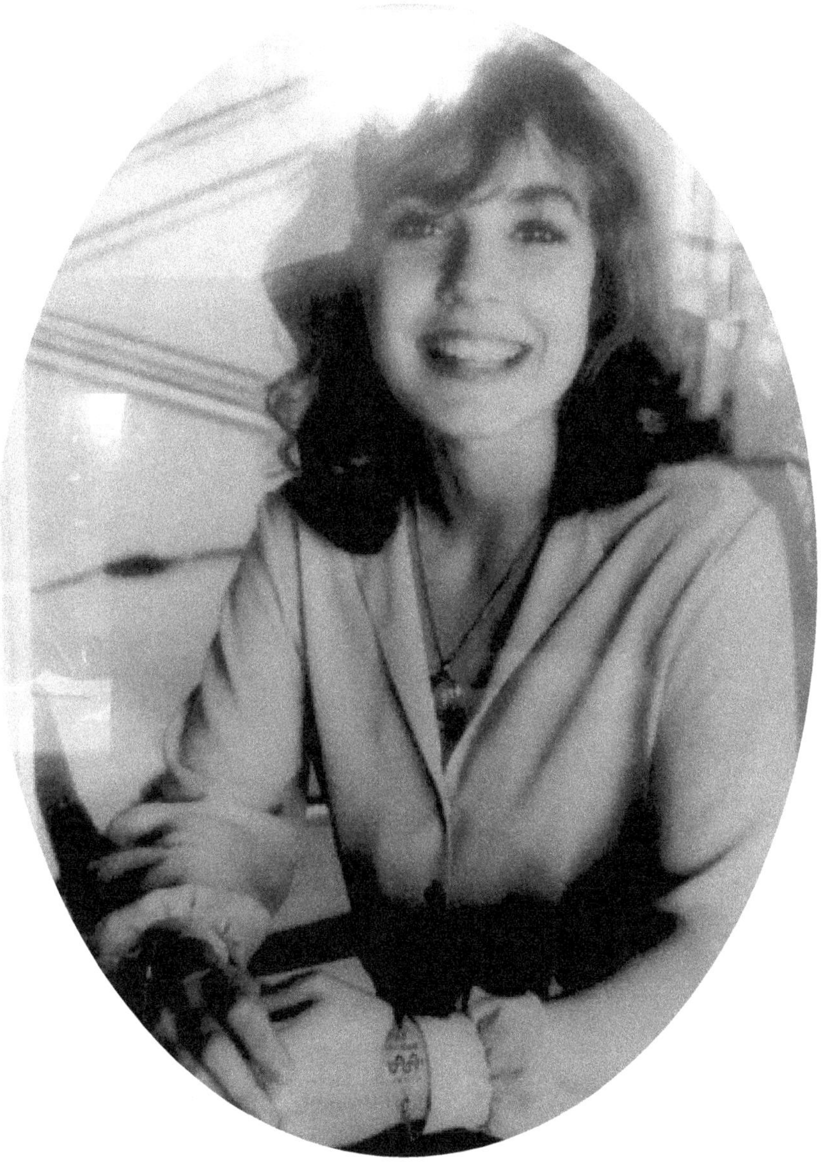

# Tragic Blondes

Blondes: a word conjuring images of gorgeous and curvaceous women, posing in cheesecake splendor, or shimmering in pure Technicolor glory on a silver screen. Descriptions such as "Blonde Bombshell", "Buxom Blonde", "Blonde Goddess", "Dumb Blonde" have been around since Jean Harlow—the first platinum blonde—blew audiences away back in the 1930s. Tragic blondes could easily be added to this list. A brunette can be stunning, but she is never referred to as a bombshell. A redhead is fiery, but she is not a goddess. Neither are ever "dumb" by virtue of the hair color. What is it about blondes that make them special/infamous/ridiculed? It's just a hair color, isn't it? Or is it? Perhaps there are more complex reasons for our cultural fascination with blondes; their lives, their figures, and ultimately, their downfalls. Blondes seem to suffer more often from tragedy than their brunette and red-haired sisters, and to top it off, they are often perceived as deserving such hardship. Society seems to run hot and cold on these women based solely on the color of their hair, and how much a part that plays in their fate can be understood by looking into the lives of tragic blondes.

Jayne Mansfield

Mention Jayne Mansfield today and the first image that pops into most people's mind in that of a headless corpse, lying beside of a two-lane highway. She is not remembered for her vibrant wit, nor her amazing curves, or her glowing platinum mane. Her few movies faded into oblivion, her tireless publicity stunts long forgotten. The woman who took the stage by storm with a single role, played classical violin, and had an IQ of 164, is sadly remembered today only for her horrific death. What's even sadder is that this image is a lie, another of the falsehoods Kenneth Anger graphically detailed in that trash heap of a book that will not die: *Hollywood Babylon*.

Vera Jayne Palmer was born on April 19, 1933, and into the quite suburban landscape of Bryn Mawr, Pennsylvania. Her mother, Vera, was a school teacher, and her father, salesman Herbert Palmer. Her father died suddenly from a heart attack when Jayne was just three years old. Some believe that this left her with emotional scars that filled her with a constant, almost unnatural need for male attention. When Jayne was still in elementary school, she showed signs of being a violin prodigy. The violin is one of the hardest instruments to master, and most children can't play it at all. Jayne probably could have been a professional violinist, had she not developed stars in her eyes just then. She was also gifted at piano, viola and bass fiddle.

One day, Jayne woke up, and realized that she had the breasts of a well-endowed, grown woman. She was barely a teen. Boys and men also noticed this, and despite her mother's struggles to keep her all buttoned up and well-hemmed in, she became popular for all the wrong reasons. She didn't seem to care about the reasons. Attention was attention, as far as she was concerned. This motto would stay with her throughout her life. An older man seduced her when she was sixteen, and Jayne panicked at the possibility of being pregnant—a huge no-no in 1950s small-town America. She immediately jumped into marriage with the first gawking, drooling, high school boy who asked her: Paul Mansfield. It turned out to be a false alarm, but the following year, she did give birth to her first child, Jayne Marie.

Domestic life bored this bursting bundle of jittery energy to tears. She loved her husband, and doted on her baby girl, but Jayne never stopped yearning to be a movie star. It's interesting that her ambitions did not include becoming an actress first. She told Paul, shortly after they were wed, that she would soon leave for Hollywood, and that he could see her starring in the movies after that. When Paul returned from a stint in the army reserves, Jayne pleaded with him to move out to Los Angeles so she could pursue her dream. He obliged. They packed up the family car, and Jayne Marie, drove out west, and bought a small bungalow in the San Fernando Valley. Jayne began to pound the pavement.

She hired an agent, who immediately had her hair dyed platinum. Hollywood did not roll over and beg. She began to spend money like a star, purchasing a hot pink Jaguar, and an expensive wardrobe, while her husband and daughter toiled away in the valley. She probably figured that if she wanted to be a star, she better look the part first: blonde ambition made manifest. She was cast in a B thriller titled *Female Jungle*, as the third or fourth lead, but it was a paying gig, and covered a few car payments.

Paul decided he didn't want to be "Mr. Jaynie Mansfield" for the rest of his life, so he ditched Jayne and his daughter, and moved back to Texas. Undaunted, Jayne continued to pose for cheesecake photos, and cut ribbons at supermarket openings. Then she met James Byron, publicity wizard extraordinaire! Byron saw a diamond in the rough in his new protégée, and assumed control of her career. He booked her on a publicity tour to promote a film she wasn't even in, *Underwater*, starring Jane Russell and Debbie Reynolds. The press seemed to lose interest in Reynolds and Russell when Jayne showed up, bursting out of her too-small red bathing suit and cooing, in that little girl voice of hers, that she just wanted to be a movie star, like Shirley Temple. Then, when she jumped into the pool, and the top of her bathing suit came off, well... cut, print it boys. A star, or something, was born.

There was no stopping her after that. Soon she posed nude for *Playboy*. Surprisingly, that didn't kill her career. In fact, Warner Bros. actually decided to give her a seven-year contract because of it. She signed with the studio on the same day she filed for divorce from Paul. She kept his name, though, saying it sounded like a star. Warner Brothers lived up to it's reputation for signing new talent and wasting them in one awful film after another. Jayne was cast as a cigarette girl in *Pete Kelly's Blues*, as a knockoff Marilyn Monroe in a knockoff of *Asphalt Jungle* titled *Illegal*. She played a gangster's moll in *Hell on Frisco Bay*. She did have a juicy second lead in a Columbia film, *The Burglar*, and got decent reviews for her role as a jewel thief's ward.

She was soon gracing the covers of every kind of magazine imaginable, from *Showgirls* to *Mr. Annual* (*Mr. Annual*?!) This was the mid-'50s, and huge breasts were "in like Flynn". Men returning from the Korean war wanted their women buxom, flirty and gravity-defyingly curvaceous. Jayne fit that bill perfectly. She wasn't coy about her assets, even posing for a photo in a director's chair with her 40-21-35 measurements printing on the back. Really? Subtle was not in her vocabulary. She did not believe there was such a thing as being overexposed, and never met a publicity stunt she didn't like. She cooed like a child, and ooooed like slut, always on cue, and in front of the cameras.

After a promising start, her career stalled. With her film career going nowhere fast, Jayne accepted the lead in the Broadway play, *Will Success Spoil Rock Hunter?*. Coincidentally, the character was a blonde bombshell. Hmm. Of course, she nailed it, and the play went on to become a smash hit, playing more than four hundred forty-four times. Suddenly, she was the toast of Broadway, and a respected comedic actress. Hollywood again took note of Jayne, and she appeared on the cover of *Life* magazine.

While living in New York, she attended Mae West's new club act in the Latin Quarter of Manhattan, out of curiosity. Jayne lit up when she saw one of the dozen beef hunks with whom West surrounded herself on stage. His name was Mickey Hargitay, and when they locked eyes, it was lust at first sight. This didn't go over well with the queen of ego, Miss West, who insisted the married Hargitay renounce Jayne—also still married, by the way—at a hastily arranged press conference. Mickey, instead, went all gaga, publicly professing his undying love for "Miss Thang", until one of Mae's bodyguard's shut him up with a right cross in the jaw.

Jayne returned triumphantly to Tinseltown swathed in mink, escorted by her new muscleman boyfriend, and talking up her new lead role in the major motion picture, *The Girl Can't Help It*. Still regarded today as pioneering in the genre of popular-music-meets-high-camp, *The Girl Can't Help It* combined Jayne's cartoonish sex appeal, with performances by some of the greatest rock-n-roll legends of the day. Jayne essentially played herself, as she had done in *Will Success Spoil Rock Hunter?*, except this time she was a singer rather than an actress. One scene had her wiggling out on stage in a skintight, red-sequined, strapless evening gown; looking for all the world like the Disney cartoon character, Jessica Rabbit. The resemblance is striking, and it's clear Jayne was the inspiration for Ms. Rabbit four decades later.

The film was a hit, and Jayne was immediately cast as the star in the movie version of her smash Broadway play, *Will Success Spoil Rock Hunter?*. The studio sent her on a forty-day, sixteen-country, European tour to promote it, which included an invitation to meet the Queen at the film's London premier in 1957. Jayne was riding high. She would never reach this level of legitimacy in her career again.

Jayne's over-the-top mannerisms mimicked her over-the-top lifestyle, which she happily shared with the entire world. No shy, reclusive

star here, folks, just a huge publicity whore willing to do absolutely anything to keep her name in the papers. She invited cameras into her pink mansion in the hills of Benedict Canyon, bought with inheritance money. It came complete with a heart-shaped pool, pink heart-shaped bed, and a pink heart-shaped tub, nestled inside a bathroom that had been covered from floor to ceiling with pink shag carpet. She even had a fountain in the foyer that spurted pink champagne. I guess pink-colored water was too ordinary. The entire house was pink, inside and out. There was usually a pink poodle wandering around as well. In case you're still in the dark, pink was Jayne's signature color. Of course, it wasn't actually her favorite color, but she felt it photographed well.

Wherever she went, she traveled with an entourage of bodyguards, photographers and animals, as well as trunks full of furs, designer clothes, and jewelry. There are numerous photos and publicity reels of her posing poolside in a bikini, sucking in her stomach so hard her bellybutton must have been pressing into her backbone. This girl was always "on", even when it was more appropriate to be "off." Fox Studios sold her to the public as "Marilyn Monroe King-sized!" and Jayne did her level best to live up to that title. When Director Frank Tashlin foolishly asked her why she wanted to be a star, pointing out it was a life of no privacy and heartaches, she smiled and said, "I like the Jaguars and minks." Well, okay then!

Jayne made one serious film before her career took a nosedive into that great empty infinity pool known as "washed up". It was called *The Wayward Bus*, and it was based on the John Steinbeck novel of the same name. This is her only performance where the words subtle and Jayne can actually be used in the same sentence without a punchline. She played a melancholy stripper who falls for a traveling salesman against her will, while traveling on a bus.

Critics praised Jayne's work, and she was rewarded with a costarring role opposite one of her idols, Cary Grant, in an insipid, poorly-written disaster called *Kiss Them For Me*. Jayne was again playing an impossibly dumb cartoonish blonde who loses out to a classy, cool redhead, played by model Suzy Parker. Her advisers told her not to take the part, but Jayne wanted to work with Grant, and besides, it was a role she knew oh so well. The movie flopped–one of Grant's few missteps– and Fox lost interest in Jayne.

In 1958, after their respective divorces were final, Jayne and Mickey were married in a small chapel, in front of thousands of gawking fans and several members of the press. Fox had decided to ignore Jayne, so she took her act to Las Vegas. Headlining at the Tropicana for weeks, she earned an unheard of $25,000 a week—ten times what Fox paid her. Take that, Marilyn! *Playboy* came knocking again, and she again posed for a photo spread. This time, the photos were only semi-nudes, and were considered more tasteful than her previous centerfold. Her sharp wit was exposed in an on-camera phone interview she granted to acrimonious nerd supreme, gossipist Hyde Gardner, in 1958. "Jayne you've been crowned Queen Of Uranium, Miss Peanut Butter and Jelly, Bluebonnet Bell of Texas. Now of all your honors, which title do you cherish the most?" he asked, with only half his tongue in his cheek. "You know which title I like?" She cooed, "I like to be called mother." The sardonic smile that flashes across Gardner's face was priceless. "Touché, dear." He replied.

Mary Hargitay, Mickey's ex-wife, was not having as much fun, and filed a petition for more child support from her stray husband. Mickey and Jayne answered her petition with a plea of poverty (yeah, you heard that right), despite the fact that they had just purchased a mansion in Beverly Hills, and Jayne still had money left over to keep her poodle dyed pink. Jayne signed a sworn statement claiming she slept on the floor of her estate because she couldn't afford to buy furniture. The judge laughed (no really, he did!), and Mary's petition was granted. The press rolled it's collective eyes, and Jayne received the first seriously negative publicity of her career.

Jayne certainly earned her favorite title, "mother" (five times over, eventually). She was this walking contradiction—her unruly boobs escaping from their almost spiritual restraints in one photograph, then posing with one baby in her arms and three at her feet in another. Fox wanted to cast her in *Bell, Book and Candle* opposite James Stewart and Jack Lemmon, but she had to turn down the role due to pregnancy. Big mistake. Her career was already on shaky ground, and that would turn out to be the last decent part she was offered for a long time. In 1959 she had a role in the western, *The Sheriff of Fractured Jaw*—a poorly received film that had the distinction of being the last mainstream film of her career. The producers of *Fractured Jaw* tried to cast her in the Paul Newman comedy, *Rally Round The Flag, Boys!*, but both Newman and

*Mansfield on the set of Too Hot to Handle (1960)*

his wife, Joanne Woodward, disliked Jayne, and made the studio cast Joan Collins instead.

The next few years were not pretty for Jayne. She left her twenties and her youth behind, entering her thirties and a period of financial and career difficulty. Three more children would follow in quick succession, while Fox loaned her out repeatedly to European studios, where she made one terrible film after another. Then something really weird happened. Jayne went missing! Two days later, she and Mickey turned up on a sandbar, apparently stranded there after a boating accident. The pictures of Jayne covered in a blanket and looking like shit were plastered all over the press, and people buzzed that it was just another one of her wild publicity stunts. Come on! This was Jayne Mansfield people! There was no way she would allow herself to be photographed looking like a chewed cat toy if she was staging a publicity stunt! For the first time in her life, she seemed hurt by publicity.

By the early '60s, Fox had dropped Jayne, her marriage flatlined, and her looks were eroding. She appeared in public visibly plumper. Her face looked puffy due to alcohol and prescription drug abuse. Seeking to bolster her frail ego, she had multiple extramarital affairs. One night, Mickey walked in his bedroom to find her with two strange men in their bed, drunk. He forgave her, maybe because they had three (soon to be four) children together, and the marriage waddled limply on for another year.

In 1962, the same year Fox dropped Jayne, Marilyn Monroe died from a drug overdose, and the era of the blonde bombshell was officially over. In truth, Marilyn Monroe had that whole fragile, girl/woman thing down, where as Jayne was seen as this crude, oversexed slut who was more object than woman. In the beginning, she really did give Monroe a run for her money, but she played it out quickly, and the public would always prefer the "vulnerable little girl" to the "aggressive sexpot."

No one was knocking on Jayne's door anymore. *Playboy* to the rescue again! Only this time, the photo spread Jayne did was so explicit, so vulgar, and so shameless that Hugh Hefner was actually arrested and booked on obscenity charges. He was forced to defend himself in a well-publicized trial that must have made Larry Flint proud. Jayne then shocked more people (as if this were possible) by appearing nude in a truly awful movie called *Promises, Promises*. She was the first well-known star to cross this barrier, and it was out of pure desperation. OMG, stop the madness!

Jayne entered a period in her life that shall henceforth be called "the supper club nudie years," in which she would appear at nearly any establishment, and do nearly anything, for money. Most of these shows were little more than striptease acts, but Jayne always referred to them as "parodies." She appeared regularly in regional theater productions of famous Marilyn Monroe films, such as *Bus Stop* and *Gentlemen Prefer Blondes*. While she was doing *Bus Stop* in some Midwestern dump, she fell in love with the director, Matt Cimber. She informed Mickey, and he obligingly agreed to a divorce. That was a long six years. She married Matt in Mexico, and returned home with bruises as a souvenir of her honeymoon.

Jayne had become hopelessly addicted to diet and sleeping pills, in addition to alcohol. She began to have a more difficult time keeping that 21" waist in check after four pregnancies and a diet rich in booze. She realized, even before the wedding cake was decimated, that she had made a mistake with Matt, but it was too late. She spent endless hours on the phone to long-suffering ex-husband, Mickey, pouring her sad heart out and lamenting her choices. "I loved her but I was powerless to do anything," Mickey said, "She was married to another man."

Baby number five came along, and Jayne temporarily cleaned up her act. Her husband took charge of her career, and she made some of the worst movies of all time during this period. She was offered, and turned down, the role of Ginger in *Gilligan's Island*, and her own television show never materialized. Disenchanted with both her career and her husband, she filed for divorce from Matt, and hired powerhouse attorney Sam Brody. She was afraid Cimber would try to take custody of their son, claiming she was an unfit mother due to her addictions and lifestyle (how silly). Brody, who was married with kids, went a little crazy over Jayne, and left his family to pursue his pink passion, showering her with jewelry and other expensive gifts. Not a wealthy man, he borrowed $250,000 from Jimmy Hoffa and the mob to win his love's heart.

In the midst of all of this chaos, her six-year-old son, Zoltan, was badly mauled by a lion during his mother's publicity shoot at a place called Jungle Land, in Sherman Oaks. The press fallout was immediate, as people were angered that the boy wasn't there on a family outing, but as a tag along on yet another of Jayne's endless bids for attention, and had probably not been properly supervised. He developed meningitis, and was given a fifty-fifty chance of survival. He did pull through, but Jungle Land didn't. Brody sued the park, and won a $1,600,000 settlement for Jayne, forcing the Jungle Land to close. Fortunately for Jayne, she had already won custody of her infant son from Matt Cimber, or things might have gone differently for her in that regard.

She went from one brutal relationship to another, moving in with Sam Brody, who was suddenly inclined to throw punches, instead of diamonds, at her. Brody had been involved in the trial of Lee Harvey Oswald, Jack Ruby's trial, and he knew how to be a bully. He didn't limit his bad guy antics to Jayne either. He harassed, intimidated and beat sixteen-year-old Jayne Marie as well. Think Nelson from *The Simpsons*, only meaner. Everything came to a head with Jayne Marie when she walked into the Beverly Hills police station sobbing, with visible bruises and welts, saying Sam beat her with a belt. As Jayne Marie told the story, both her mother and Sam had been as drunk as two Irish Rovers on Sunday, and while Sam wailed on her, her own mother egged him on by saying "Beat her more! Beat her like you beat me!" Wow. Jayne Marie was placed in protective custody, and the press held another Jayne Mansfield BBQ.

In 1966, she invited herself to the San Francisco Film festival, and the event chairman was not pleased. He held a press conference in which he stated, "She was not invited. She came by herself. I finally approached her and said, 'Madam, I don't know how much a pound you are charging, but I will pay it if you will leave.' I suppose it would be nice to have some sexy starlets at the festival, like they do in Cannes. In my opinion, Jayne Mansfield does not fit the bill." Ouch. Yes, because the San Francisco Film Festival can afford to be picky, being so prestigious and all.

While in San Francisco, she decided to stop in at The Church of Satan, and get herself ordained as High Priestess. The church's founder, Anton LeVey, took a shine to our Miss Mansfield, but he didn't care for Brody, placing a death curse on his head for supposedly "abandoning" the church. Jayne kept her high priestess certificate framed and hanging in her pink bedroom at her pink mansion. True story.

Amazingly, during this E-ticket, meteoric free fall, Jayne was offered a small role in A-list Hollywood movie, *A Guide for the Married*

*Man*. She gave a truly charming performance opposite wonderful British actor, Terry Thomas, as a (what else) busty dumb blonde who, after her and Thomas's illicit tryst, can't seem to locate her bras. "Oh don't worry!" she chirps, "If your wife finds it, she'll just think it's hers!" Thomas gives her huge cleavage a sideways glance and replies, "Don't be ridiculous." Tsk tsk, Jayne. This temporary career reprieve did not last, and soon she found herself in England, playing coal and stockyard venues for money. The shows were verged on porn, with Jayne playing Jayne, which she again insisted was a parody. She became a caricature of her own ridiculous image, now sad and outdated in the age of Twiggy, Bob Dylan, and the feminist movement. Admittedly, she did try to update her look, with huge bouffant wigs and heavy, exaggerated '60s eyeliner, but it all just looked pathetic and artificial. When she returned to the states, only supper clubs were offering her jobs.

On the evening of June 29, 1967, Jayne wrapped up another highbrow striptease at the prestigious (tongue in cheek) Gus Stevens Supper Club, in Biloxi, Mississippi. She, Sam, three or four Chihuahuas (seriously, what's with the Chihuahuas?), three of Jayne's children (Miklos, Zoltan and Mariska) and a twenty-year-old driver named Ron Harrison, all piled into the borrowed 1966 Buick Electra (owned by Gus Stevens himself!) for a long overnight drive to New Orleans, and a scheduled local television appearance there the following morning. Jayne made one last phone call to Mickey, telling him not to worry about the kids, that they would be asleep in the backseat the whole trip.

Thirty miles outside Biloxi, on highway 90, they ran into a dense fog caused by a pesticide truck spraying for mosquitos ahead of them. Directly in front of the Buick was an eighteen-wheel truck. When the truck entered the pesticide fog, the driver threw on his brakes because he was suddenly blinded. Unfortunately, Ron Harrison didn't, and the Buick smashed into the back of the semi with such force, the entire top of the car was sheared off as it became wedged underneath the trailer section. Estimates put The Buick at around eighty miles per hour. Jayne, Ron and Sam were killed instantly, as was at least one of the dogs. Incredibly, all three children survived with minor injuries. Accident photos circulated the world over, depicting what appeared to be a blonde head wedged in the windshield wipers on the dashboard of the mutilated car. Thus, a gruesome urban legend was born. Another, lesser-known photo shows Jayne, her body lying on the side of the road; her

*Jayne Mansfield on stage just hours before her death.*

head still on her shoulders, but horribly crushed. The blonde "head" on the dash was either a wig, or her actual scalp. Jayne was thirty-four. It was good riddance to Brody, sad for Harrison, who probably had a hard time keeping his eyes on the road while sitting next to busty Jayne, and a tragic sayonara to the last of the screen's blonde sex bombs.

"The movie star, well she crashed her car. Everyone said she was beautiful, even without her head. Everyone said she was dangerous." So goes the opening line to song "Movie Star", made popular in the '90s by a band called Cracker. Was that a cryptic reference to poor Jayne? Probably.

How disappointed the Blonde dynamo would be to discover that only her death is talked about today, not her life. How frustrated she would be to find out that all those publicity-seeking, attention-grabbing efforts were a huge waste of time, and that the single headline she did not solicit was, in the end, the only one that mattered.

*Rare newspaper photo of Jayne Mansfield's body with her head still attached.*

Sharon Tate

The news crackled across radios and spread across television screens, all over the sprawling chaos of Los Angeles. With the revelation of each grisly detail, shock and fear spread as well, starting in the posh living rooms of the rich and famous, then trickling down into the ordinary family rooms of the rest of the city. Three people had been found murdered, no four, no five! Five souls horribly butchered in a gated estate in Benedict Canyon, surrounded by a high wall and a sophisticated security system! Holy crap! If those people weren't safe in their own home, who was?

They weren't merely murdered either, but mutilated, stabbed and shot over and over and over again, and their blood was used to scrawl cryptic messages all over the house. One of the victims was lovely Sharon Tate, an actress who just made a big splash in the highly publicized film, *Valley of the Dolls*. It got worse. Tate, wife of the Polish director Roman Polanski, was eight months pregnant. The horror! Why? Why this house? Why her? Just why?

Sharon Marie Tate was born in Dallas, Texas in 1943 (why does Texas get all the pretty girls?) to Doris and Paul Tate. Her father was in army intelligence, and spent most of his time away from the family. Doris got bored one day and decided to enter her six-month-old daughter in the "Miss Tiny Tots of Dallas" contest (this was years before "Toddlers In Tiaras"), and of course, Sharon won. As the years passed, Sharon realized the power that the attention her beauty commanded, and began modeling. She even appeared on the cover of *Stars and Stripes* magazine in a bathing suit and straddling a missile. Colonel Daddy was not pleased, but also never home, and Sharon carried on with her activities without any long, boring speeches or moral comeuppances.

The colonel moved his growing family—with two newly added daughters—to Italy in 1959, where Sharon blew the boys away at Vicenza American High School in Verona (where Romeo and Juliet are 'buried'). She was a cheerleader—with endless offers from lovestruck admirers to carry her books—and she reigned supreme as the glittering homecoming queen, a position the school created for her. She was the girl that most other girls really wanted to hate, with her perfect skin and knockout body, but because she was so damn nice, they ended up being her best friend, and basking in her aura instead. Sharon enchanted everyone everywhere she went.

In the early '60s, American movies were using exotic European locales as backdrops for period pieces. She snuck herself into a crowd scene in *Barabbas*, and got hired as an extra on *Hemingway's Adventures of a Young Man*. A costar in that film, Richard Beymer, was so smitten that he took her out few times. He also gave her his agent's card.

Once home in California, Sharon wasted no time dialing Hal Gefsky to arrange a meeting. She convinced her family to let her move to Hollywood by herself, at the tender age of nineteen, to pursue her dream. Despite having nearly zero acting experience, Gefsky signed her on the spot. See, pretty girls really do get all the breaks. She started with a little fashion modeling and a few commercials. Photographs of her then clearly show the mod, waif-thin, '60s vibe she had going on, with just a touch of whimsy. There were a lot of candid photos of her and Mr. Gefsky, who looked uncomfortably like a dirty old man, frolicking in his fancy backyard pool.

She tried out to play one of the sexy daughters on the television show, *Petticoat Junction*, but her lack of experience got her rejected. The show's producer, however, contacted the head of Filmways Pictures, babbling away about the dewy neophyte beauty who had just walked on his set. She signed a seven-year contract with Filmways, just like that,and must have been one of the last actresses to sign a bonafide studio contract before that system went the way of the dinosaurs. She got the full studio treatment: acting lessons, paid rent at a place called The Studio Club—run by the YWCA—and charm lessons on how to walk, how to dress, and how do her hair and makeup. According to Gefsky, her first female roommate at The Studio Club put the moves on her, forcing her to switch rooms. Well, it was the YWCA. Even women couldn't resist her.

It didn't take long for the girl with the Midas touch to ditch her shabby digs, and move into a swanky apartment off the Sunset Strip, within walking distance of the famed nightclub: The Whisky A Go Go. It was at a party there that Sharon met Jay Sebring—hairstylist to the stars—and Warren Beatty, star of the hit film, *Splendor in the Grass*. Sebring—a notorious philanderer—plied his wares up and down the strip, and was that rare breed: a genuine heterosexual male stylist that his bluehaired, well-heeled clientele had a hard time resisting. He was impossibly good looking, and could have been an actor himself, if he had showed the slightest interest, which he didn't. He and Sharon became seriously involved, and she eventually moved into his spooky house on Easton Drive in Benedict Canyon, the former home of Paul Bern and his wife, another blonde babe: Jean Harlow.

Everyone knew the story that Bern, despondent over not being able to consummate his marriage to Harlow, blew his brains out in the upstairs bedroom way back in the early '30s. Sharon spent long hours alone in the German cottage-style home, and claimed to have met the ghost of Bern himself one night. Sharon had always carried a fascination with the paranormal, and also told friends that the ghost of Valentino haunted the home she lived next to on Cielo Drive, Falcon's Lair.

Sharon's film career was in limbo. Filmways had her doing a small reoccurring role on *The Beverly Hillbillies*, where she had to wear a black wig. She wasn't credited and was barely recognizable. They tried to cast her in a small role on the Elizabeth Taylor/Richard Burton film, *The Sandpiper*, but Liz was entering her fat years, and didn't want to share even a second of screen time with the hypnotic Sharon. She had to travel to England to get a decent part, in the witch story, *Eye of the Devil*. Sharon took this role seriously, even meeting the High Priest and Priestess of Wicca, Alexander and Maxine Sanders. As fate would have it, Filmways President Martin Ransohoff introduced Sharon to his good friend, hot new director Roman Polanski, in hopes that Polanski could put her in his new film, *The Fearless Vampire Killers*. Roman was reluctant at first, fearing she wasn't experienced enough. Her charisma was too much for him, though, and she got the part. Following in the tradition of all good actresses, Sharon fell in love with her director, and by the time the film was over, the two were inseparable.

Photos of the couple striding down fashionable London streets during the swinging '60s show a carefree Sharon, stunning, radiating happiness and looking the epitome of the mod princess in her giant bell-bottoms and miniskirts. Jay got word that his girlfriend was keeping company with another guy, and flew to London to win Sharon back. He ended up meeting, and liking, Roman and the three of them became best friends. I think this scenario could only have happened in the '60s. Polanski later said that despite his popularity with the jet set (is that still a term?), Sebring was in truth very lonely, and thought of he and Sharon as his family. He kept wearing Sharon's college ring around his neck for the rest of his short life.

Sharon and Roman set up house together in LA, and while he got busy directing the film that would define horror for years to come, *Rosemary's Baby*, she was cast in the film version of one of the most successful novels of all time, Jacqueline Susanne's *Valley of the Dolls*. The book depicted, with scathing realism, the deviant, shallow existence of those who choose show business as their way of life. It was shocking for its time, though it seems fairly tame today. *Shades of Grey* need not worry. Not a critically acclaimed novel, *Valley* was even less acclaimed on film. Sharon played the role of Jennifer North: a struggling Broadway actress who has little talent and is admired only for her beauty. Wow, that sounds familiar.

Director Mark Robson was not a pleasant man and according to Patty Duke, who played Neely O'Hara in the film, he directed most of his unpleasantness towards sensitive Sharon, treating her horribly in front of the rest of the cast and crew. Lets face it–Sharon was no great actress. Her delivery was wooden and amateurish. She seemed to be dancing on the surface of her roles, rather than digging deep within herself to become the part. Either she didn't have that capability, or she hadn't met the director that could get such a performance out of her yet. If you listen to her in *Valley of the Dolls* with your eyes closed, her acting is cringe worthy. *The New York Times* reviewer, Bosely Crowther, wrote of the film, "All a fairly respectable lover of movies can do is laugh at it and turn away."

Sensing her limitations, or perhaps lamenting them, Sharon began referring to her roles and her career trajectory as "sexy little me". Meanwhile, *Rosemary's Baby* was almost causing riots around the theaters, and there was Oscar talk for it's young costar, Mia Farrow. Sharon couldn't help but resent it. She had hoped Roman would use her as his star, (after all, what's the point in having a director boyfriend if you can't get preferential treatment when he's casting his films!), but Roman felt their personal relationship would make for a professional conflict of interest, and left it up to Paramount to bring up her name. They never did.

Roman and Sharon's beach house become party central in the late '60s. Everyone from movie stars to politicians gathered in their living room to drop acid and eat Sharon's home cooked polish dishes. The more successful Roman became, the more his eye (and other things) wandered. They weren't married, and Sharon pretended to be too liberated to care about it, but when Roman's tomcatting peaked, she may have had second thoughts. She accompanied him to London for the European premiere of *Rosemary's Baby* in 1968, and they tied the knot there. Gotcha!

The press reel shows her beaming in a very '60s wedding minidress, hair caught up in orange blossoms, cutting a huge slice of wedding cake with her new husband. Sadly, wedded bliss was not on the table.

Roman, not particularly large on oath-keeping, kept sleeping around, and Sharon kept tolerating it, because she didn't know what else to do. She was still hopelessly in love with this man and his thick, Slavic accent, who had to stand on his tiptoes to kiss her. On top of that, in early 1969, she discovered she was pregnant. Hoping that having the baby would settle Roman down, activating his partnership instincts with his paternal ones in a kind of "wonder twin powers activate!" moment, she searched for a home to rent that had a nursery. The couple had been living in the posh Chateau Marmont Hotel for months, after leaving the Santa Monica beach house they rented. Sharon longed for a home of her own with a proper environment to raise her child. Candice Bergen, her close friend, suggested that she move into the house that she and Terry Melcher had just vacated. Sharon thought the house was perfect. On February 15, 1969, she and Roman moved into 10050 Cielo Drive in Benedict Canyon, a few miles from Sebring's home on Eastman Drive.

Terry Melcher, the son of actress Doris Day was a well-known record producer. He had once planned to promote a struggling musician/drifter by the name of Charles Manson. He had even recorded some of Manson's songs at the behest of Brian Wilson of The Beach Boys. Wilson befriended Manson, but Manson became unsettlingly violent during an afternoon recording session one day, and Wilson cut all ties with him.

The month after Sharon and Roman moved into Melcher's old house, a strange man walked past the gate and up the driveway, eyeing the pretty blonde in the doorway. Photographer Shahrokh Hatami asked him what he wanted. The man said he was looking for Terry Melcher. Hatami didn't know Terry, but told him that this was now the Polanski residence, so the man left.

The last photos of Sharon, taken over the following few months, are heartbreaking. One photo shows her beaming in the backseat of car, holding up her hands with a baby booty on one finger, her lap covered with baby things. In another, her hands cross under her growing belly, looking down wistfully from a staircase. One of the very last photos taken of her shows her in profile in the backyard, her belly peeking out from her loose top, hands shielding her face from the sun. Everything in the photo is in bright sunlight, except her face, which is in deep shadow. It's as if she's peering into her future, but there's nothing there.

Sharon was happy about the baby, but Roman was not. He spent his childhood in a Polish Nazi concentration camp, and he did not believe in bringing children into such an evil world. Sharon waited until she was four months pregnant before she told him. Of course, he was furious, and if she thought it would stop his philandering, she was mistaken. Just as a wedding ring hadn't changed his ways, neither did a pregnant wife.

Sharon managed to squeak in a French comedy before she began to show, a film called *Thirteen Chairs*, costarring Orson Wells. Sharon was thrilled to be working with the legendary director/actor, and she did a pretty good job in the limited role she was given. After filming was completed in Italy, she flew to London to be with Roman while he worked on his latest picture, 6. By July, she was seven-and-a-half-months pregnant, and returned to Los Angeles to prepare for the birth while Roman stayed behind to tie up loose ends with his film. She left a copy of the classic novel, *Tess of the d'Urbervilles* on his nightstand, suggesting he might want to consider the story for his next project. Roman would later remark that he had a feeling he would never see her alive again. Maybe he should have asked her to say?

August in Los Angeles is brutal. It's hot, sticky and just plain miserable, especially if you're eight months pregnant. August of 1969 saw a particularly vigorous heat wave hit the city, with temperatures into the high 90s, and even the triple digits in outer suburbs. On the morning of August 8, Sharon woke around 9:30 AM, and spent the morning on the phone with her husband and her mother. Her mother asked if younger sister, Debra, could come over for a swim and a sleepover. Sharon politely declined, saying she was just too hot, tired and miserable, and would be lousy company. She did entertain two actress friends for lunch around the pool, and then had a nap. She was not alone in the house. Roman's two friends, Wojciech Frykowski and Abigail Folger (of Folger's Coffee) were staying at there, at Roman's request, until he could return from London for the birth. In the late afternoon, as the cool sea breeze wafted across the valley and up into the hills, Jay Sebring left his home and drove up to Sharon's to take everyone to El Coyote—Sharon's favorite Mexican restaurant—for dinner. Everyone had a good time at El Coyote, spending about three hours there before returning home around 10:30 PM. Abigail retired with a book, Frykowski fell asleep on the sofa, and Jay and Sharon spent the next few hours talking in her bedroom. What did they talk about? Did Sharon confess her disappointment with the marriage, and how she wished her husband loved her as much as she loved him, and how she wished he wanted their baby as much as she did? Did Jay sympathize with her—the love of his life—whose high school ring he was still wearing around his neck? Did he confess his undying love, how he wished things had turned out differently? Were regrets shared on both sides? We will never know.

The next morning, echoes of horrified screams bounced through the hills, the source being one lone housekeeper, Winifred Chapman, who entered the house on Cielo drive to discover a blood bath of epic proportions. Five bodies, brutality stabbed, beaten and shot, were scattered throughout the property. Folger and Frykowski were on the lawn outside. Frykowski had really been through hell. He had been stabbed more than sixty times, pistol-whipped repeatedly, and shot twice. The handle of the gun used to beat him had broken in the process. Inside, Sharon lay covered in her own blood, wearing only a bra and panties, a rope around her neck. She was twenty-six. The other end of the rope was tied around Jay Sebring's hooded neck. He was just a few feet away, shot in the head twice. The words "Death To Pigs" and "Helter Skelter" were scrawled on the front door and walls, in Sharon's blood. The sight was so gruesome that seasoned cops were retching on the front lawn. To this day, this scene plays over and again in peoples minds, remaining the most notorious multiple murder in Los Angeles history. In death, Sharon got what she desperately strived for in life: real lasting fame.

The next day, two more people would also be found dead in their homes, Rosemary and Leno LaBianca. A band of true counter culture hippies led by Charles Manson, and known to local law enforcement as The Family, were rounded up and jailed on unrelated charges a few months later. One of them, Susan Atkins, bragged to her cellmate about how she and four others "killed those people up in the canyon", and how, when Sharon Tate had begged for her life and that of her baby, she had coldly told her "Look Bitch. You might as well face it. You're gonna die and I don't feel a thing." Then she began stabbing her. She said Sharon kept repeating "Mother" until she stopped talking... forever. What a nice, young, well-raised, middle-class psychopath.

Roman was, of course, horrified and grief-stricken when he learned of the murders. He returned immediately to a media frenzy. All of LA, and the world, were stunned that such a brutal crime would happen to such a sweet and lovely girl on the cusp of a bit of honest happiness. Many have said that the carefree innocence of the '60s died with the Tate/La Bianca murders, and the world was never quite so idealistic again. Sharon was buried in the Grotto at Holy Cross Cemetery, in Culver City. It is widely believed that her unborn son was placed in her arms, and buried with her. The headstone carries his name: Paul Richard Polanski.

*Sharon and Jay's bodies in the living room of the Cielo Drive house.*

Roman went on to make more amazing movies, including the classic, *Chinatown*. He didn't waste much time in replacing Sharon, and was linked with a number of leggy starlets throughout the '70s, until he got himself indicted on child molestation charges, and had to flee the country.

He had one last gift for Sharon, though. He took her advice and made the film version of *Tess of the d'Urbervilles*, then bedded its unknown teenage star, seventeen-year-old Nastassja Kinski. Sharon would have been proud, or perhaps not. She's safe now, from her disloyal husband, from critics, and from soulless madmen and the drooling freaks that follow them.

You won't be forgotten, Sharon. Rest in peace.

*The Tate family grave at Holy Cross Cemetery, Culver City, California*

Jean Harlow

The girl on the screen barely contained her enthusiasm at being slapped by the well-dressed man. "Do it again! I like it! Do it..." Throwing herself on him, she passionately kissed him. Excuse me! That's not very ladylike, Miss! She didn't care, and knew that no one else cared either. She was something more than a lady; she was a bombshell: a term invented to describe her when all existing terms proved inadequate. This was Jean Harlow.

In 1991, a beautiful baby girl was born in Kansas City, Missouri. Her mother, Jean, named her Harlean Harlow Carpenter. Jean was from a wealthy family, and had never been happy in her arranged marriage to Harlean's father, Mont Clair Carpenter, as she considered him beneath her class. Those who knew Jean said she was one of the most beautiful women they ever saw, even prettier than her daughter one day became.

Mama Jean doted on her little girl, and for the rest of her life would refer to Harlean as "the baby." Harlean was a beautiful baby, who grew into an even more beautiful child, with shocking white hair—helped along by a few chemicals courtesy of Mama Jean—and huge green eyes. She lived in splendor and a huge house complete with nannies, chauffeurs and maids. While Mama Jean doted on her, Harlean's affection for her mother bordered on worship, as demonstrated in this handwritten thank you note Harlean penned to her mother after receiving a bracelet from her for her eighth birthday. "Dearest dearest Mother: Your gift was the sweetest of all. The little bracelet you gave me is to bind our love still tighter than it is, if that is possible. For I love you better than anything that ever its name was heard of. Please know that I love you better than ten lives. Yours forever into eternity, your baby." Seriously, did an eight-year-old actually write this, and why is an eight-year-old writing a thank you note to her mother anyway?! This note sounds strangely like a love letter.

When Harlean was eleven, Jean divorced her bourgeois husband, took Harlean, and tried to make a go of it alone in Hollywood. For two years she pounded the pavement, but at thirty-four, Hollywood didn't bite. Defeated, they returned to Kansas city.

Harlean's grandfather felt the level of attachment between his daughter and her daughter was unhealthy, and tried unsuccessfully to separate the two. He sent Harlean to a summer camp that lasted the entire summer, to which she would later refer as the "worse nightmare of my life". She lost her virginity there, and came down with scarlet fever. Mama Jean to the rescue! Would a little quarantine keep her from her baby? Hell no! She bowled through the protests of the camp director, got into a boat, and rowed herself across the lake to the camp, where she found Harlean in an isolation building far from everyone else. She spent the next three weeks tending Harlean, and would not leave her side. Later, it came to light that the illness triggered a dormant virus that would, in eleven years, lead to kidney disease.

On the way back from camp, they stopped in Chicago to dine at a posh restaurant. A suave man, sporting an Italian accent and gigolo-like manner, introduced himself as Marino Bello. It must have been love at first site for Mama Jean, for the penniless Bello became her new boy toy. Harlean was less impressed, but tolerated him for the way he made her mother smile (and smile and smile). Harlean herself was soon smiling, when she met Chuck McGrew—a boy with high social standing and a sizable inheritance in his future. She dropped out of her oppressive private high school and got married. Mama had already married Bello, eight months prior to Harlean's wedding, without her daughter's presence. Ouch.

Harlean now had money to play with, as her husband came into the first installment of his vast fortune just a few months after the wedding. Chuck loved Harlean, but had no use for her meddling, clingy mother and her Italian gigolo husband. So in 1928, he moved his new bride clear across the country to a lavish mansion in Beverly Hills. They lived like Zelda and Scott, in true Jazz Age decadence. Chuck loved booze as much, or more, than he loved his wife, and the ever-accommodating Harlean tried to keep him company in this regard. It was not pretty. They were seen drunk and carousing in all the fashionable nightclubs of the day, and their parties were legendary.

If Chuck thought a little thing like six-teen hundred miles could deter Mama from being with her baby, he was sorely mistaken. Within months, Mama and her gigolo were standing on Harlean and Chuck's doorstep, suitcases in hand. Sigh.

When Mama learned that Harlean was noticed at Fox Studios while waiting for her actress friend, and had turned down extra work in the movies, she nearly had a heart attack. To top it off, Harlean had not used her real name at central casting, but that of her mother. There was no stopping Mama Jean after that, and Jean Harlow was born, or remade...however you want to look at it.

Mama immediately took the reigns and ordered Harlean to accept the next studio offer that came her way. Soon, she was appearing as an extra and in bit parts all over the place, and getting noticed by those with influence in the business. Colleen Moore recalls the first time she saw Jean on the set: "This beautiful girl with white hair and a white dress was just sitting there, nonchalantly. People were passing by to look at her and asking who she was." With attention like that, it was not long before someone with real clout, Hal Roach, offered her a five-year contract at one hundred dollars a week. Mother was thrilled, husband Chuck less so, and a classic tug-of-war began.

Betcha can't guess who won there? While in San Francisco, Harlean (now going by Jean) and Chuck had a violent argument over her career and her mother. He got drunk, trashed their hotel room, and she threatened divorce; a threat she eventually made good on, but not before she got pregnant, and got an abortion to save her career. Guess whose idea that was?

With Chuckie out of the way, Mama was free to pilot Jean's career as she pleased, while her unemployed mooch of a husband tagged along and did as he was told. Jean broke her contract with Hal Roach, and worked as an extra again, being the sole breadwinner for her little family (Mama, Bello and herself). As she would later put it, "I turned to motion pictures because I had to work or starve." Quite a come-down for the high society lady.

*The Hell's Angels Premiere, Grauman's Chinese Theatre, Hollywood, CA, 1931*

Howard Hughes, wealthy playboy turned movie director, was making the big-budget war epic, *Hell's Angels*, and cast Harlow as the female lead. This film made her a household name. *Hell's Angels* had already been completed as a silent film, but Hughes knew the era of silents was over, so in 1929 he completely remade the picture with sound, and a new leading lady. He immediately recognized the gem he had, and signed her to an exclusive, five-year contract, at only one hundred dollars a week. The movie was full of stunning cinematography and cutting-edge special effects. Hughes had poured every last dime he had into it, and it showed. When the film premiered at Grauman's Chinese Theater in Hollywood, on May 27, 1929, the town went nuts. Fifty thousand people lined the streets to catch a glimpse of the stars in their limousines, especially the young unknown, Jean Harlow, who managed to shock a bootleg-gin-soaked, depression-fearful audience in her barely-there satin dresses and come-hither banter. A squadron of real fighter planes screamed overhead, and one hundred and eighty-five arc lights lit up the boulevard.

The National Guard was called in to keep the peace. And there she was! She materialized amidst all this chaos, draped in white fox and diamonds, kissing the microphone as she thanked Howard Hughes for her stunning success, looking every inch the star she now was.

*From left: Jean Arthur, Clara Bow, Jean Harlow, Leone Jane in The Saturday Night Kid*

Hughes wasted no time in loaning his new ingénue out to every studio that asked. Like all smart producers of the day, he was paid thousands for her services, but paid her only a fraction of that, even though she did all the work. She suffered tremendously during the filming of *Hell's Angels*, due largely to her inexperience. Her acting was considered subpar, and to salvage his investment in her, Hughes filmed a scene in a new colorized technique called Technicolor, to accentuate her stunning eyes, milky skin and white hair. The effect made Jean a sensation, but caused her to suffer from "burned eyeballs" from the harsh light she was forced to stand under for hours. Acting was not so fun anymore.

She was loaned out to one mediocre film after another, and her acting did not improve. She was often mocked by film critics for her stilted delivery, but they had to acknowledge that, although she couldn't act her way out of a paper bag, she was so stunning no one really cared.

She met the fella that would become her second husband while the rushes for *Hell's Angels* were still being previewed. He was MGM executive, Paul Bern. Paul was on the rebound from the untimely, drug-related death of his first love, The Girl Too Beautiful: Barbara La Marr. He became Jean's friend and confidant, much to the alarm and disapproval of guess who?

You're right! Mama Jean thought Paul was a weasel who just wanted to use Baby Jean for his own conniving, self-centered purposes. Pot calling the kettle black much? Mama still had her hands full, fending off Jean's soon to be ex-husband, Chuck McGrew, who continued to petition for reconciliation with Baby Jean, who was still Harlean, as far as he was concerned. She really wanted to go back to the hubby and the domestic life, but Mama would have none of it, eventually managing to separate the two for good and ever. A nasty breakup scene occurred, with a very drunk McGrew calling Jean something vile, then slapping her so hard that her head snapped back. He left the house, never seeing his wife again. Jean remarked to her aunt, "Nothing on Earth is worth what I go through when I don't let her dominate."

With Bern in her corner, Jean was given the part of a true slut in the MGM gangster film, *The Beast of the City*. She wiggles, shimmies, and double entendres her way into the reluctant heart of a stiff-lipped police detective, much to the delight of the audience. Jean is at her free-spirited best in this film, touching herself seductively while dancing, messing up her hair, then throwing herself on her shocked suitor, all in an attempt to extort money for sex. It doesn't get more pre-Hayes, office-risqué than that. Bern booked her on an East Coast promotional tour for the film, and every theater where she appeared sold out. MGM saw the light, and bought out her contract from Hughes.

Jean was soon paired with new hottie, Clark Gable. They became the new "it" couple, at least onscreen, and worked in more than five films together. They became fast friends offscreen as well, and rumors swirled of romance. Gable had that boy/man vibe, with eyes like a child, and a body that flung women over the edge. Maybe that's why people were truly shocked when she up and married the balding, ordinary, middle-aged Bern in July of 1932, instead of the niftier, dreamier Gable.

That wedding night must have been fascinating, as Mr. Bern was allegedly hiding a little secret about himself, a wee, itty-bitty little secret. As Leatrice Joy Gilbert, ex-wife of John Gilbert, explained after she had seen Bern naked by accident in the house he shared with her husband, "His penis was no bigger than my pinky." Bern was rumored to have had a physical deformity resulting in permanent, hopeless impotence. But like a horny priest who lusts after the ladies in the confessional chamber, he was strangely obsessed with sex, concealing his lascivious, unfulfilled desire beneath a suave, controlled demeanor. Oh, the iro-

*Jean Harlow and Paul Bern outside the Benedict Canyon home that Bern would later commit suicide in*

ny. This man, who was sex-obsessed yet unable to do anything about it, finds himself married to the very embodiment of sex, and still unable to do anything about it.

Because of this defect, Bern became a bitter little man who belittled his sex goddess wife, putting her down in public as uneducated and stupid, even striking her occasionally, which makes what happened that fall seem like not such a bad thing after all. On the evening of September 4th, two months into this marriage which had not been, and would never be, consummated, Bern killed himself in the upstairs bedroom he shared with Harlow in their new Bavarian-style house in Benedict Canyon. He and Jean had argued, supposedly about Mama Jean and Bello, who were pressuring Jean to deed them her mansion and invest with them in a Mexican gold mine. Seriously? Could these two be any more clichéd? Jean stormed off home to mother, leaving him to his own, dark thoughts. At least that was one story. He stripped naked, doused himself in her most expensive perfume, and shot himself in front of a full-length mirror. Nice touch, the mirror, just to remind himself of why...

Husband and wife domestics, Winifred and John Carmichael, arrived at Eastman drive late the next morning, discovering Bern's corpse. Did they call the police? No. Did they call an ambulance? No. Winifred called Mama Jean, who in turn, informed Louis B. Mayer, head of MGM. Did Mr. Mayer call the police? No. He called studio chief, Irving Thalberg, who told his wife, Norma Shearer, who then called producer, David O. Selznick. Mayer, Selznick, Thalberg and Shearer all headed over to Bern's house. Had anyone bothered to inform the police at this point? No, but two official MGM photographers received orders to get over to the scene, as did MGM head of publicity, Howard Strickling. MGM party at Bern's house! Last one to the suicide is a rotten egg!

Strickling and photographers arrived first, and had a blast contaminating evidence and jumping to conclusions. Strickling waffled through Paul's address book, finding a hastily written suicide note on page 13. It read "Dearest dear; Unfortunately this is the only way to make good the frightful wrong I I've done you and to wipe out my abject humiliation. I love you. Paul P.S. You understand last night was only a comedy." Hmm. Wonder what that last part could mean?

People would speculate about this for decades. If Mayer had his way, no one but he and Strickling would ever see the note; he intended to destroy it before the cops ever got there. Strickling talked him out of it, as its very existence cleared Jean of any wrongdoing. Makes you wonder what was destroyed. The three musketeers—Shearer, Thalberg and Selznick—arrived. Reporters gathered outside, and word of a coverup began to spread. Had anyone called the cops yet? Nope. That wouldn't happen for another hour. Bern must have been getting pretty whiffy by then, but the studio hot shots needed time to concoct a believable story that would protect their investment (Harlow), and their company from scandal. Talk about balls.

When the story did break, the headlines exploded with the words "Paul Bern kills self in Jean Harlow's bedroom. Bern Impotent!" Jean refused to confirm the impotent stories, even though they were true. She would not be a part of dragging poor dead Paul's reputation through the mud.

Then another unpleasant fact came to light.

The body of a woman was found floating in the Sacramento River, five days after Bern's death. Her name was Dorothy Millette, and she had been Bern's secret, common-law wife for ten years. Ooops. Yet an-

*Paul Bern's body*

other secret Mr. Bern kept from Jean before he married her. Millette was mentally unstable, and had been stalking Paul and harassing him over his marriage to Jean. He, on the other hand, had been supporting her financially and trying to keep her under wraps. That all went to hell on the night of Bern's death, when Dorothy showed up at Eastman Drive, and was still there when Jean came home. This brings us to the second version of what happened that night.

This is probably what really happened. Dorothy wailed outside the house at Paul, who tried to calm her down and get her to leave, when Jean comes home. An awkward exchange among all three parties ensued, and ended when Jean told Bern to call her when he figured out to whom he was actually married, before storming out. Dorothy left shortly after Jean. All of this upset Bernsie enough to ice himself early the following morning, after spending an interesting night prancing around naked and putting on perfume. "You understand, last night was only a comedy." Ah, now that makes more sense. Millette didn't see the point of hanging around without her sugar daddy, so she bought a one-way ticket on a paddleboat, and jumped off into the Sacramento River, mid-trip. What's that again, Mr. Mayer, about avoiding a scandal? Not a chance.

> Dearest Dear,
> Unfortunately this is the only way to make good the frightful wrong I have done you and to wipe out my abject humiliation, I love you -
> Paul
>
> You understand that last night was only a comedy.

*Paul Bern's suicide note*

    The hard-boiled streetwise little tramp became the wronged party in a tawdry love triangle she had no knowledge of. Jean came out smelling like roses in springtime after a pleasant afternoon shower. Mayer himself couldn't have manipulated the public's reaction better. And what better way to capitalize on the whole thing than to have Jean star in a movie that eerily resembled her real life tragedy? Gotta hand it the studio. They sure knew how to turn something ugly into a profit. The movie, *Reckless*, was a huge hit.

    Harlow tried to put the whole thing behind her by throwing herself into her work. She entered her golden period, with movies such as *Red Dust, Hold Your Man, China Seas* and *Wife vs. Secretary*. Mayer forced her into a sham marriage with cinematographer Harold Rosson, just as she was about to be dragged into an alienation of affection suit by the wife of a man with whom she had a brief affair. The marriage was annulled seven months later. But then, she met William Powell, with whom she fell passionately in love, and remained so, until her death.

Jean had completed three important films between 1932 and 1934: *Red Dust*, *Bombshell*, and *Dinner at Eight*. In *Red Dust* she played another hooker who falls for Clark Gable, himself a rough-and-tumble entrepreneur trying to make a go of a rubber plantation in Indochina. Jean really shines as the trash-talking hussy who continually tries to shock the prim and proper Mary Astor with her potty mouth, while trying to win over Gable. In one scene, as a tropical storm is raging, she stands in a window, the wind blowing back her shock of white hair, her bow-mouth pursed like a pouting child's, watching Gable carry her foe to an isolated cabin. She never looked more vulnerable or lovely.

*Bombshell* may as well have been a biography, it was that close to her real life situation. Her character is a movie star being worked to death while her moochy family lives in her mansion and spends all her money. Hey Bello, I'm looking at you.

*Dinner At Eight* surrounded her with the finest actors of the day—Marie Dressler, John Barrymore, Lionel Barrymore, Billie Burke and Wallace Berry—in a comedy of errors revolving around a high society dinner party. Jean not only held her own among the illustrious company, she stole the show. In the final scene, as she is slinking to dinner beside Marie Dressler, she remarks that she was reading a book. Marie, obviously shocked, stops dead in her tracks and turns to Jean, "A book?" Jean continues, "A nutty kind of a book. Did you know the guy says machinery is going to take the place of every profession?" Marie slowly looks Jean up and down, then tosses her head back, and says, "Oh my dear. That's something you need never worry about." Classic.

By the mid-1930s, Jean Harlow was the biggest star on the block. The depression raged, theaters went bankrupt and shut down, studios hemorrhaged money, but MGM stood alone in its profitability, due almost entirely to the Blonde Bombshell. Audiences couldn't get enough of her. Her face graced the covers of countless magazines all over the world, and women went crazy trying to dye their hair the same distinctive platinum color that was her stock-in-trade. Her signature color was ice white, to emphasize her white hair, and she was a vision in white satin and white fur, shimmering at movie premieres and on the screen. There had never been anything like her, and there never would be again. The party, however, was coming to an end.

The Legion of Decency, a Catholic organization intending to spoil all the pre-censorship Hollywood fun, forced studios to rethink their "loose moral values" in certain films, mostly the ones with Jean Harlow. Suddenly the sexually-charged blonde slut was out, and the good girl with discerning leanings was in. Jean had to make the switch, which, unbelievably, she was able to do with relative ease. In the film, *The Girl from Missouri*, she appears with her as a flirtatious tease who holds out until marriage.

She even made a smattering of films with her new brown tresses. This was supposed to be an improvement. Later, it would come out that her hair had actually fallen out during filming, due to over processing, and the only alternative was a nice brown rinse. That's what happens when you mix peroxide with ammonia, girls.

Meanwhile, Jean and William Powell were burning up the sheets and tearing up the nightclubs together. He gave her an impressive, 98-carat star sapphire ring—in lieu of an actual engagement ring—in the hope that she would stop asking him to marry her. It didn't work. She kept pestering him to distraction, and he kept politely refusing, then bedding her like the gentleman he was. The only time they ever stood before a justice of the peace was on film.

In 1937, Jean began work on what was to be her final film, *Saratoga*, at the pinnacle of her career. She had never been more popular with fans or critics, was with the man she loved, and she was being offered quality parts in quality pictures, for which she was well-paid. What should have been a happy, triumphant time was somehow miserable. Her one true love, William Powell, still refused to make an honest woman of her, and it ate her up inside. Another untidy fact, this one concerning her family, was also causing her anxiety. Her stepfather, Bello, had been skimming 25% of her salary, for what he said were investments. He was actually supporting his mistress south of the border. Sheeze! Someone arrest the guy! Mama Jean finally saw the light, and bought his absence from their lives for the tidy sum of twenty-two thousand dollars.

A few months before filming on *Saratoga* began, Jean and her mother attended a plethora of events in Washington DC, including lunch with Eleanor Roosevelt—as well as twenty-two other functions—all within a two-day period. Exhausted, both mother and daughter returned to Chicago with severe influenza. Jean still had to complete *Personal Property* though, and was on her feet and at the studio within days.

Everyone noticed a change in her appearance. Where there had always been a perfect figure was now a bloated one with a puffy face. Lacking her previous energy, she often seemed confused and out-of-it. Her relationship with Powell consumed her, and she remarked to a friend, "I can't stand it anymore. He's driving me crazy. He's breaking my heart." Binge drinking surfaced pent-up rage at how her life had turned out, and the rage was unleashed on Mama Jean—who often served as her verbal punching bag—railing at her until she passed out. Jean would have no memory of what she had done or said after she woke, and her physical deterioration was mostly blamed on alcohol.

When filming on *Saratoga* started, people couldn't help but notice how ill Jean looked. She brushed off their concerns, saying she never really got over the Washington trip and her bout with the flu. A persistent oral infection from a botched wisdom tooth extraction two months earlier would not leave her alone, itself a constant reminder of the operation in which her heart had stopped and she nearly died. Saturday, May 29, was her last day on the set, and she was so ill—dripping with sweat and doubled over in pain—they tried to take her to the hospital, but she wouldn't allow it. Fevered, bloated, infected, and yet there she was, grinding away, trying to do everything that was expected of her, just like she had done her whole life.

By Monday morning, Mama Jean summoned a doctor to Baby's bedside in their Beverly Hills home. On Tuesday, Jean did something she had never done, and called in sick to work, spending the rest of the day fretting over it. On Wednesday, delirious with pain, she fell asleep, then woke up refreshed, seeming much improved. She had a light meal and read. Everyone breathed a sigh of relief, then things went all to hell.

Thursday, Jean's pain intensified, and she became delusional. Mama Jean desperately sought a second opinion, fearing the attending physician, Dr. Fishbaugh, was fumbling in his attempts to make her well. She was right. He had misdiagnosed her. What she didn't realize was that all the doctors in the world couldn't make Baby well. She was dying from acute nephritis, kidney failure, and in the days before dialysis machines, that was a death sentence. She had been living on borrowed time for a decade, since the scarlet fever virus caught her at camp all those years ago, and quietly left her with permanent hypertension and kidney disease. Another doctor was finally called in, who correctly concluded that the situation was hopeless before bursting into tears.

By Saturday, she had stopped urinating and was excreting her bodily toxins through her pores. She reeked of ammonia, and was in excruciating, unrelenting pain. Clark Gable was horrified, ashamed of his own inability to suppress the revulsion when he saw her. Her body was doubled in size from fluid retention, and her breath was a shocking blast of noxious corpse air. "It was like kissing a dead person, a rotting person," he lamented.

Powell didn't even show his face until Sunday, probably because he was busy going out with another actress, Bernadine Hayes. Jean was happy to see him, but complained that he looked blurry, before she lapsed into a kind of fevered trance. An ambulance was called, and she was admitted to the hospital. By Monday, her brain was swollen, and pressing against her skull. Powell dropped by on the way to work, so kind of him to find the time. He emerged from her room, a changed and devastated man. His eyes were swollen shut from crying. Her aunt Jetty urged her to get better, to which she replied, "I don't want to." Aunt Jetty left in tears. Two-and-a-half hours later, at 11:38 AM on June 7, 1937, Jean Harlow was dead. She was twenty-six years old.

Headlines around the country blared "Jean Harlow Dead", "Harlow Dies", "Illness Takes Harlow", but the most poignant one, from *The New York Daily News*, showed gorgeous Jean in profile, throwing back her head and laughing, as if she didn't have a care in the world. It simply read, "Beautiful Jean Harlow Dies". The funeral was a star-studded, MGM-produced circus, complete with celebrity singers and tributes. Powell arrived, barely sitting through the service successfully, before losing it completely and having to be escorted away. Guilt is a powerful thing. Mama Jean saw to it that he paid for his transgressions towards Jean, thirty grand to be exact, to fund the white marble mortuary chamber, located in the priciest dead real estate neighborhood in the country, the Grand Mausoleum's Sanctuary of Benediction at Forest Lawn, Glendale. Of course, the room was big enough for more than one, so rather than waste the space, she saved a spot for herself.

PETE M'DONOUGH TAKEN TO JAIL

7 SPORT COMPLETE BASEBALL

THE CALL BULLETIN

RACE RESULTS NIGHT FINAL

Di Maggio Hits Home Run

DEATH TAKES JEAN HARLOW!

BAIL CZAR LOSES PLEA FOR WRIT

DYING KISS TOLD IN TUB TRAGEDY

Mourned Star Before Demise

POWELL AT HER BEDSIDE BREAKS INTO TEARS LEAVING HOSPITAL

Jean's Film Life Began On Bet

JOE DI MAGGIO HOMES AGAIN

Students Battle Lansing Strikers

The tragedy of Jean Harlow isn't only that she died so young, or that she never seemed to find lasting happiness. The real tragedy is that she didn't want the movie star life at all. She really wanted the house with the white picket fence, the nice husband and kids. Other people wanted it for her. The studios wanted to make money off her, her mother wanted to live vicariously through her, and the public just wanted to want her. Fame sought her out, not the other way around, and she was too passive to fight it, too sweet to just say, "Fuck it!" and walk away. That's the real tragedy.

If you manage to talk your way past the bulldogs that guard the Grand Mausoleum at Forest Lawn, and the treasure trove of celebrity tombs locked inside, you will find her, hidden down a short hallway, resting in all her white marble splendor. The crypt doesn't bear her name, just two little words—simple words ripped from the grieving core of she who chose them—mark the resting place: "Our Baby".

OUR BABY

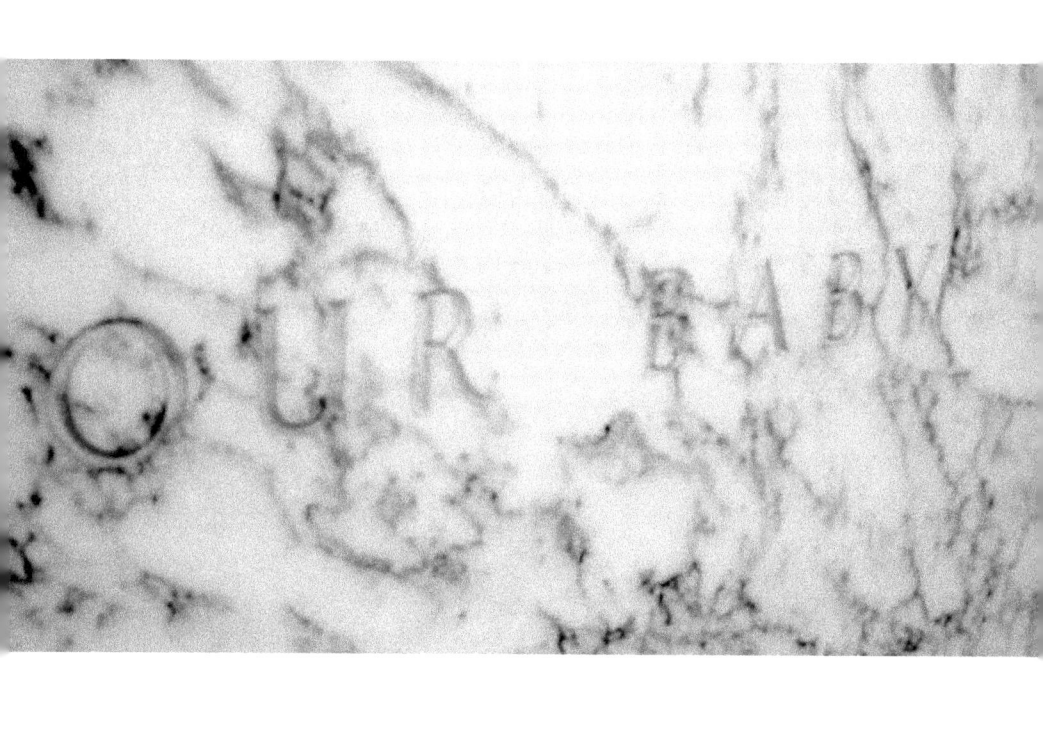

# Dorothy Stratten

It had been one of those insufferably hot August days in the San Fernando Valley, a suburb of Los Angeles. Something didn't smell quite right in the downstairs bedroom of one of the nondescript tract houses in a certain nondescript, middle-class neighborhood. When the room's locked door was broken open at 11 PM, the aftermath of a nightmare unfolded before shocked faces. Two nude human bodies lay inside: a woman face down across a low waterbed, most of her head blown away, and a man on the floor whose head bore a gaping hole, and whose eye dangled from its socket. A 12-gauge shotgun was under him, blood and ants were everywhere. Just a few days ago, the pulpy mess that now lifeless and strewn across the bed had been celebrating the honor of being *Playboy*'s Playmate of the Year. Her name: Dorothy Stratten. The man whose brains oozed lazily onto the floor: her husband, Paul Snider. What the hell happened?

Born on February 28, 1960, in Vancouver, British Columbia, Dorothy grew up in a rough, lower middle-class environment. When she was three, her father left her mother, Nelly, for another woman. When she was eight, Nelly married a violent man who broke her younger brother's arm in rage. Nelly left that man, finding herself on her own with three kids to raise, and not many options. Dorothy performed the role of surrogate parent to her brother and sister while Nelly toiled most of the day, and part of the night, away in menial jobs. She was especially close to her little sister, Louise, whom she had cared for since infancy. Dorothy was not a particularly beautiful child, and she grew into an average-looking teen with average dreams.

One facet of her appearance would command attention, however, and when small time hustler, Paul Snider, walked into the Dairy Queen where she was working, he spotted it in an instant. Dorothy had an amazing body, and even under her Dairy Queen uniform, her youthful breasts swelled atop her long, slim torso. They were the breasts of a curvaceous babe paired with the lithe form of a model, and best of all, she seemed completely unaware of it! Visibly shy and naive, she was a perfect victim. Paul said to his companion, "That girl can make me a lot of money!"

Paul Snider was a promoter, shady entrepreneur, pimp, and an avid reader of *Playboy* Magazine. In addition to ogling the centerfolds, he actually read the articles (shock!), and when it offered a twenty-five thousand dollar reward for the discovery of an unknown of the "girl next door" type to pose for the 25th anniversary edition, a bounty hunting he did go. He never waited for opportunity to knock; he actively sought it out. There it was, quietly taking burger orders and avoiding eye contact, in all its doe-like glory: a towering blonde with gorgeous grey eyes and a boatload of potential that only he could see, or so he thought. He silently thanked fate for kindly dropping it into his lap, and began putting the older man moves on this innocent, doe-eyed Bambi.

Dorothy was so utterly, so completely, unprepared for this, and along with her total lack of experience in romance, she fell hard for Paul's rather hackneyed lines and laughably transparent come-ons. Paul always kept his eye on the prize, keeping his own interests front and center, while keeping his cash cow passive and prone by feigning genuine love and protective instincts for Dorothy.

After checking out the merchandise and deflowering her, he promised to pay a professional photographer to shoot nudes of her for the *Playboy* contest. Dorothy, a decent girl with a real mother and a genuine middle-class upbringing, was horrified at the suggestion that she remove her clothes in front of a stranger, then have the resulting photographs sent off so more strangers could see them. But if Paul was anything, he was persistent. Endless hours of cajoling and pleading gave way to angry tantrums and threats. Eventually, he bullied her into submission. She was probably just too tired to argue any more. Paul forged Dorothy's mother's signature on the photographer's permission form, and the resulting spread was sent off to *Playboy*. Dorothy's life would never be what it had been again.

Hugh Hefner, editor-in-chief of *Playboy*, spent most of his adult life as a connoisseur of beautiful women. He had an uncanny ability to recognize a diamond in the rough, to see beyond the awkwardness of inexperience, and realize the commercial potential of a girl that could easily be overlooked by others. When Hef set eyes on the corny layout of Dorothy's photos in the darkroom at *Playboy* headquarters, a sly smile must have taken shape on his lips.

Eighteen-year-old Dorothy was flown out to Los Angeles the very next day. It was the first time she had ever been on a plane. Alas, Paul was not invited. It was against her mother's wishes, and at Paul's urging, that Dorothy threw herself into a lifestyle that epitomized decadence in the post-disco era of the late 1970s. One of the main temples of decadence was Hugh Hefner's Mount Olympus in Beverly Hills: the Playboy Mansion. Dorothy, with her hickish naiveté, exhibited a Marilyn Monroe-esque quality that had the famous—and her potential rivals—paying close attention. The mansion had no shortage of beautiful girls, yet Dorothy stood out, and not just for her looks. In fact, she wasn't exceptional in that sense when compared with the other Playmates and models. Her face was ordinary, taking on a kind of over-the-top, '80s-style glamour only when in professional makeup. Her figure was fantastic, but the other mansion bunnies had great figures as well. No, Dorothy stood out in ways much harder to convey in word. She possessed an ethereal innocence best captured with the still camera, as Marilyn did, an effect far less pronounced on video. To say the camera loved her is a terrible understatement. The image of a woman-child posing in sexually explicit ways is tremendously appealing to a lot of men. Hefner knew this, and he exploited Dorothy's appeal like the brilliant businessman he was. During an interview with *A&E Biography* on Dorothy in 2000, he spoke in tired clichés that nonetheless seemed heartfelt. "She was the sweetest person I ever knew; the epitome of the girl next door. She lit up a room. All the corny phrases were true about Dorothy."

Back in Vancouver, Paul stewed, bitterly second-guessing the decision to let Dorothy move to L.A. without him. Incessantly pestering the photographer of the original photo shoot for any word on her, the photographer finally shut him up by doing a complimentary shoot of Paul, playing to his boundless ego. Paul looked like a '70s pimp in the photos, wearing white bellbottoms, flowery polyester shirts (buttoned down to unleash his chest bush, ugh!), a heavy gold chain, and pants so tight they could have been paint. He peers into the camera with a stomach-churning come-hither look, his upper lip curled up ever so slightly beneath that awful, porn star mustache. Yet there was a darkness in his eyes that the camera captured perfectly, a blackness that sets ones teeth on edge. Three months after Dorothy moved to Los Angeles, so did he.

Dorothy must have been so deflated when he showed up, insinuating himself into her new, glamorous life. Spending time at the Playboy Mansion, she had rubbed shoulders with movie stars and directors, been treated like a princess by Hugh Hefner—who was grooming her to be August's Playmate of the Month—and here comes Mr. Weasel, with his awkward, cheap looks, his appalling social skills and his possessiveness. Video of Paul's first visit to the mansion shows him trying to be cool, but coming off pretentious and creepy.

By 1979, through Hefner's connections, Dorothy had a Hollywood agent and was appearing in bit parts on television shows such as *Buck Rogers* and *Fantasy Island*. She also had a small role in a motion picture titled *Skatetown USA*. Not exactly the big time, but she was still darling de jour of Hef's inner circle, and she was August's Playmate of the Month. She paid the bills by serving cocktails at the Playboy Club in Century City.

Paul busied himself by pretending to be busy and getting the brush off from Dorothy's A-list circle of friends. Paul was a lot of things, but stupid wasn't one of them. He knew Dorothy was pulling away, and he was not about to let the greatest thing ever to plop into his pathetic existence just walk out. He guilted her into marrying him by pointing out that if he hadn't walked into that Dairy Queen back in Vancouver, she'd still be working there. He might have been right. Behind even the most vile assertions usually lies a kernel of truth. The wedding photos show him, dressed in a brown prom tuxedo, grinning like the Cheshire Cat, while she towers over him in her halter style wedding dress, forcing a smile, no A-listers in attendance.

Soon the shy Dairy Queen began to come into her own, posing for publicity shoots and conducting interviews to promote her upcoming centerfold. During one interview, an unbelievably rude reporter asks her if she would take her clothes off for him. She is sitting on the grass in a tight red tank top that has a *Playboy* Bunny emblem embossed in sequins on the front, no bra, and hot pants. Her bright smile vanishes, and she says "no." Looking hurt at the suggestion, she manages to come off both sad and absurd at the same time, though she has a hard time explaining why she wouldn't remove her clothes.

Paul had been toiling on a project of his own, his own a brilliant idea (no really!) for an all-male erotic nightclub act consisting of beefcake dancers wearing skintight pants, white collars, cuffs and nothing else. Obviously inspired by the uniform Dorothy wore as a cocktail waitress at the Playboy Club, the concept had nonetheless been previously unexplored. And so The Chippendale Dancers were born. This act was shear genius, and it's hard to believe that the notion had not been tried sooner. Paul recognized that women had sexual appetites just as much as men, yet there were precious few outlets (still aren't)— other than romantic entanglements—that catered to those needs. The act, as well as the club that showcased them, was an instant success, but due to low business acumen, Paul found himself on the outside looking in when his investment partners cut him completely out of the action.

Not nice. Tick-tock, tick-tock. The clock began to count down in Paul's head. Dorothy was all he had now.

The two love birds made a nest of a tract house along side the 405 freeway, and took in renters to help make ends meet. Guess the pay at the Playboy Club wasn't much better than at the Dairy Queen. A modest income did not stop Paul from trying to live immodestly. He purchased himself a used Mercedes with what little money Dorothy managed to bring in, hanging a customized license plate on it which read "Star 80": a reference to the bright future he was securing for Dorothy in the coming year. The newlyweds never basked in the warm fuzziness of their honeymoon period though, as the same old issues kept coming between them—namely that everyone loved her and couldn't stand him. He accompanied her on publicity gigs and to parties, and it was always the same story. She'd charm everyone with her gentle, unassuming ways, and he'd shadow her like the stalker he was, embarrassing her with his ridiculous clothes and hustler demeanor. He even picked up a cheap imitation of Hefner's satin pajamas. He was quite the walking freak show.

Then one day, when she managed to shake Mr. Goodbar and sneak off to the Playboy Mansion by herself, she met Paul's opposite in famed movie director, Peter Bogdanovich. Here was a man of wealth and fame, a gifted filmmaker who broke into the Hollywood scene a few years prior with the gritty, hauntingly beautiful movie, *The Last Picture Show*. He was fresh off a seven-year relationship with the star of that movie, supermodel turned actress, Cybill Shepherd. Seeing this wide-eyed newcomer off in a corner, he made a beeline for her, and when she had no idea who he was—even after he introduced himself—he became even more intrigued. The two began seeing each other. How their relationship could be explained to Paul in a way he would accept was a problem, so Bogdanovich cast Dorothy in the film he was currently working on, *They All Laughed*. She had to be on the set every day, and there was nothing Paul could do about it. Perfect!

Though Dorothy now had a real part in a real movie, was carrying on with a famous director, and was about to be Playmate of the Month, she was still living with Paul in their sad freeway shack. Marilyn Grabowski, former photo editor for *Playboy*, said in her interview for the Biography Channel's profile on Dorothy that she had given Dorothy a puppy, only to hear a week later that the puppy was dead. Grabowski said she just knew Paul had murdered the dog out of jealousy, after Dorothy had mentioned that Paul accused her of loving the dog more than him. Um, red flag much?

The August 1979 issue of *Playboy* hit the stands, with Dorothy on the cover, and suddenly the world knew who she was. It was the best selling issue of the year. Hefner began grooming his protégé for Playmate of the Year. The calendar turned from 1979 to 1980, the year Paul's license plate promised a new star, and it looked like that promise might become reality. Dorothy jetted off to New York to shoot scenes on location for *They All Laughed*, leaving Paul to obsess about her back in LA, while she and Peter carried on their affair as if he did not even exist.

While Dorothy was away, Paul had another idea, and began feverishly working on it in the garage. It was to be a workout bench, with leather straps that could be adjusted to support all kinds of bizarre sexual positions. He hoped to sell his invention to The Pleasure Chest, a kinky sex and bondage shop on La Brea Avenue in West Hollywood (it's still there), then mass produce it for the sex toy industry. The Pleasure Chest said thanks but no thanks. Apparently the device was too B.K.T., even for them. Another failed venture for Paul...Tick tock, tick tock. When Dorothy returned to LA, things went from bad to worse for her and Paul. He had her tailed by a private detective, who just confirmed what he already knew: she was in love with another man.

Hefner held a lunch in her honor, where he announced that she would be Playmate of the Year, attended by Dorothy and Paul. Dorothy, in a really ugly, brown, shapeless dress, went up to the podium to accept the honor. Her face radiant, her blonde hair a mass of gorgeous curls, she thanked Hefner and her photographer, but not Paul. Hint hint.

While in Vancouver on a publicity tour, Dorothy began to cut ties with her Paul. She closed their joint bank account, sent a formal request for a separation, and planned to leave him. Desperate and angry, Paul flew out to Vancouver, and went to Dorothy's family's house. He took her to a club, and put her on display while he collected a buck a piece for signed glossy photos. When they got back to LA, she was done, and moved into Bogdanovich's Beverly Hills mansion. It's a wonder Paul let her go. Oh that's right! He didn't have a gun yet.

Dorothy and Bogdanovich wrapped up the final scenes of *They All Laughed* in New York, over the summer of 1980, and returned home in late July. Paul bought a gun, and waited all night in the shrubbery of Bogdanovich's yard for the couple to return, so that he could kill them both. Fortunately for Bogdanovich, Paul got the day wrong. That twist of fate saved Peter's life, but it only delayed the inevitable for Dorothy.

On the morning of August 14, Dorothy told Peter that she was off to see her attorney, then go to a photo shoot at the mansion afterwards. Dorothy's little sister Louise was visiting, and she wanted to tag along, so the two of them got into the car and left. In truth, Dorothy had agreed to meet Paul at the house they used to share, to make her break with the psycho final. She had a thousand dollars in an envelope and hoped it would buy her freedom from her tormentor. En route, she changed her mind about bringing Louise, and dropped her off at the beach instead. Would Paul have carried out his sick plan if Louise had

*Paul Snider's house at 10881 Clarkson Road, Los Angeles, California.*

been there? Would they be dead today? Would he just have waited for another time? We will never know.

Dorothy arrived at Paul's house around 12 PM. Exactly what transpired in the next few hours will never be known, and detectives were only able to construct a likely scenario. At some point, Snider snapped, making her a hostage. He brutalized, beat, and raped her, repeatedly. He put the shotgun to her cheek and blew her face away, also taking the tip of her index finger as her hand rose defensively. No one knows if she was alive or dead when he strapped and taped her to his sex bench prototype, and proceeded to brutalize her in unspeakable ways. His bloody handprints were stamped on her buttocks. He tore out a hunk of her hair, which was still clutched in his fists when the bodies were found. He took her off the bench, tossed her onto the bed, and killed himself. He fell on the gun, and the bullet had left his right eye dangling from the socket. Dorothy Stratten was dead at the age of twenty.

Strange events followed Dorothy's death. Bogdanovich had what they used to call a good old fashioned nervous breakdown. He still had to edit *They All Laughed*, and after spending months in the dark, alone with his dead Dorothy flickering onscreen, he pretty much lost it. He spent the next four years writing a book about it, *The Killing of the Unicorn*, where he laid the blame for her death squarely on the shoulders of his old friend, Hugh Hefner.

Sorry, but honestly, there was plenty of blame to go around. Hefner didn't appreciate this, and did news conferences and interviews where he pointed out that it was Dorothy's affair with Bogdanovich that pushed Snider over the edge, not her work with *Playboy*. He also called Bogdanovich out for seducing Louise Stratten, who was only sixteen at the time. All of this controversy helped book sales tremendously.

Dorothy's mother and sister filed a multimillion dollar lawsuit against Hefner for libel, hotly denying there was anything between little sister and the bigshot director-turned-author. Hefner insisted that Bogdanovich was really behind the lawsuit. Everyone went to court, and lots of lawyers got rich. The charges were dropped, and Bogdanovich declared bankruptcy. Four years later, he and Louise were married.

This turn of events put most people off. It seemed that Peter was unable to move on from Dorothy, and just wanted to hang onto her in any sick way he could. No one gave the marriage more than a year, but they were wrong, it lasted eleven. Peter never regained the stature in Hollywood that he had enjoyed before Dorothy's murder, and was divorced in 2001.

Dorothy's final resting place is at Westwood Memorial Park, just across the lawn from another tragic blonde, Marilyn Monroe. A few months before her death, she told an interviewer who asked whether or not she was worried that her life would end as tragically as Monroe's due to the nature of her business, "I just try to take life one day at a time." Her epitaph, from the Ernest Hemingway novel, *A Farewell to Arms*, reads, "If people bring so much courage to this world, the world has to kill them to break them. So of course it kills them. It kills the very good and the very gentle and the very brave impartially. If you are none of these, you can be sure it will kill you too, but there will be no special hurry." No special hurry indeed.

> **DOROTHY STRATTEN**
> FEBRUARY 28, 1960 — AUGUST 14, 1980
> IF PEOPLE BRING SO MUCH COURAGE TO THIS WORLD
> THE WORLD HAS TO KILL THEM TO BREAK THEM, SO
> OF COURSE IT KILLS THEM. IT KILLS THE VERY GOOD
> AND THE VERY GENTLE AND THE VERY BRAVE IMPARTIALLY
> IF YOU ARE NONE OF THESE YOU CAN BE SURE THAT IT
> WILL KILL YOU TOO BUT THERE WILL BE NO SPECIAL HURRY
> WE LOVE YOU, D.R.

*Dorothy's epitaph is from the novel A Farewell To Arms by Ernest Hemingway.*

Barbara Payton

The prostitute cruising for free drinks in the Sunset Boulevard dive was distinguished only in her complete lack of distinction; just another forty-dollar whore, willing to trade sex for a drink, and not very selective about with whom she bargained. Grossly overweight, she was in dire need of a bath, and her slurred speech often impossible to decipher. At the end of the bar, patron leaned in to another and whispered, "See that drunk prostitute over there? She used to be movie star." The drunk prostitute was more than a movie star; she was an enchanting blonde vision, making ten grand a week, and playing her many drooling admirers for fools. Before she became the neighborhood pump, staggering up and down the Strip, looking for tricks and passing out on public benches, she was Barbara Payton: Queen of film noir. Her fall from grace was so darkly profound that it is not an exaggeration to say that she put the "Tragic" in *Tragic Hollywood*.

    In 1927, she was born in Minnesota, but grew up poor in Odessa, Texas, spending her days dreaming of stardom in a darkened movie theater. Like many striking but obscure young women in small towns, she married the first boy who asked her, handsome Air Force pilot, John Payton, and they moved to Hollywood so she could try her hand at stardom. The year was 1943, and World War II was raging in Europe. Barbara was too pretty and too restless to stay cooped up at home while her husband attended USC under the GI Bill. She began modeling, appearing in print ads for cars and fashionable clothes. Soon, she was a fixture in the clubs around town, and her husband began to grumble. They had a son by then, but Barbara seemed more interested in self-promotion than in being a wife and a mother. The marriage ended, and Barbara found herself a single mother on her own in Hollywood.

    Soon Universal noticed her, and gave her a contract for a hundred dollars a week. Agent Phil Feldman described her as possessing "that blonde goddess shine that can't be described as anything but a radiance that makes a movie star." Her first film was *Trapped*, costarring Lloyd Bridges, for which she received decent reviews. Now the ultimate party girl had the money to party in style. She was known as the "Queen of the Night Clubs", and when she wasn't working, or sleeping, she was drinking and dancing her nights away. This became habit quickly, and Universal eventually dropped her contract.

She so impressed James Cagney that after her screen test for his new film, *Kiss Tomorrow Goodbye*, he immediately signed her with his own production company. The film was a huge success, and is still considered one of the best noir films ever made. Barbara plays Cagney's moll/girlfriend, who ends up killing him after he betrays her with another woman. *The Hollywood Reporter* said of her performance, "Barbara Payton, in the difficult role of a basically good girl who turns to evil in spite of herself, makes a vivid appearance. She manages the subtle transition with polished artistry." The world took notice of the blonde with legs to the moon, pouty full lips, and babydoll, blue eyes. Barbara was at the top of her game. Just ten years later, she would be working in a dry cleaners just to make ends meet, and that wouldn't even be as bad as it got.

True to form, Hollywood did not realize the potential staring them in the face, and cast Barbara in a second-rate Gary Cooper film as a third lead. The film was titled *Dallas*, and Barbara played the villain's girlfriend. The movie did nothing for her career, and rumors swirled of a romance between her and Cooper, who was a renowned skirt chaser. She also had a brief affair with notorious womanizer, Bob Hope, who set her up in an apartment as a "kept woman." The deal ended when Barbara became too demanding, and Hope's attention span ran out. A new man entered Barbara's life, however, and he did not take no for answer.

Many who knew Franchot Tone thought him one of the most handsome men in film. He was suave, and exuded class and refinement, though he preferred the opposite in women. He was once married to volatile Joan Crawford, who was called many things, but classy was not one of them. He was often seen at the Hollywood supper clubs with one busty nobody or another as his escort. He became truly obsessed with gorgeous Barbara, following her on her *Kiss Tomorrow Goodbye* tour, and begging her to marry him. He sent her roses and champagne every day, and soon they were a fixture at all the chic Hollywood clubs.

Warners, together with Cagney Productions, owned Barbara's contract, and they proceeded to kill her career by casting her in one bad western after another. She would have benefited from a better manager who believed in both her potential and her abilities. Instead, she was left to flounder in second- and third-rate parts in B-westerns that disappeared from theaters almost as quickly as they appeared. The only variation from this theme was the movie *Only the Valiant*, in which both

Gregory Peck and Gig Young duked it out for the glamorous blonde's affections. It was her last A-list film.

Barbara was subpoenaed to testify at the murder trial of bad boy extraordinaire, Stanley Adams, as it seemed she had been in his company the night a narcotics dealer found himself shot dead. Though she was not implicated in any wrongdoing, the press nonetheless had a field day with the story, and Warners' was not amused. She was loaned to yet another substandard production, *Drums in the Deep South*, costarring Guy Madison, with whom she instantly began yet another affair. Three leading men, three affairs, but who's counting? Well, Tone was. He had Barbara tailed by a private eye, and burst in on Madison and his wayward "fiancé", catching them in the act. You know the one. He threatened to punch Madison out, saying, "I'm engaged to this girl and I'm going to marry her! Are you?" to which Madison replied, "No. I can't. I'm already married." Oops. Again, the press lapped it up, and more negative publicity swirled around Barbara, who was by now developing something of justified reputation as a drunken floozy.

Tone was called out of town for a few days, and as soon as his back was turned, Barbara hooked up with hunky B movie actor and fellow boozer, Tom Neal. She claimed it was love at first sight, after she encountered him and his ample charms at a Hollywood swim party. The feeling was mutual, and soon Neal and Barbara were messing up beds all over town. Tom was a jock, a former amateur boxing champ at Northwestern, and had pecs you could hang a side of beef from. He was the bad boy to Franchot Tone's good guy, and Barbara began playing a dangerous game of hot and cool love between them. Neal was fond of Barbara, but Tone was impassioned and possessive of her. After all, they were technically engaged. It wasn't hard to see an epic showdown on the horizon, with lovely Barbara cast as the bag of gold.

On the night of September 13, 1951, Tone confronted Neal outside Barbara's home in Beverly Hills. He hit Neal in the jaw, and Neal responded by knocking him off his feet, leaping on his chest, and pummeling his face repeatedly. Shocked, Barbara tried to intervene, receiving a backhanded black eye from Neal for her trouble. The attack was so violent that neighbors cowered inside their homes, watching Neal pummel Tone for ten full minutes. When it was over, there was blood everywhere. Franchot Tone lay unconscious on the ground while Barbara screamed at Neal, "You've killed him!" Not quite. Tone was in a

*Deer-in-the-headlights, Barbara Payton*

coma for eighteen hours, and hospitalized for another two weeks. He had a smashed cheekbone, a broken nose and a serious concussion.

The press went wild. Headlines screamed "Tom Neal Knocks Out Tone In Love Fight," and the public took sides, mostly against Neal and Barbara. No one cared that Barbara thought she loved Neal, or that Tone had actually thrown the first punch. It was all about that two-timing blonde slag and her lowlife bully of a boyfriend ganging up on that nice fellow, Franchot Tone, who was obviously much too good for Payton. Barbara knew she'd be finished in Hollywood if she didn't make it right with her bruised and battered fiancé. Upon his release from the hospital, she married Tone in the town where she was born: Cloquet, Minnesota. She said that this marriage was forever, but added later that "forever was just a weekend or so." That sounds about right.

Fifty-three days, one suicide attempt (by Barbara), and several ugly arguments later, forever was over. Barbara just couldn't forget Tom Neal, who soaked his sorrows in booze, lamenting the loss of his love. Years later, in a futile attempt to rescue Barbara from total self-destruction, Tone offered to marry her again, "I'll be young for you again. I'll become a boy again." Barbara was far too gone by then. It never happened.

Neal and Barbara got back together, also teaming up for another forgettable western, *The Great Jesse James Raid*, wherein a bloated, pathetic Barbara attempted to keep it together as a torch singer in a saloon. Blessedly, the film was quickly forgotten. Unable to get film work, they began touring the country in a stage production of *The Postman Always Rings Twice*. How appropriate. Two actors, fresh off an adulterous love triangle that turned violent, tour in a play about adultery and violence. The problem was, Barbara no longer looked the part of the sexual temptress, and Neal had never been a great actor. When it became clear that the terrible reviews of *Postman* were not going to turn around, Payton crossed the pond to England to make even more bad movies.

Of her time there, she said, "I was a smash hit. It paid loads of money. Countless lords begged me to be their little pussy wussy. I gave a couple of them a thrill or two but when Tom came over to London, they all looked like shadows instead of men. That Tom rocked my haunches every time I looked at him." With such a strong foundation at the heart of their relationship, it's not surprising that Payton and Neal split up four years after their international love affair began. Neal went on to marry twice more, though he never again deemed Barbara worthy of another proposal. He was eventually tried and convicted of shooting and killing his last wife in her sleep, and spent six years in prison. He died of a heart attack in 1971, six months after he was paroled. Barbara didn't even make it that far.

Back in Hollywood, during the early '60s, Barbara found herself unable to provide for her own basic needs or feeding her appetite for alcohol. What's a girl to do? She tried legitimate jobs, but would get herself fired every single time by showing up drunk. It's hard to blame her. How hard it must have been, working as a hostess at a fancy restaurant and seating her former celebrity friends, who would then spend the rest of the evening laughing behind her back and rubbing it in. She wrote bad checks to buy booze, getting fined and lectured by unsympathetic judges who criticized her for wasting the opportunities she had, yet never offered help. Barbara enjoyed a brief respite in the late '50s, when she spent some time living with a fisherman on his boat off the coast of Mexico, but the ever-restless Barbara just had to return to Hollywood for one last shot at the big time. She should have stayed on that fishing boat.

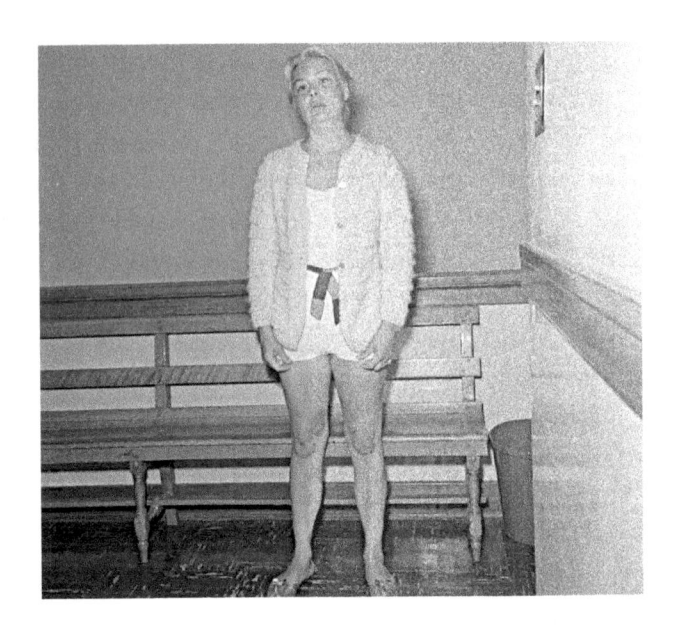

By 1962, she was working as a three hundred dollar a night prostitute, living hand-to-mouth on the Sunset Strip. Three hundred became one hundred, then forty. She was arrested for vagrancy repeatedly, and for being passed out on bus stop bench wearing only a bathing suit and a sweater, and for dancing naked in front of an open window, and for being drunk and disorderly. In 1963, she was rushed to the hospital having been stabbed by a john, scoring thirty-eight stitches. In February of 1967, she was found unconscious, under a pile of garbage by a dumpster, barely alive, covered in bruises, and missing several teeth. She was estimated to be around sixty, she was thirty-nine. She'd slept there for days. Someone offered to take her to a detox center, but she shook her head: "I'd rather drink and die." Doesn't get much more self-destructive, does it? The hospital kept her a few days, then sent her to her parents house, where she died of heart and liver failure three months later.

Barbara's most memorable film was *Kiss Tomorrow Goodbye*, and that's exactly what she ended up doing. She was gorgeous, with a commanding screen presence, and that elusive quality that only the few who became stars possess. Barbara's biggest love was not a man, or stardom, or her son—her biggest love was booze. That was one love affair that never waned. But alcohol is a greedy lover, and it took everything away from her: it took her beauty, her money, her self-respect, and finally, it took her life.

Before she died, ghost author Leo Guild propped Barbara up long enough for her to dictate her autobiography to him, for which she was paid a paltry thousand dollars. The book remains the only time Barbara's story was told in her own words, and is suitably revealing. In the prologue, she laments the time she tried to warn younger actresses not to fall victim to the traps that she had, but that they just brushed her off. "I know I'm an old coot for now—almost thirty-five, wine soaked, prey for men's five dollar bills but I can still write poetry." Barbara had a gift for poetry. One of her compositions is particularly poignant:

> "Love is a memory
> Time can not kill
> The cherished tune
> Gay and absurd
> And the music unheard."

There is a profundity in understanding that some people do not want to be saved, but prefer that their cherished tune be silenced and their music remain unheard. Such a person was Barbara Payton.

Marilyn Monroe

A woman and a boy, clad alike in nondescript black sweaters, walked side by side down 57th street in New York. They moved along the crowded sidewalk without incident. The woman leaned over to the boy and whispered, "Do you want to see her?" He looked puzzled. "See who?" She gazed at him with a mixture of amusement and disbelief, and replied "HER!" A metamorphosis washed over her, a transformation that had less to do with the physical than the psychological, and it came from so deep within her that it could have easily been perceived as a physical change. If it weren't for the fact that she did it right in front of him—in seconds—he might have thought it was someone else standing there. She tilted her head back, thrust out her chest, ran her fingers through her flaxen hair, put on a beaming, artificial smile, and began to walk with a kind of half-swish, half-wiggle (something that most women wouldn't be able to pull off even if they spent years practicing). Immediately, people on the sidewalk began to stop and stare. A crowd gathered, and an excited murmur slowly grew in intensity. "Look! Do you know who that is? It can't be! Miss Monroe! Miss Monroe!" Strangers that had not given her a second glance mere seconds before began to reach out to touch her, and beg her autograph. They swept the boy aside and swamped the woman. Miss Nondescript had become Marilyn Monroe, the most famous actress in the world, in less than five seconds. She did not need make-up, clothes or wigs to accomplish this. All she needed was to summon her alter ego from within.

This small, insecure woman would become not only the most famous actress of her time, but the most enduringly famous actress of all time. Her visage is even more recognizable today than it was when she held court on the screen for ten brief years, sixty years ago. The story of her life has been written about countless times. She has been portrayed on screen more than any other star, most recently in the acclaimed film, *My Week with Marilyn.* Recently, Macy's department store launched a new juniors clothing line based on her iconic style. Macy's belief that a star who died fifty years ago can still sell clothes to modern teenage girls is remarkable. She did not have a happy beginning, and it ended badly as well, but for a magical period in the middle, she was the very essence of beauty, ethereal innocence, and sex.

Norma Jeane Baker was born in June of 1926 to a mentally unstable woman named Gladys Baker. As for the identity of her father, well, that's anyone's guess. Gladys was married to Martin E. Mortensen at the time, but Monroe said her mother named Charles Stanley Gifford as the sire, and as he bore a slight resemblance to Clark Gable—someone Marilyn had a mad crush on—she clung to this story her entire life. Gladys worked full-time, and wasn't really into motherhood anyway, so she left her baby daughter in the care of foster parents Ida and Albert Bolender. Norma Jeane would remain with the Bolenders for seven years—the most stable period of her childhood. In 1933, Gladys bought a small house near the Hollywood Bowl, and brought Norma Jeane back to live with her. Her stability was fleeting, though, and she sank into complete insanity the following year, eventually being placed in the same mental hospital where her own mother had died. Norma Jeane spent the rest of her life haunted by the specter of insanity. Her mother's friend, Grace—a huge movie buff and Jean Harlow fan—adopted Norma Jeane briefly, instilling in her a love of movies and Harlow—the first blonde bombshell. Grace got married, and felt there was no place in her new life for the child, so she stuck Norma Jeane in an orphanage overlooking the Paramount Studios water tower, where she remained for nearly two years. Norma Jeane didn't understand why she was there, and was dragged inside, kicking and screaming that she had a mother and didn't belong there.

She was sixteen when she wed Jimmy Dougherty, and already a beauty, with thick, wavy hair, perfect skin and a perfectly proportioned body. She was also thoroughly scarred from her traumatic childhood, and wrestled for the rest of her life with the insecurities and inner demons it left in her. Dougherty probably couldn't believe his luck, but Norma Jeane was less interested in marital bliss than she was in following the footlights of the movie premieres she lived next door to in Hollywood. It wasn't long before Dougherty left for the fun of WWII, leaving his new bride with his mother. Norma Jeane went to work in a munitions factory with her mother-in-law. One day, photographer David Conover came to the factory to photograph the women doing their part for the war effort, and spotted the lovely brunette right away. David spent most of the afternoon shooting her, ignoring the rest of the women at the plant. The camera's love affair with Norma Jeane had begun.

David got her an audition with the Blue Book Modeling Agency, and she began modeling for print ads. She asked a hairdresser to add some zing to her hair for a shampoo ad, which turned her hair strawberry blonde. She loved the effect, and returned to the salon to have them take it even blonder. Her next series of modeling photos got significantly more attention, the blonder she got, the more the phone rang. Twentieth Century Fox saw her modeling photos, and offered her a standard, six-month contract at seventy-five dollars a week in 1946, with the stipulation that she change her name to Marilyn. She chose her new last name as an homage to her grandmother. Years later, she said she wanted to keep Jeane as her first name, but Ben Lyon, head of talent at the studio, had insisted on changing both. She also divorced her husband that same year, as he did not approve of the trajectory her life had taken.

*Rare photo of a young Marilyn Monroe posing semi-nude*

After nothing but bit parts, Fox dropped her option, and Columbia picked it up. This was due in large part to her relationship with Joe Schenck–Fox Studio mogul and good friend of Columbia boss, Harry Cohn. Columbia put her into her first real film role in *Ladies of the Chorus*, where she shined. She also met two people who would become two of the most important influences in her life and career: drama coach Natasha Lytess, and powerful agent, Johnny Hyde. Marilyn was not above showing powerful, older men a good time between the sheets, and most were wise enough not to take it beyond the bedroom. Hyde, however, fell hard for her. He left his wife and children, and pleaded with Marilyn to marry him. Despite receiving great reviews for *Ladies of the Chorus*, Columbia dropped her option anyway. Bet someone got fired over that decision.

Needing to eat during this lull, she posed nude for photographer, Tom Kelley. Her milky white body was laid against a deep crimson velvet background, to stunning effect. Several photos were snapped, and Marilyn received fifty dollars for her time. Wifey was there the whole time, and all three went out to Barney's Beanery afterward for coffee. No kidding. Of course, the photos would come back to haunt her. One of them, showing Monroe laying on her side, with her torso stretched out and her arm above her head, would make its way to a pinup calendar, creating a sensational scandal when it came out during the pinnacle of her success. It would become the most famous nude photograph ever taken of a star, and go on to achieve pop culture status as a definitive timestamp of that era. Astonishingly, it did not end her career, but rather only enhanced her popularity. A young upstart named Hugh Hefner would use the photos in the very first edition of a new magazine called *Playboy*, but all of that was in the future.

With Johnny Hyde going to bat with the studios for her, she began appearing in small but memorable roles, such as the dumb blonde starlet in *All About Eve*, in which she has the memorable line "Why do they all look like unhappy rabbits?" (a reference to movie directors). She had a meaty role in the gritty crime drama, *The Asphalt Jungle*, and critics loved her in it. Things were going well, but there was one problem: Johnny Hyde, who was already married, was still pressuring her to marry him. He had become obsessed with Marilyn, but she did not return his passion. Hyde was wealthy, powerful, and kind, but she did not love him, and felt her career would stall if she married him. She did fall in love with her voice coach, Fred Karger, who rejected her pleas to get married. After the rejection, she attempted suicide, the first of many attempts. Though she didn't marry Hyde, she let him keep on lavishing her with expensive gifts like jewels and furs, and taking her to many elite Hollywood schmoozefests. She also didn't mind that he alone stood between her and two-bit roles in subpar films. That gravy train would have screeched to a halt when Hyde dropped dead of a massive heart attack in 1950, if he had not secured a long-term contract for her at Fox beforehand.

Fox's publicity department went into overdrive, displaying Marilyn in all kinds of ridiculous poses, everything from a stocking stuffer for GIs to a "pastry chef" in a bathing suit and six-inch heels preparing to slice a (cheese?) cake. The studio began to see her as a viable replacement for the glamorous, multitalented pinup queen, Betty Grable, who was nearing her mid-thirties (gasp), and thus, the end of her career. As Grable had dominated musical comedies, that's where Fox saw Marilyn's future. She was cast in a series of light comedies, which took advantage of her dumb blonde persona, and her ample physical assets.

*Marilyn doing her part for troop morale in Korea*

When Marilyn signed with Fox, she insisted that Natasha Lytess be present during all of her scenes, and that Lytess—not the director—have the last say on whether her performance was good enough. This put her costars in an awkward position: they knew they had to be "on" no matter how many takes they did with her, as the one take that favored Marilyn most would be the one used. She was barely beyond bit parts, yet her reputation for being difficult was already preceding her.

Marilyn was soon working on the film that would catapult her into major stardom, *Niagara*. The movie was a suspenseful thriller, set against the backdrop of the majestic Niagara Falls. Monroe played a married woman of slight moral character, who fooled around on her very jealous and shell-shocked vet husband, played by Joseph Cotton. In one scene, she had to walk down the street... sounds simple enough, yet when Marilyn walked down that street, it was an event. The camera kept focus squarely on her as she did that half-wiggle, half-swishing thing, for an entire minute. This was the longest single tracking shot in a major film thus far. As she made her way toward the falls, it was as if everyone and everything else faded away—so riveting was her image—even as that image got smaller and smaller as she moved further and further down the street. Marilyn literally walked into stardom right then and there. Of her performance, *The New York Times* wrote, "Perhaps Miss Monroe is not the perfect actress at this point. But neither the director nor the gentlemen who handled the cameras appeared to be concerned with this. They have caught every possible curve both in the intimacy of the boudoir and in the equally revealing tight dresses. And they have illustrated pretty concretely that she can be seductive—even when she walked. As had been noted, *Niagara* may not be the place to visit under these circumstances, but the falls, and Miss Monroe, are something to see."

*Monroe in Niagara*

As Marilyn seemed poised on the edge of major fame, two stories broke that could have derailed it. The press—having been fed that she was a poor orphan who struggled against adversity to achieve the American dream—one day got wind that she had a mother, who was not only alive, but wasting away in a mental institution. The story broke around the same time that the nude photographs resurfaced. It's astonishing that Fox Studios didn't kick her to the curb. Instead, they went into full damage control, hastily arranging two news conferences, in which Marilyn explained these things to the public. She claimed that in all that time she spent in an orphanage, she did not know her mother was still alive (pants on fire, Marilyn?), but having learned about it when the press did, she had already begun trying to help her in any way she could. As for the nudie pics, she said that she was desperate for money at the time, felt they were artistic and in good taste, and that the photographer's wife had been present the entire time. Astonishingly, not only did the public accept her explanations, she was seen as even more vulnerable and appealing than before. Kudos Marilyn! Thus began the public's perception of her as a woman/child who exuded sex and fragility at the same time.

How did she top all this? She dated the wholesome hero of that all-American pastime, the epitome of respectability and apple pie, Yankees slugger, Joe DiMaggio. Marilyn fell for the lifestyle DiMaggio dangled before her: the proverbial white picket fence and the feeling of really belonging to a family. He came from a tight-knit, Italian clan—complete with domineering Italian mama and gobs of siblings—and she loved it. A discrepancy exists between what she appeared to yearn for later, and what she initially wanted back when she ditched her first husband—and her own picket fence—for the Hollywood hamster wheel.

Marilyn entered a period generally known as her golden years. She did a handful of films that would forever be associated with her, films that exploited the perception of her as a silly, clueless, yet overtly sexual, child. The first of these was *Gentlemen Prefer Blondes*, and it was during this production that she really leveled up her reputation for being difficult. Problems started from day one, when, as usual, her acting coach, Natasha Lytess had to be present on the set for Monroe even to come out of her dressing room to perform. Speaking of dressing rooms, Marilyn complained years later that her dressing room was half the size of Russell's. She described going to the producers and saying, "The film is called *'Gentlemen Prefer BLONDES'*". They gave in, giving her a larger dressing room, and she remained there for hours, until Jane Russell came and escorted her to the set. This happened almost every day.

*Marilyn in New York, 1956*

Director Howard Hawks was on the verge of a nervous breakdown. Jane just shrugged, and kept walking her to the set. Russell later said that she did not believe Marilyn was being difficult on purpose, but that she was just had a severe case of stage fright and a fear of failure. Whatever. Monroe only started this nonsense after she had a bit of clout. If she had behaved this way when she was still struggling, she would have never gotten further than bit roles.

*Gentleman Prefer Blondes* was a huge success, and contained some of the most enduring Marilyn moments on film. She dazzled in a sleeveless pink velvet gown—dripping rhinestones—in the musical number *Diamonds Are a Girl's Best Friend*—one of the most well-known and parodied songs in film history. She exhibited a flair for comic timing, and she and Russell played off each other beautifully. Add the sugar overload of gorgeous Technicolor, and the recipe for a film classic was complete. To promote the film, Russell and Monroe were asked to leave their foot and handprints outside Grauman's Chinese Theater. Newsreel footage of the two busty bombshells, side by side on their stomachs, holding up their cement-covered hands, remains an iconic image of 1950s Hollywood. Marilyn hung out at Grauman's as a child, placing her tiny feet into the prints of movie stars. It must have felt like all her dreams were finally coming true.

Marilyn played another dumb blonde in *How to Marry a Millionaire*. Her costars, Betty Grable and Lauren Bacall, were old Hollywood veterans. Monroe had actually replaced Grable in *Gentlemen Prefer Blondes*, so, awkward much? It was well-known that Monroe was Fox's answer to Grable's forced exit from the screen. The studio made up a story about a feud between the two blondes, but it was bullshit. Betty Grable was one of the nicest actresses in a town not known for nice people, and she became fast friends with Monroe, a friendship that lasted until Monroe's death ten years later. Monroe continued showing up to the set hours late, when she showed up at all. Hollywood was beginning to notice, but as long as she continued to drive smash hits, which *How to Marry a Millionaire* was, her behavior was tolerated.

In 1953, Marilyn received *Photoplay*'s Gold Medal Award for *How to Marry a Millionaire*, and the occasion would include the first public indication that there was trouble in paradise between her and DiMaggio. Marilyn insisted on wearing the daring, amazing, and now iconic, gold lamé halter dress from the film to the awards ceremony. Everyone who is even a rainy-day Monroe fan knows this dress; it was handcrafted from a single exquisite piece of pleated gold lamé, and she had to be sewn into it. The dress did not leave much to the imagination, and since it hugged every curve, she obviously could not wear underwear with it. She and DiMaggio must have gotten into a terrible argument over it, because he refused to accompany her to the Beverly Hills Hotel, where the awards were being held, if she insisted on going out in public like that. So, she went with old flame: syndicated columnist, Sidney Skolsky. By all accounts, she created quite a stir with her swishy walk sans underwear, prompting Joan Crawford to label her as vulgar. Marilyn knew what she was doing. The following morning, entertainment columns could talk of nothing else.

Marilyn did one more film before she decided to play hardball with the studio, going on strike for something non-dumb-blondish. *River of No Return* was a trying, demanding shoot, that required her to spend hours drenched from head to toe. She and the director, Otto Preminger, were constantly butting heads. He had the balls to ban Natasha from the set for her meddling, infuriating Marilyn, but making him a hero to everyone else. She responded by making his life a living hell on the set with her signature chronic tardiness and production delays. Preminger later said, "I would not direct her again, ever. Not for a million dollars, tax-free."

Marilyn grew frustrated with the measly fifteen hundred dollars a week that had been negotiated before she was a star, and grew increasingly displeased with the roles she was offered. She finally just didn't show up for her next silly movie, *The Girl in Pink Tights*, and the studio suspended her. She responded by marrying Joe DiMaggio in his hometown, San Francisco. The studio was forced to lift the suspension because on this happy news, which was widely reported in every major newspaper from coast to coast.

They sent her the script for *The Girl in Pink Tights*, and she refused it again. They suspended her again. She held firm, went to Korea, and made more history entertaining the troops wearing that beaded, purple spaghetti strap number in sub-zero temperatures. Finally, she got a new contract, and was promised a role in *The Seven Year Itch*, but she first had to make another so-so film, *There's No Business Like Show Business*. The movie was an epic tribute to Irving Berlin's music, featuring an all-star cast of the best musical stars in the business. Monroe held her own against the likes of Ethel Merman, Donald O'Conner and Mitzi Gaynor—three of Hollywood's greatest musical stars—and decades later Mitzi even said that she probably stole the show.

Then she was off to New York, to film what would be the most infamous Marilyn Monroe scene ever: the subway skirt-blowing scene in *The Seven Year Itch*. The now-famous white dress had been bought at a secondhand shop, and altered to fit her. She wore shear underwear that was even more transparent in the glare of the set lights. A huge crowd gathered to watch, including Joe. Things were not going well for the newlyweds. Joe wanted her to give up movies, and just be his wife.

He was intensely possessive, controlling, jealous, and they quarreled often. He didn't like the way she dressed, the way men fell all over her, and he really didn't like feeling humiliated by what he saw that day—in full public view—on the streets of Manhattan: his wife standing over a subway vent with her skirt blown up over her head, as she cooed and oohed with delight in front of thousands of people. They reshot that scene over and over, all day long. When it was finally over, so was their marriage, sealed with a violent argument back at the hotel, where an enraged Joe allegedly hit her. Seriously, who marries the biggest sex bomb on the planet, and then gets angry when she acts like a sex bomb? Pathetic video of a distraught Marilyn, cowering in tears outside her lawyer's house during a press conference about the divorce, followed. Again, the public just wanting to give her a big hug.

Marilyn felt it was time to turn over a new leaf, so she gave Fox the finger, moved to New York, enrolling at the Actors Studio. That's right, this girl was serious about her craft. Tired of being typecast and disrespected, she was out to be taken seriously as an actress, or die trying. She wanted to distance herself from Hollywood types, and immerse herself in a more intellectual, literary culture full of method actors, writers and theater. Living at first in a tiny Manhattan apartment, she next moved to the Connecticut home of photographer Milton Greene and his wife, Amy, spending her days studying acting and her evenings hobnobbing with the New York intellectual elite. She met Andy Warhol, Truman Capote, Tennessee Williams and, of course, Arthur Miller.

She must have felt like a human being for the first time since she locked herself into that plastic image of a mindless blonde goddess, ten years earlier. She went out in public in bulky sweaters, dark glasses, and a scarf tied around her hair, and absolutely no one cared! She dated celebrated dramatist, Arthur Miller, who had just received the Pulitzer Prize writing one of the greatest American plays of all time, *Death of a Salesman*. Emboldened by her new sense of independence, she held a news conference at her Connecticut retreat, with Milton and Amy Greene by her side, and announced plans to go into partnership with Greene to form her own production company, Marilyn Monroe Productions. "I'm tired of sex roles. I don't want to play sex roles anymore. I would like to play Grushenka in *The Brothers Karamazov*," she stated. Fox was not amused, but others had a hard time keeping a straight face.

Fox lured Marilyn back with a new contract that allowed her to make an independent film once a year. They also dangled the role of Cherie, the gentle saloon singer who captures the heart of a simple cowboy, in a movie version of the play, *Bus Stop*. Marilyn jumped at the chance to sink her new method acting chops into the role.

Some felt that power and studio concessions had begun to go to Marilyn's head. She was unreasonably difficult during the filming of *Bus Stop*, insisting that Hope Lange dye her hair a darker shade, so as not to compete with her own hair, and her chronic lateness continued to frustrate everyone on the set. She had a hard time remembering her lines, something that had been an issue for most of her career, but had steadily grown worse as her drinking and pill-popping increased. She wanted so badly to be taken seriously, but her unprofessional behavior was at odds with that desire.

Arthur Miller, having finally obtained a Reno divorce, was now openly courting Marilyn, and the public was intrigued at the juxtaposition of the brain and the bimbo. On the day they planned to announce their engagement, something so terrible occurred that it could have easily been interpreted as a foreshadowing of the awfulness to come. A press car containing *Paris Match* reporters Ira and Paul Slade, along with Mara Scherbatoff, failed to negotiate a hairpin curve along a narrow country road, slamming into a tree. They had been trying to follow Arthur Miller and Marilyn, but Miller cut his teeth driving that road, and accelerated to daredevil speeds in order to shake the reporters (sort of a reversed version of the Diana vs. the paparazzi catastrophe). His plan worked nicely. Mara, who did not fasten her seat belt, was thrown through the windshield and impaled on the hood of the car. Her face was sliced open from the center of her upper lip to the top of her forehead. Miller and Monroe pulled over, running back to find an awful scene they could not have imagined. They pulled Scherbatoff off the car and laid her on the ground. She was alive, but not for much longer, suffering for three hours—most of that time spent lying on the ground while photographers took pictures of her. Less than an hour later, Monroe and Miller stood on the front lawn of Miller's parents home, trying to act happy, announcing their engagement, and failing miserably. Marilyn looked lovely in a simple blouse and black skirt, but was clearly distraught and said very little. Looking like a frightened bird, she clung to Miller and avoided eye contact with the media. They eloped that night. Marilyn said that the accident was a bad omen, and she was right.

*The Prince and the Showgirl* was the first and only movie made by Marilyn Monroe Productions. Filmed in the UK, with the esteemed Lawrence Olivier serving as both costar and director. Marilyn wasn't doing well on a day-to-day basis. Plagued by chronic insomnia, handfuls of Nembutal were needed to get her to sleep. Champagne and Vodka flowed through her all day. She replaced Natasha with Susan Strasberg, Lee Strasberg's daughter, so it was Susan who was required on the set at all times. Her punctuality worsened from an hour or two late to four, five, and six hours late. When she did show up, she didn't know her lines, requiring multiple takes. It was as if she hadn't tried to prepare at all, and just rolled on the set, half-drunk, expecting things to go her way.

She didn't like it when Olivier told her to be "sexy", yet at the joint news conference to promote the film, a spaghetti strap snapped, flashing her boob to a sea of flashbulbs, and she didn't seem to mind. She whined about wanting to be taken seriously, but still acted the dumb blonde she claimed to hate, and still played in all her films. After the film wrapped, she had a miscarriage. That's what happens when you pump your body full of barbiturates and booze and get pregnant. Her marriage got worse, as Miller didn't like being Mr. Monroe any more than the others had, but the difference was that—being a writer—he wrote this shit down. She read his notes—his regrets about marrying her, how her constant need for attention and reassurance was stifling his creativity. Things were never the same after that.

Despite all of this, the Marilyn magic shone through in *The Prince and the Showgirl*, and she scored some of the best write-ups of her life. Even Olivier, who was very disenchanted with her during filming, grudgingly admitted that the final product had been worth the torment. How long would people keep saying that? How long would the magic be worth the inhuman effort it took to extract it, and the terrible physical and psychological toll it took on those involved? The clock was already ticking.

A year passed before Marilyn began another film, and that time was spent having another miscarriage—this time the result of an ectopic pregnancy—and supporting her husband as he was convicted of contempt of court for refusing to name names during Joseph Stalin's—oops—I meant Joseph McCarthy's communist witch-hunt hearings. Monroe was depressed. Her marriage was failing, she'd had two miscarriages, and her husband was staring down jail time. She took an overdose of sleeping pills—her second suicide attempt (in case anyone is counting)—but Miller discovered her in time, and rushed her to the hospital. Miller's legal problems worked themselves out, but his other problem, his marriage, only got worse.

Miller encouraged her to take the role of Sugar Kane in the Billy Wilder directed film, *Some Like It Hot*, another dumb blonde role that she would play to perfection. Wilder and Marilyn worked together four years earlier on *The Seven Year Itch*. Apparently that movie went relatively well, so Wilder had no qualms working with her again. He soon regretted this decision. On the very first day of wardrobe fitting, Marilyn showed up four-and-a-half hours late, spent another two hours in makeup, then skipped onto the set at 6:10 PM, where she was met with a deserted building. Wilder and the entire cast and crew had gone home at 6 PM, after waiting for princess to show her face for six hours. That's pretty much how the entire shoot of the movie went. She would be hours late every single day, and she would not be prepared when she was on the set. She fancied herself a method actress, and forced Wilder to redo the simplest scenes, take after take after take, until she felt she had done it just right. Other times, she couldn't remember the simplest line. Wilder recalled one scene in which she was simply required to ask "Where's the bourbon?" but she kept flubbing this simple line over and over again. Bet if it had been "Where's the champagne?" she'd have nailed it.

She drove Wilder to drink, and made an enemy of former friend and lover, Tony Curtis, who quipped kissing her was like kissing Hitler. She caused the film to run five hundred thousand dollars over-budget, and delayed its completion by several weeks. Wilder threw a lavish wrap party at his Beverly Hills home for the cast and crew. Guess who wasn't invited? Aubrey Wilder—Billy's wife—who had feared for her husband's health during the making of the picture, conspicuously left the Millers off the guest list. Wilder would later acknowledge that while she was hell to work with, the end result was some of the finest work he'd ever produced on film. He told a reporter for the *New York Herald Tribune* at the time "I'm the only director who ever made two pictures with Monroe. It behooves the Screen Directors Guild to award me a Purple Heart."

*Some Like It Hot* was one of the highest-grossing comedies of all time, proving once again that Ms. Monroe still had it going on. She was luminous, like a glowing butterfly flitting from scene to scene as the brokenhearted Sugar Kane, who played with the emotions of two men in drag, hiding out from the mob. When she sang, "I'm Through With Love," her inner turmoil spilled over into the song, making that scene one of the most poignant she had ever filmed. It's a good thing she was damn near poetry on film, and the picture such a resounding success, or she might have found people were tired of her shit and too afraid to work with her anymore. She sacrificed a lot for *Some Like It Hot*, including another miscarriage that occurred right in the middle of everything, which destabilized her marriage even further. After it was all over, everyone went to their separate corners and licked their wounds. No one associated with the movie could have foreseen that it would later become a Marilyn Monroe masterpiece that has stood for of six decades as one of the greatest comedies of all time, and sealing her legacy as an icon for the ages.

She was next cast in the trite musical comedy, *Let's Make Love*, co-starring French heartthrob, Yves Montand. Showing up for the first day of filming looking distinctively chubby and bloated, creative camera angles and costumes had to be designed to camouflage these irregularities. In addition to her usual chronic lateness and line amnesia, she also had a passionate affair with her costar, while Arthur retreated to New York to finish a screenplay he had written especially for her: *The Misfits*. She and Montand carried on right under the nose of his wife, French actress Simone Signoret, who seemed to just accept her husband's transgression with true French laissez-faire. Ah, to be French! The movie was not a success. For once, the Marilyn magic fizzled. She looked fat, and she seemed to be going through the motions.

Marilyn did not have a break between *Let's Make Love* and *The Misfits*, and she sure needed one. Now completely dependent on drugs to get her through the day and night, as well as an alcoholic, she had a very hard time just getting it together on a daily basis, much less getting to a movie set and putting in a full day of work. Her marriage was completely demolished, they only stayed together to finish the picture they started together. She had this fantasy that he, by creating *The Misfits*, was simply using her just like everyone else did, for his own personal gain, when in fact he had begun the project to prove his love for her. This was typical. In her mind, everyone was using her, but she never used anyone else. Today they call this a persecution complex, back then, they called it paranoid.

Considering all the adversity *The Misfits* faced, it really is a miracle that it was ever completed. It's hard to imagine a more dysfunctional group of individuals trying to come together to make a movie, and actually succeeding. John Huston, the legendary director, was a notorious alcoholic and compulsive gambler who spent most of the time either drunk, or severely hungover, while losing all his money in the casinos. Montgomery Clift had been slowly trying to kill himself with booze and pills for years, ever since his near fatal car accident, and was notoriously hard to work with. Marilyn famously remarked that Clift was the only person she ever met who was in worse shape than her (and that pretty much says it all). Gable was in his late 50s with a heart condition, and found himself staring down the monster that was his costar. She kept him and everyone else waiting for hours in the one hundred and ten degree desert heat, then couldn't remember her lines when she did show, if she showed. Marilyn was in very bad shape. Her marriage was over, her addictions were consuming her, and her mental state was deteriorating. She suffered a complete breakdown during the middle of filming, and had to be confined to a hospital for ten days.

Seriously, how did this thing ever happen? It should have been finished before it even got started. Instead, it's this beautiful vignette, a moving and breathtaking tribute to the troubled stars who made it, and to the brilliant man who directed it. Monroe's character, Roslyn, is about as close to being the real her as it gets. No other actress in a major motion picture had ever played it so close to the bone. She was painfully vulnerable and lovely, even though she was slightly overweight and puffy from the booze and pills. It just didn't matter. In the stills as well as the film itself, she looks ethereal, like a heavenly body, a tragic caricature of herself. Huston fully exploited in her what other directors were only able to touch on: the magic of childish innocence, extreme vulnerability and sublime sensuality, a combination that has not been seen to the extent Monroe possessed it ever again.

The film got a mixed reception upon its release, mostly due to its stark, avant-garde style, and the fact that audiences were not used to seeing Clark Gable in such a morally ambiguous role. He dropped dead of a heart attack just days after filming wrapped, and many in Hollywood, including his wife, blamed Monroe for creating the intolerably stressful environment that led to his death. Of course, that three pack a day habit of his couldn't have had anything to do with it.

Marilyn received glowing praise in the film's reviews, even though she detested the role, and no longer had use for the writer. She felt her husband had betrayed her most intimate feelings by weaving them into the screenplay, on display for the whole world to see, while failing to reveal her inner depth. Miller had been reduced to playing errand boy and pill counter, a demeaning role for one of the country's greatest dramatists. They separated soon after, divorcing within the year. Marilyn, at thirty-six, was a three time loser, and alone again.

She grew ever more dependent on her psychiatrist, Dr. Ralph Greenson, who had been treating her since the *Lets Make Love* days. He had tried to get control over her pill addiction, without success. She would make a little progress, then slip back when she couldn't cope with a new crisis. She could not fall asleep naturally at all anymore, and needed the Nembutal just to function.

In February of 1961, she checked herself into psychiatric hospital, which was the closest thing they had to rehab back then. It didn't go well. She called up ex-husband, Joe DiMaggio, begging him to come get her. He galloped back into her life as a knight in shining armor, rescued her from the "nut house", and was a shoulder for her to cry on for those dark, final days.

She befriended Peter Lawford and his wife, Pat Kennedy Lawford, and at one of the many parties they held at their Santa Monica beach house, she allegedly met John and Bobby Kennedy—the bad news bears for any messed up woman. What was Marilyn thinking? Surely, she didn't believe the president of the United States would actually leave his wife, Jackie Kennedy, and marry her, did she? She must have known it was just sex for him, and perhaps a little bit of a fantasy thing. Yet, when he supposedly ended it, she mostly lost it, leaping from the frying pan and into the fire by hooking up with the Attorney General. Some accounts have her fucking both of them simultaneously. Ok, so her judgment was impaired, but if any of this is true, seriously, what was she thinking?

Marilyn moved into her very first, and very last home, on 12305 Fifth Helena Drive in early 1962, and began work on *Something's Gotta Give*. Poor Marilyn would try to push out another dumb blonde right up until the end. Filming had barely begun when she fell genuinely ill with a severe sinus infection with fever, and stopped showing up for work. Due to her reputation, people thought she was just crying wolf, and rumors began to fly that she was up to her old antics. She managed to drag herself onto the set sporadically, and the few bits of resulting film once again proved how much the camera adored her. She was stunning. She had lost at least twenty pounds since *The Misfits*, a fact that was gorgeously detailed in her first filmed nude scene, where she playfully skinny-dips in Dean Martin's swimming pool. There aren't enough unique adjectives in the English language to describe her onscreen magic in that scene. A few who knew her have said of her appeal that she was pretty in person but that it was the camera, whether still or moving, that turned her into a goddess.

Yet, on April 8, the weekend after she had stunned everyone with her on camera magic during the costume shoot, producer Henry Weinstein found her unconscious in her home, nearly comatose from an overdose of sleeping pills. This would prove a harbinger of things to come.

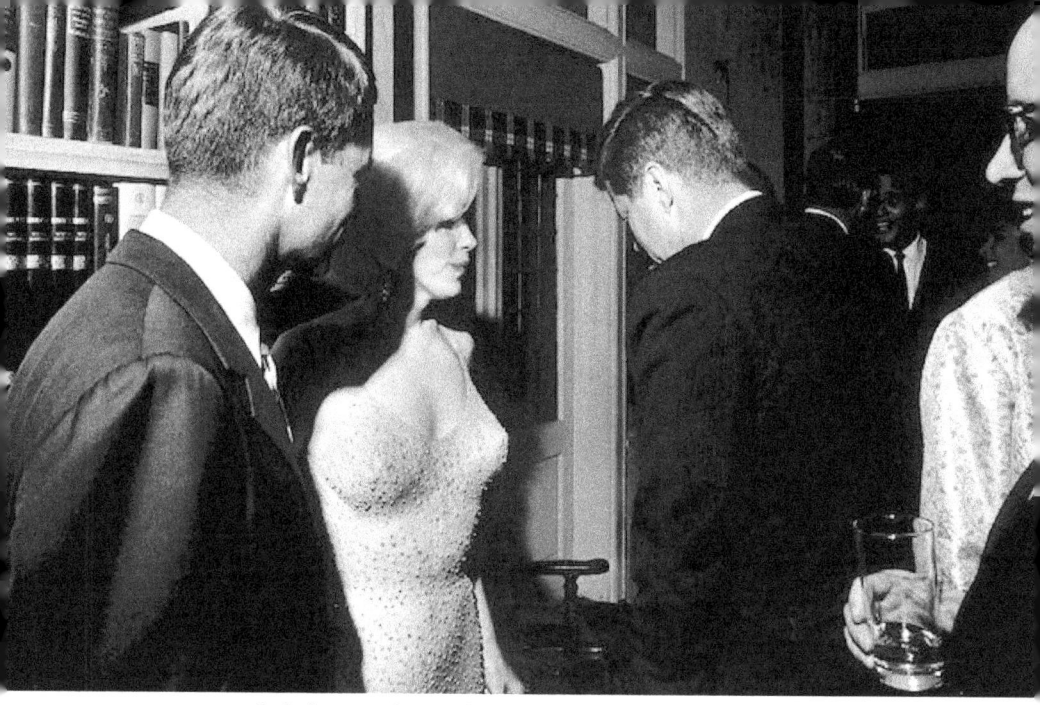

*Only known photo of Monroe and the two Kennedy brothers together*

She failed to show up for work for most of the month of April, due to various colds, sore throats and fevers. She was not, however, too sick to fly to New York and get herself sewn into a flesh-colored, heavily-beaded wiggle dress and sing "Happy Birthday" to the President. Fox took note of this.

After the event and its resulting publicity blitz, she returned to the set of *Something's Gotta Give*, and to her old habits of calling in sick or simply not coming. On June 1, she celebrated her thirty-sixth birthday with a cake and presents on the set. That was a Friday. The following Monday she again called in sick, and again the day after that, and the day after that, and the day after that. Fox finally just shut down production, firing her ass. Marilyn boo-hooed to the press about mean studio executives, and shut herself up in her house.

Dean Martin refused to continue the picture unless they hired her back, and they finally did, with a salary increase to boot! Meantime, she spent her days drinking, and her nights taking pills and talking on the phone.

Just three weeks before her death, she and photographer, George Barris, created photographic history with the poignant images they created during a Santa Monica beach shoot. She is wonderfully natural in these pictures, less plastic and false than she appears in so many other photos. She is smiling in nearly every picture, but her eyes betray the inner turmoil in such a stark manner, the effect is heartbreaking. In the very last photo ever taken of her, she is sitting in the sand with her arms resting on her knees, pursing her lips in a kiss. Goodbye Norma Jeane.

On the night of August 4, she locked herself in her room with a brand new bottle of Nembutal and the telephone. Six hours later she was found dead of a fatal overdose. Was it murder? Was it suicide? Was it an accident? Trying to answer that would require another book. Marilyn was a desperately unhappy person who tried to kill herself at least three times before she succeeded, and that's just the ones we know of. She was mixing booze with barbiturates, and eating almost nothing. She was clearly on a very self-destructive spiral that would have ended badly even if she had not OD'ed that August. How many more years could she have gone on? How many more months, even?

Maybe she could have cleaned up her act, sobered up, and found love again. Then again, she was staring down middle age. Her looks weren't going to hold out forever, and lets face it, she based her self-worth on her looks. Worse, she didn't seem to possess the strength of will to help herself. It seems she was destined to be this shooting star in our mediocre sky, streaking through just long enough to make us gasp, before vanishing into the night.

Marilyn once said, "I'm just a small girl, in a big world, trying to find love." Marilyn was possibly the most beloved screen star of all time, but in the end, even this wasn't enough. In the end, nothing was enough.

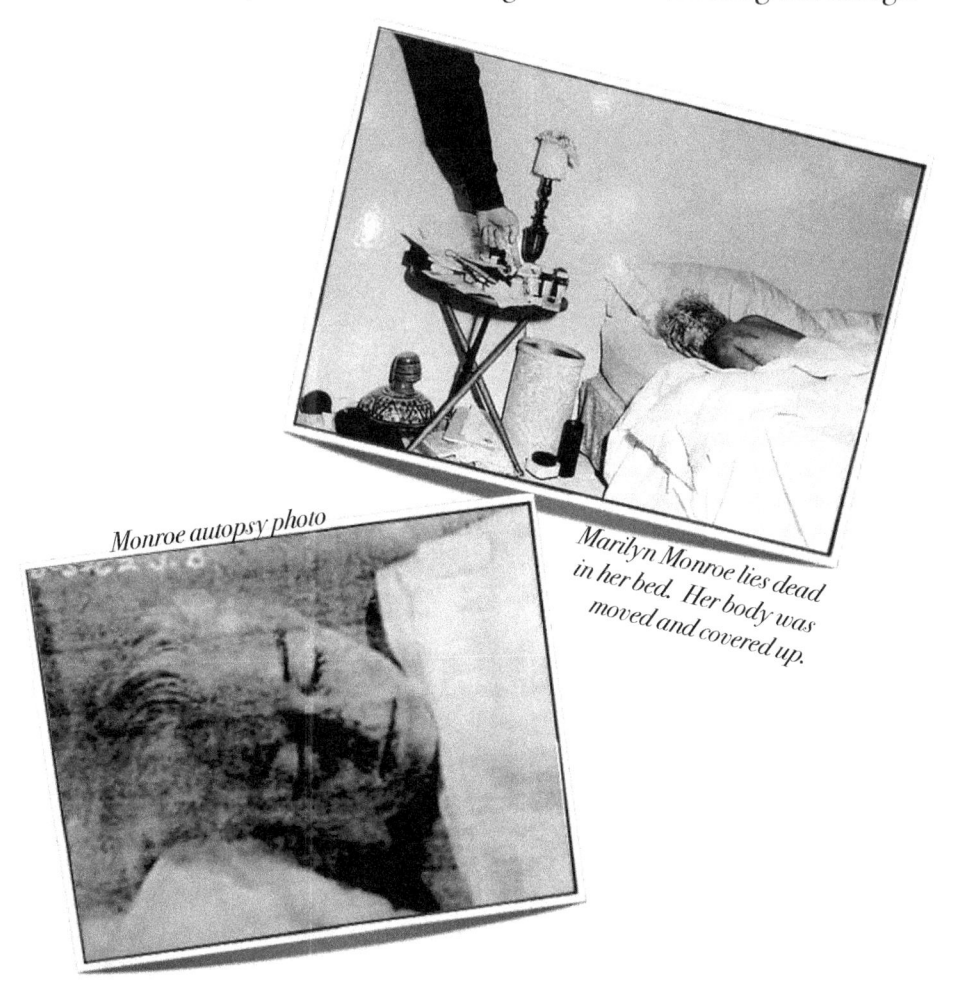

*Monroe autopsy photo*

*Marilyn Monroe lies dead in her bed. Her body was moved and covered up.*

# Hauntingly Tragic: Spectral Tales of the Famous and the Infamous

What would a book about the dark side of Hollywood be without a chapter on the hauntings attributed to the famously departed? Though the subject of the tragically famous, and stories of their earthbound souls, do not always go hand in hand, there seems to be enough interest in the combined subjects to warrant several television specials, and a multitude of publications. Whether you believe in ghosts, or simply can't get enough of the subject of tragedy and fame, the idea that somehow the show never ended for some of these people is more powerful and compelling than your run-of-the-mill ghost story.

# The Paul Bern/Jay Sebring/ Sharon Tate House

*Rare photo of Sharon Tate outside Jay Sebring's House. This is also the house where Paul Bern killed himself thirty-two years earlier.*

Tucked in a very tight canyon, at the base of a steep hill, sits a picturesque Bavarian-style cottage that looks as if it belongs in a fairy tale. It has a sloping slate roof, dark wooden crisscrossing accents, honeycomb-patterned windowpanes, and a neglected swimming pool. Facing the pool, carved into support beams that hold up the back of the house, are the gargoyle faces of four long-dead movie stars from the golden age of Hollywood. This is the home that was built by MGM studio executive, Paul Bern.

Bern built the home in the early '30s, bringing his new bride, Jean Harlow, to live there in early 1932. Four months later, on the night of September 5, following an argument with his new wife, Bern went up to the master bedroom, stripped naked, doused himself with Jean's best perfume, and shot himself in front of the full-length mirror. In his book, *Bombshell: The Life and Death of Jean Harlow*, David Stenn suggests that Harlow walked in on Bern and his (oops!) common-law wife, Dorothy Millette. Harlow told him to call her when he decided who he was married to, then left. Stenn also said that Bern was physically unable to have sex with anyone, due to a genetic defect that left him with a stunted penis. Reason enough to kill yourself, I suppose.

The house changed hands many times after this tragedy. A man supposedly drowned in the swimming pool, and a maid reportedly killed herself in the home as well. Jay Sebring, hairstylist to the stars, purchased the home in the early 1960s, and Sharon Tate moved into the home with him in 1965. She lived with Jay for about a year, often staying alone at the cottage while he traveled on business. She related something she experienced during this time to reporter Dick Kleiner a few years after the fact. One night, she had gone to bed, in the upstairs master bedroom where Bern had killed himself decades earlier. She had just fallen asleep when she was suddenly awakened by a strange noise. She looked up, and saw the figure of a "creepy little man" walk quickly into the room. She described him as being short, completely naked, and having a mustache. He did not acknowledge her presence, but began riffling through the dresser drawers, looking for something. She waited for him to disappear, as she felt certain this was the ghost of Paul Bern, but he simply kept searching the room. Frightened, she got out of bed and fled down the hall. She was headed towards the hidden bar downstairs, but as she approached the landing of the stairs, she stopped. The sight that met her eyes was beyond disturbing. A figure of a person, she could not tell if it was male or female, was tied to the banister. The figure had a hood over its head, with one end of a rope tied around its neck, and the other end looped over the banister.

Of course, this was exactly how Jay Sebring's murdered body would be found, four years later, at Sharon's Cielo Drive home, after the Manson killers' slaughter fest, in August of '69. Did Sharon not only meet the ghost of Paul Bern, but also experience a premonition of the horror that was to come, in her and Jay's own future? This is one of the more unusual ghost stories, as it is not strictly about ghosts, and the person relating the tale is, herself, dead. I visited this home last year. It is still gorgeous, if a little neglected. There is definitely an eerie vibe when you stand near the pool and gaze up at the darkened upstairs bedroom window. It's a sad house with a sad history, but given half the chance, I'd live there in a heartbeat.

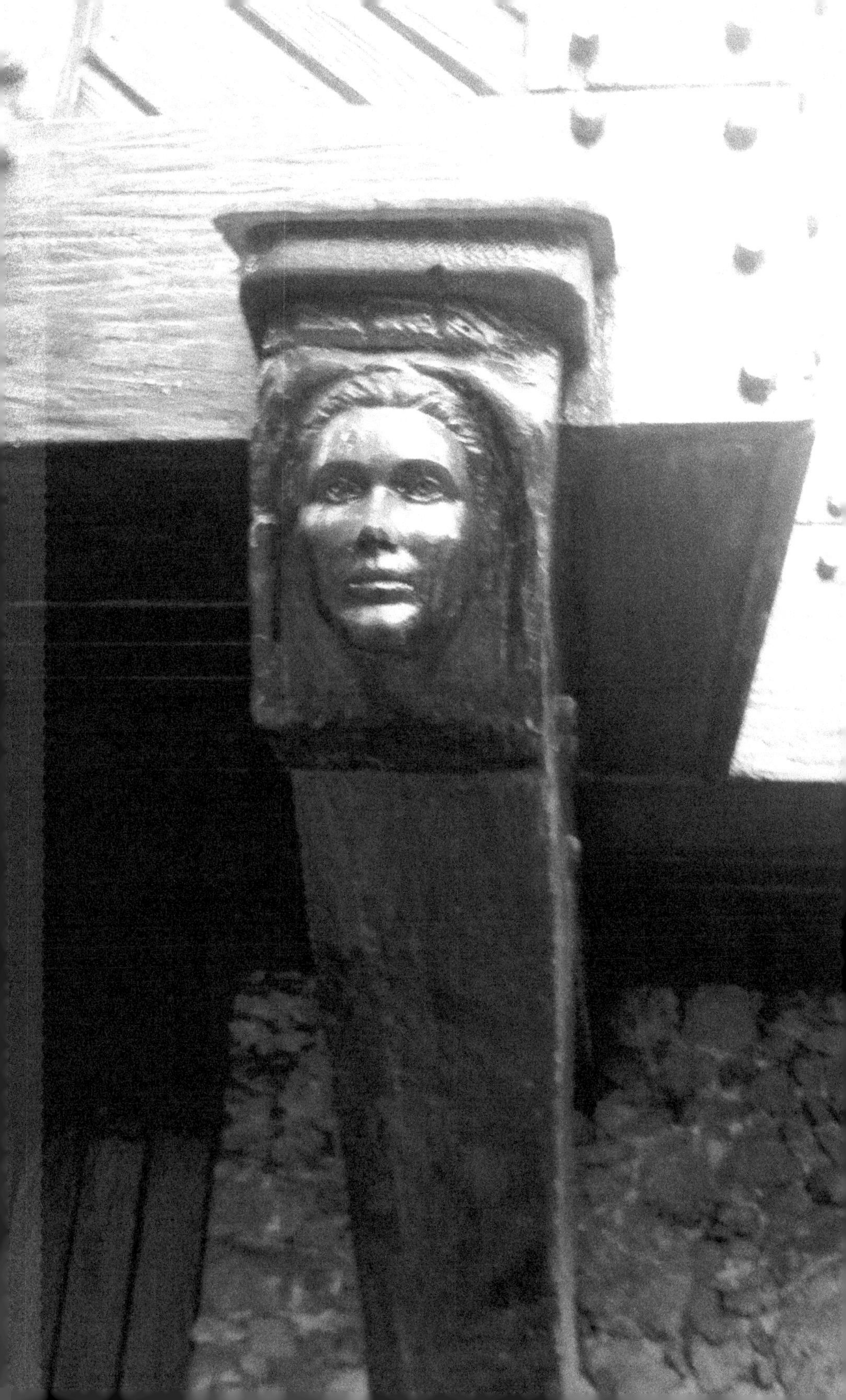

# Superman Just Won't Die
# George Reeves' Ghost

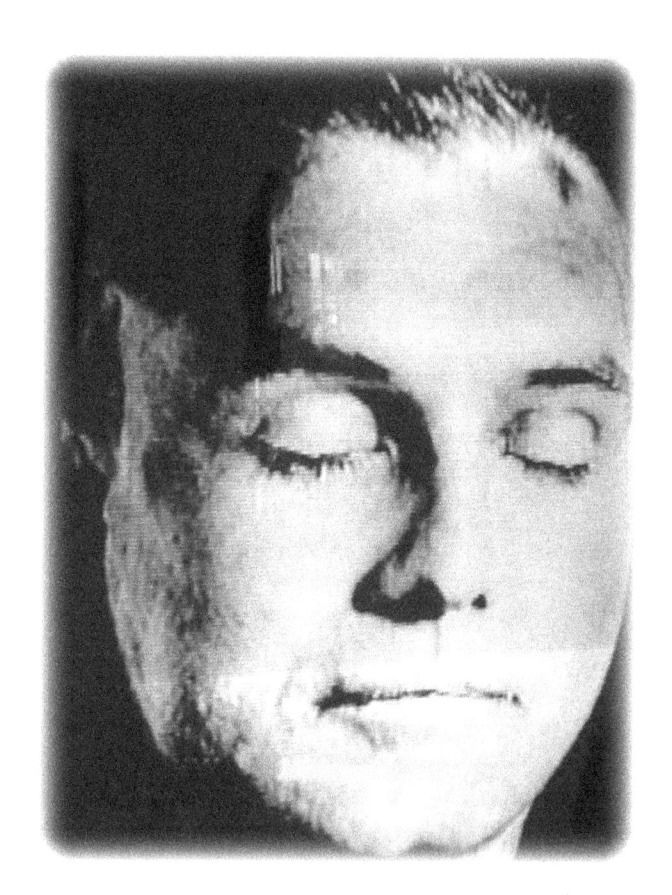

*George Reeves' autopsy photo*

It's a bird! It's a plane! No, actually its George Reeves, dead of a self inflicted gunshot wound. George Reeves played Superman on television for eight years, from 1951 and to his untimely death in 1959. The circumstances surrounding that death have been debated almost as much as those of Marilyn Monroe's. He was involved with an older woman, wife of a studio executive, Toni Mannix, and had just broken off the relationship. He was living in a large home in Benedict Canyon (does everyone in Hollywood live in Benedict Canyon?) with his fiancée, Lenore Lemmon. He was having financial problems, and was reportedly frustrated over the fact that all his career options revolved around playing Superman forever. On the evening of June 15, 1959, Reeves and Lemmon were out drinking with friends at a restaurant. They got into an argument. Later, they returned home, and Reeves went to bed. Lemmon was downstairs, entertaining three uninvited guests that had dropped by to continue the party. Reeves angrily came downstairs and told everyone to shut up, then went back to his room. It was shortly after that, at around 2 AM on June 16, that he shot himself in the head.

Conspiracy theorists insist that Reeves was murdered. They point to inconsistencies about the entry wound, the fact that Reeves supposedly could not use his right hand due to an injury, the position of the body, and the fact that there were five other bullet holes found in the room. Whatever. A formal inquiry was conducted, and the conclusion was suicide, though Reeves's mother never accepted this.

The ghost stories soon followed. Subsequent owners and occupants reported hearing all sorts of strange noises in the upstairs bedroom when no one was in there. When they investigated, the room would look like an angry whirlwind had torn through it! One tenant claimed that after hearing noises and fixing the room, they returned downstairs to find their drinks moved from the living room to the kitchen. Dogs barked furiously at the threshold of the bedroom, at something only they could see, and people reported smelling the distinct odor of gun powder. There are numerous reports of Reeves appearing to tenants and their guests, dressed in his Superman uniform, leaving no doubt as to who he is. A television crew in the '80s, while using the house as a backdrop, claimed to have encountered Reeves. Several crew members saw his apparition hanging around the set.

The most famous documented paranormal occurrence happened when no one was actually living there. Neighbors called the sheriff's department one night after hearing a loud argument going on at the house, followed by a scream and the sound of a gunshot. They also reported lights were turning on and off. The house was unoccupied and the neighbors thought someone had broken in! Two sheriffs deputies responded. They searched the home but found nothing out of the ordinary. Weird. Poor George Reeves...victim of the ultimate typecasting monster—television.

# The Ghost of Marilyn Monroe

Just as people couldn't get enough of Marilyn when she was alive, her legion of fans, which has grown exponentially over the years, also refuses to allow her to rest in peace. Ghost sightings of the blonde phenomenon are so numerous, they border on the ridiculous. Many claim to have seen her, appearing in mist form, near her tomb at Pierce Brothers Memorial Park in Westwood. Her grave is a popular tourist site, and her tomb is usually littered with red lipstick kisses. One fan claims to have photographed her misty image at the site. Others have felt tremendous sadness overwhelm them when paying their last respects.

The most famous sighting of Marilyn's ghost occurred at the iconic Hollywood Roosevelt Hotel. A maid was cleaning a mirror when she claimed to have seen the image of a blonde woman, wearing older style clothing. She then jumped to the conclusion this must have been Marilyn Monroe, as she had spent time living at the Roosevelt and modeling there when she was younger. The story has persisted ever since. Several tourists claim to have seen her image in the same mirror, which now hangs in the lobby of the Roosevelt. She has also been seen lounging at the pool, then disappearing before startled observers.

Marilyn's spirit is rumored to still linger at her former home, where she died. Since this is a private residence, the story is hard to verify, though she is reportedly still haunting the bedroom where she was last seen alive. Sadly, this home was once rented to another tragic blonde, Anna Nicole Smith. Smith claimed to feel Monroe's presence when she lived at the home.

Even in death, Marilyn is still the center of attention.

MARILYN MONROE
1926 — 1962

# Heath Ledger's Visit From Beyond

Heath Ledger's sudden death shocked everyone, but it affected his loved ones the most. Michelle Williams, his girlfriend at the time, claims to have been visited by Heath's spirit twice. The first time, she was awakened at 3 AM to the sound of furniture moving in her living room. When she went to investigate, nothing was out of place, but she felt Heath's presence. The second time, she was sleeping when she awoke and saw the outline of a man standing at the foot of her bed. She knew it was Heath and she felt that he spoke to her telepathically, telling her he was sorry he would not be there to help her raise their daughter.

The famous psychic medium, James Van Praagh, said in an interview that he had also seen Heath, though they never met when he was alive. He says Heath's image appeared in the reflection of his shaving mirror and that the troubled actor told him he (Heath Ledger) had screwed up. Again, he communicated with Van Praagh telepathically. Van Praagh claimed this encounter occurred two weeks after Heath's death from an accidental overdose of prescription drugs.

# Pickfair and the Haunting that led to a Demolishment

Once, there was a magical place: a sublime testament to silent Hollywood decadence christened Pickfair. Hollywood's king and queen—Mary Pickford and Douglas Fairbanks—transformed a modest hunting lodge into a magnificent, four-story, twenty-five room mansion in the early '20s, and held court there over the lords and ladies of film for over fifteen years. Divorcing in 1936, Mary continued to live there until her death in 1979, after which Pickfair was vacant for many years. A rich doctor, Jerry Buss, bought it and restored its former glory. All seemed well...until it wasn't.

In 1988, singer Pia Zadora had her millionaire husband, Meshulam Riklis, purchase the property for her and their two kids to stay in while he was away on business (which he usually was). They lived there less than two years before they had the structure demolished—allegedly due of termites—and a new, tasteless palazzo built in its place. That's right. They had the unimaginable gall to purchase a Hollywood icon, then bulldoze it, because they couldn't deal with a few termites. At least, that was Pia's story at the time.

Twenty-four years later, a much older, less in-demand Pia Zadora went on the popular television show, *Celebrity Ghost Stories*, and told the world the "real" reason she and her husband tore down Pickfair: it had a ghost! Pia said her daughter was frightened one night by a very tall woman in a long, white gown, floating above her bed and laughing. This so upset the child that she refused to sleep in her room. Pia said it was too much to handle, so her solution was simply to tear the house down. Yeah, cause that makes perfect sense, if you have a billion dollars, I guess.

It would be easy to dismiss this if not for the fact that the other two owners of the home also reported seeing the same woman, including Mary's last husband, Charles "Buddy" Rogers. Rogers believed it to be the spirit of Mary Pickford, which may be why he moved out shortly after Mary's death. Jerry Buss, who purchased it from Rogers, also claimed to have seen the woman in the flowing gown, as well as other apparitions.

Maybe Mary loved Pickfair more than anyone realized. Still, was that really a good enough reason to tear down such a historic home? Why not just move? Donate the place to a museum—anything, just don't tear it down! Seriously, I hope Mary continues to haunt Pia's nightmares for decades.

# Ozzie Nelson's Still at Home

Here come the Nelsons! That was the catch phrase for one of the most popular family shows on television, *The Adventures of Ozzie and Harriet*. The show featured a real life family, Ozzie and Harriet Nelson, and their two sons, David and Ricky. The exterior shots were filmed at their real life residence in Beverly Hills, located at 1822 Camino Palmero Street, a home they purchased in 1948. Though the show ended in 1967, Ozzie and Harriet continued to live there until Ozzie's death from cancer in 1975. Harriet then sold the residence, and subsequent owners have been reporting ghostly encounters with Ozzie Nelson ever since.

Ozzie's apparition is often seen in the bedroom of the home, or stalking the hallways. Witnesses report that he does not look happy either. He seems melancholy or restless. One female witness claimed to have been the victim of unwanted sexual attention in the middle of the night, but when she turned on the lights, no one was there. Hmm. Not nice Ozzie! What would Harriet say? Others have reported hearing footsteps, faucets turning on and off, and lights flickering for no reason. Poor Ozzie just doesn't seem to want to leave his beloved home.

*Lucille Ball outside her house on Roxbury Drive in Beverly Hills.*

# Lucille Ball & Roxbury Drive

We all loved Lucy, especially the bus loads of tourists who drove by her home on Roxbury drive in the flats of Beverly Hills several times a day, hoping to catch a glimpse of the Queen of Comedy puttering in her garden, or waving to her neighbor, Jimmy Stewart. Lucy lived at Roxbury Drive for more than two decades, and by all accounts, she loved it there. She died in 1989, but the current owners claim she still makes her presence known. The home has undergone extensive remodeling and barely resembles the house Lucy loved so much, which might explain the recurrent broken windows, loud voices coming from the attic, and poltergeist activity of moving furniture and misplaced objects. Seems Lucy doesn't like the changes.

# Errol Flynn Still Sailing

If Lucille Ball was the Queen of Comedy, Errol Flynn was King of the Hellraisers. His shameless, hedonistic lifestyle has been thoroughly chronicled in several biographies, including his own, aptly-titled *My Wicked, Wicked Ways*. His notorious taste for extremely young women, some might say illegally young, got him into serious guano when two underaged girls accused him of snatching their virtue while they were onboard his infamous floating pleasure palace, The Zaca. Flynn managed escape that one, and enjoyed many "happy" times aboard, right up until his death in 1959. After that, the Zaca entered a period of decline, passing from owner to owner, finally ending up in a boat yard in Villefranche, France. Locals began passing stories that the ship was haunted. The sounds of gay parties, the tinkling of ice in tumblers, laughter, and the sound of champagne bottles popping were heard. Lights were seen burning brightly, and the silhouettes of party goers were seen moving past the portholes, even though the Zaca was empty and had not been hooked up to electricity in years. The ghost of Flynn himself was often seen pacing the deck, usually at dusk, smoking his pipe and gazing out at the horizon. This unnerved the Zaca's owners to such a degree that they contacted the Catholic church, who recommended exorcism. Rather than mess up the yacht with such a ceremony, a replica of the ship was brought into a church and the exorcism took place there. Guess it worked, because shortly afterwards, the yacht was bought, restored, and now sails the seas off the Mediterranean coast of Monaco as a private yacht for hire. Somehow I think Errol is still at the helm.

*Zaca Livingroom as it appears today*

# Phantoms at the Phantom Of The Opera Set

Lon Chaney was known as the man of a thousand faces. He was one of the biggest stars ever to come out of Universal Studios, and his premature death at the young age of forty-seven, only heightened his fame and mystery. His greatest performance was as the hideously deformed recluse, living deep within the bowels of the Paris catacombs, in the film, *The Phantom of the Opera*. A specially constructed, elaborate set was built inside sound stage 28, on the Universal backlot, to replicate the baroque style of the Paris Opera House. The set took months to complete and was so expensive, the studio chose to keep it rather than break it up after the film was complete. Amazingly, in a town and industry known for brushing aside its heritage and embracing the fleeting allure of mediocrity, this beautiful set is still intact on the Universal lot.

The set is creepy enough all by itself, without the added ghost stories to add to the atmosphere. The intricately carved walls are two stories high, and the stage is massive, stretching three hundred sixty feet long by one hundred forty-five feet wide. The huge chandelier, an exact replica of the one that hangs in the Paris Opera House, was removed in the '60s, as were all of the seats, but the skeleton remains, harboring dark nooks and shadowy corners.

Movies are still made here, though infrequently. Those who have worked inside, and a few lucky enough to visit the sound stage, have spread the word about the strange goings-on inside. Unexplained noises are heard, as well as doors opening and closing of their own accord. Lights go on and off, and footsteps and voices are heard when the stage should be empty.

For decades, people have reported seeing the disturbing specter of a man in a black cape. He is described as appearing in the shadows, silently observing before fading away. More significant, he has been spotted running along the catwalks above the stage, then vanishing. These descriptions read like a page from the 1925 Lon Chaney film, and there are those who claim the apparition is the spirit of the dead actor. Perhaps Chaney is still filming his greatest cinematic triumph, and is unaware that almost a hundred years have passed. There is a theory that sometimes energy from the past can be trapped and played over the present, when conditions are just right. This is called a "residual" or non-intelligent haunting. No one has come forward to claim they have chatted with this caped man to confirm his identity, so it is left to speculation and conjecture as to what is actually going on. It could be just the result of overactive imaginations, but isn't it much more fun to believe that Lon Chaney, in his Phantom costume, is still wandering around the old sound stage, keeping an eye on things?

# Jayne Mansfield and The Haunting of The Pink Palace

Jayne Mansfield was larger than life in many ways, which might explain why she simply refused to move on from her beloved custom-Beverly-Hills mansion-on-steroids masterpiece, lovingly nicknamed The Pink Palace. This house had to be seen to be believed. Jayne purchased a traditional Spanish style home with money she inherited from her grandfather. She then proceeded to mutilate the interior in a kind of perverse tribute to her signature color: pink. Interior photos taken during the time she lived there reveal wall to wall pink carpet, a pink bathroom, a water fountain in the foyer that spurted pink champagne, pink wallpaper and well, just pink everything. There was even a pink, heart-shaped bathtub, nestled in the pink shag carpet walls and floor of the master bathroom. Lots of pink.

After Jayne's death, the property changed hands, and rumors of Jayne's ghost appearing to subsequent owners began to trickle out. Engelbert Humperdinck, who purchased the home in 1976, claimed to have encountered Jayne's ghost roaming the upstairs rooms, as if searching for something. He also claimed to have smelled her rose perfume many times.

Ringo Starr, who owned the home prior to Humperdinck, tried to paint over all the pink but for some reason, the color would just keep seeping through! Layers and layers of white could not erase it.

Jayne's second husband, Mickey Hargitay, claimed that Jayne appeared to him in the mansion shortly after her death. He quickly moved out, declaring that the mansion died when Jayne died.

In 2002, the home was sold again, and the new owners did what a lot of rich people do in Beverly Hills. They tore down a piece of history and built an ordinary piece of crap in its place. Welcome to Hollywood.

# Peg Entwistle and The Haunting of the Hollywood Sign

Poor Peg Entwistle. Coming to Hollywood with stars in her eyes, she left with the lights of that city reflected in them as she fell into oblivion, where she found what had eluded her in life: lasting fame. The only person known to have used the iconic sign as a suicide prop, and people have talked about her ever since. September 16 was a Friday, and that afternoon, Peg hiked up rugged Mount Lee toward the sign—which at the time still read "Hollywoodland"—in heels and a skirt. By the time she reached it, night had fallen, and the lights must have been blinding. Climbing the "H" via a service ladder, she stood with the lights of Hollywood below her—chiding her—before leaping to a rocky death in the ravine below. Her broken body was found two days later.

Ghost stories began to crop up almost immediately. The area around the sign is a popular for hiking, and many people claim to have seen the apparition of a young woman— dressed in white—walking effortlessly up the hill. When she is approached, she vanishes, leaving the scent of gardenias in air, a scent Peg was known to favor. Animals behave strangely on the trail, and sometimes refuse to go past a certain point. Motion detectors were placed on the sign years ago to prevent vandalism. Park rangers have claimed that often the motion detectors are set off, yet nothing is there when they check, but the scent of gardenias hovers.

On a recent episode of the popular series, *Paranormal Witness*, four people told of a harrowing encounter they had with this apparition when they were teenagers in the late '80s. They climbed up the mountain and felt triumphant at reaching the sign, and they all celebrated with hoots of joy. On the way down, however, they encountered something that would haunt their nightmares for decades to come.

They all saw her at once. She was slowly making her way up the path as they were coming down. She did not seem to be having any difficulty whatsoever, yet she was hardly wearing appropriate hiking clothes. She was dressed in a skirt and high heels! As they got closer, one of them called out to the woman, but she did not respond. Then, as she came within only a few feet of where they stood, they recoiled in horror. Her face was a hideous skeletal blob. They all went tearing down the mountain. One of them claims the apparition followed, and even pursued them to the fence.

This is the only truly frightening encounter of the ghost of the Hollywood sign that I have come across. Most people who have seen the ghost say she is shy, not aggressive, and seems to be doomed to repeat her last desperate moments in life over and over again. The Hollywood sign is truly impressive, but if you are brave enough to hike up Mount Lee on a windless fall night, by yourself, you might encounter something even more daunting.

Haunted Hollywood Forever

There once was a glamorous place where the rich and famous went to spend eternity. It was called simply Hollywood Memorial Park, and it had a very prominent neighbor. The cemetery backed right up to Paramount Studios, thus making the commute from work to death quite convenient for many of its notable occupants. The famous who are buried there are too numerous to list in this short chapter, but they include notorious Paramount studio boss Harry Cohn, Rudolph Valentino, Cecil B. DeMille, and the list goes on and on.

When Forest Lawn Glendale reared its pretentious head in the 1930s, poor Hollywood Memorial Park fell out of favor, soon falling on hard times as well. Sprawling lawns and a serene pond became overgrown, neglected, and clogged with weeds. It took on the look of a rural cemetery, rather than the impressive final resting place of some of the most famous stars in entertainment history. The long, echoing columbarium, adorned with amazing stained glass roofs, became dirty and shabby. Glass panels were broken and never replaced. The marble floor became chipped and cracked.

The cemetery continued to decline for the next seventy years, until it was sold in the late '90s to Tyler Cassity, who came from a prominent family of mortuary owners in St. Louis. Tyler was a lover of old Hollywood, as well as an experienced funeral industry insider. His passion for both saved Hollywood Memorial Park from a terrible fate of complete obscurity. He poured money into the park, and soon it was restored to its former glory. He renamed the newly restored cemetery Hollywood Forever, which has to be the coolest name for a cemetery ever.

Hollywood Forever has earned a reputation for hosting some very famous ghosts throughout the years. It is said that Rudolph Valentino haunts his modest tomb, tucked away inside the beautiful Cathedral Mausoleum towards the back of the cemetery. For decades, a woman in black has appeared on the anniversary of Valentino's death, bearing one red rose, which she lays next to the tomb. Over the years, many women have claimed to be the woman in black, but the original has no doubt been dead herself for many years. Many claims of seeing the specter of a woman in black, kneeling at Valentino's tomb, have been recorded. People also claim to see red roses suddenly appear in the brass vase when there were none a second before. One woman claimed that she turned and walked away from the tomb, only to turn and see red roses in every vase in the hallway, where there were none before. I had my own ghostly experience at this tomb. I heard the distinct sound of 1920s music playing softly while I was there.

Along the side of the cemetery is the impressive columbarium known as The Abbey of the Psalms. This is where famous director, Victor Fleming, is said to make his otherworldly appearance known. Many have reported hearing the sound of hard-soled shoes echoing behind them, as they stroll the endless corridors lined with human remains from floor to ceiling. I had this experience, when I first visited this cemetery, when it was still in desperate need of saving. The columbarium was quite spooky back then—so neglected and deserted— free of the throngs of tourists that visit it today. As I wandered the corridors, I heard the distinct sound of someone with hard-soled shoes following me, though I was the only one in the building.

Towards the center of the park lies the grave of Virginia Rappe, another actress who achieved her cherished desire for fame only after her gruesome death. Rappe was little more than a bit player back in the '20s, but she developed quite the reputation as a woman of loose morals. She was known as the ultimate party girl, and frequented the same wild social events the stars did. It was during one of these gin-soaked, cocaine-dusted shindigs at San Francisco's St. Francis Hotel—hosted by *Keystone Cops* golden boy, Roscoe "Fatty" Arbuckle—that she found herself suddenly dying from a mysterious ailment. Within days she was dead, and soon rumors began to fly about why. Many of those rumors centered on Arbuckle, a champagne bottle, and an unnatural sexual act.

Arbuckle found himself smack dab in the center of a good old-fashioned Hollywood scandal. Witnesses claimed that he and Virginia left the common area of the hotel suite, and retired to the private bedchamber, where Virginia would be found barely coherent and moaning in pain, hours later. Arbuckle claimed she got sick immediately after they entered the room, and that he had put her to bed and rejoined the party. The truth likely lies somewhere in-between. Arbuckle was put on trial for murder THREE TIMES! Two trials ended in hung juries, but the third time was truly a charm for the comedian, as he was acquitted. His career was over by then, and he himself died alone and forgotten, at the young age of forty-six.

From such epic tragedy are born the ghost stories. Many have reported hearing the sound of a woman weeping softly at Virginia's grave. Some have even seen an apparition of a woman in white, quietly sitting at the grave and sobbing.

Hollywood Forever is welcoming and friendly to celebrity grave seekers. This is a rare thing in Los Angeles, where being caught holding the wrong book (i.e. a guide to where the famous rest in sweet repose) is grounds for expulsion from many of the city's memorial parks. I find it ironic that a town so dependent on celebrities and their fans for its culture and economy would suddenly turn off the charm to those same fans who wish to remain loyal to the very bitter end, and pay their final respects. After all, as one macabre Hollywood death tour states, it's the closest they are likely to get to their favorite stars, or any stars, for that matter.

*A view of the Hollywood sign from inside the Hollywood Forever cemetery.*

# The Tate Murder House & the Haunting of a Neighborhood

There have been no murders more gruesome or terrifying than those that occurred nearly forty-five years ago at 10050 Cielo Drive in Beverly Hills. The Tate murders, as they have came to be known, still haunt our collective consciousness and stalk our nightmares. Is it any wonder that, despite the original house being razed, and the passage of four decades, Sharon Tate's horrific end is not forgotten and tales of the restless dead still linger here?

Vincent Bugliosi, the prosecuting attorney in the murder trial, and author of the bestselling book on the subject, *Helter Skelter*, wrote about an incident that happened a few weeks before the murders, when Tate was still in London. Homicide detectives found a videotape of casual dinner party at the house, including Abigail Folger, Wojciech Frykowski and two of their friends. The couple were housesitting for Sharon and Roman. Nothing seemed out of the ordinary on the tape, except for the astonishing incident Abigail described having happened to Frykowski one night while they sat gazing into the living room fireplace, stoned out of their minds. She said he suddenly jumped up and grabbed a camera, looking really freaked out, and said he saw a flaming pig's head in the fire.

10050 Cielo Drive had many subsequent residents after that terrible day, yet none reported anything paranormal. Until recently, when a man who bought land and built a home just down the road from the infamous address came forward with spine-chilling tales of unexplained events in his home. His name was David Oman, and he has been telling his story all over the media. He even made a movie about it called *House at the End of the Drive(2014)*.

According to David, it started almost immediately after he had moved in. He describes unexplained knocks on his front door, and wine glasses flying off counters in front of dozens of witnesses. He even claims to have been woken in the middle of the night by a male apparition standing in his bedroom, that he later identified as Jay Sebring. One night, as friends gathered in the movie room, they all reported hearing strange, mournful voices coming from the intercom system. They were so clear that Oman thought there were intruders in the home, he immediately searched the house. While he was upstairs, his friends said that the voices moved from the intercom to inside the room with them. The witnesses claimed the voices sounded panicked or distressed, but that they could not make out what was being said.

A séance was held at the home. The medium, while trying to contact the spirit of Sharon Tate, became incapacitated with abdominal pain, as if she were being stabbed. All of the lights went out, and a candle flame bent at a weird, right-degree angle. One woman's chair was pulled back by unseen hands, and everyone heard a bone-chilling, female scream.

Mr. Oman does not know why his home, which was built long after the murders occurred, would be attracting the spirits from 10050 Cielo Drive, but he puts forth an interesting theory. In an interview for the SyFy show, *Paranormal Witness*, he said that perhaps these poor, doomed souls did not realize they were dead, and were simply running to his house to get some help and escape their fate.

Whatever the causality, if you are inclined to walk alone in the quiet streets of Benedict Canyon on a windless August night, listen carefully. Was that a scream, or just the summer wind bouncing off the hills? Can you ever really be sure?

# Conclusion

*Rudolph Valentino's funeral in New York*

Once again, we return to that mythical place, that magical, mystical town called Hollywood, where illusion is a business, and tragedy an unfortunate side-effect. The few whom this town blessed with her fickle gifts of fame, fortune, and glory found they were a mixed blessing, at best. Why does fame seem to result in a relentless stumble into the same vices and pitfalls that befall all of us? Because stars are not allowed to be unhappy! In the eyes of the fans, those people out there in the dark (to roughly quote Norma Desmond) must be happy, because they are stars. They are beautiful, rich and beloved. They have achieved everything that is of value (or so it would appear) in this shallow, paper-doll culture, and if that isn't enough, then fuck it, we are all doomed. There is an almost mocking hostility when we watch them fall, as if their failure was somehow our victory.

In reality, of course, none of it is true. Stars aren't special, unique, plucked from the masses and forever destined to live rarified, happy lives devoid of everyday problems. Stars are just people, people who chose to make their living entertaining other people. They are no less inclined to mental breakdowns and substance abuse than anyone else, and in many cases, due to their artistic temperament and talent, are often more inclined to fall victim these issues. They don't fail in obscurity like the rest of us. Their failures are public, humiliating and unforgiving. Their mistakes are debated, written about ad nauseam, and discussed for decades. It's hardly surprising that tragedy is woven through the mansions, the sound stages, the Bentleys, and the Ferraris to the same extent that contentment is. In Hollywood, all that glitters is not gold, and lasting happiness is, by default, a mirage.

*A young Barbara La Marr*

# Bibliography and Credits
## Books & Periodicals

CRIVELLO, KIRK. *Fallen Angels*. Berkley Publishing Group, 1990.

DAVIS, RONALD L. *Hollywood Beauty: Linda Darnell and The American Dream*. University of Oklahoma Press, 1991.

FARLEY, TOM, JR. & COLBY, TANNER. *The Chris Farley Show: A Biography in Three Acts*. Viking Adult, 2008.

FINSTAD, SUZANNE. *Natasha: The Biography of Natalie Wood*. Three Rivers Press, 2002.

GILMORE, JOHN. *L.A. Despair: A Landscape of Crimes and Bad Times*. Amok Books, 2005.

HASPIEL, JAMES. *Marilyn: The Ultimate Look at the Legend*. Henry Holt & Co., 1991.

HEYMANN, C. DAVID. *Liz: An Intimate Biography of Elizabeth Taylor*. Carol Publishing, 1995.

HYAMS, JOE. *James Dean: Little Boy Lost*. Random House, 1994.

NASH, ALANNA. *Baby, Lets Play House: Elvis Presley and the Women Who Loved Him*. It Books, 2010.

OGDEN, TOM. *Haunted Hollywood: Tinseltown Terrors, Filmdom Phantoms, and Movieland Mayhem*. Globe Pequot, 2009.

OTFINOSKI, STEVEN. *Latinos In The Arts (A to Z of Latino Americans)*. Facts on File, 2007.

PARSONS, LOUELLA. "The Real Life Story of Clara Bow" *The San Antonio Light*, May 15 - June 4, 1931.

PAYTON, BARBARA. *I Am Not Ashamed*. Holloway House, 1963.

SNAUFFER, DOUGLAS. *The Show Must Go on: How the Deaths of Lead Actors Have Affected Television Series* McFarland, 2008.

STENN, DAVID. *Bombshell: The Life and Death of Jean Harlow*. Doubleday, 1993.

## Television & Radio

*Dana Plato*. Documentary. A&E Productions.

*Dorothy Stratten*. Documentary. A&E Home Video, 2005.

*Final 24:* "River Phoenix". Documentary. Cineflix, 2006.

*The Howard Stern Show:* "Dana Plato". Radio Program. NBC Universal, May 7, 1999.

*Harlow: The Blond Bombshell.* Documentary. Turner Pictures, 1993.

*Making The Misfits.* Documentary. Image Entertainment, 2002.

*Marilyn on Marilyn.* Documentary. British Broadcasting Corporation (BBC), 2001.

*Reel Life:* "Marilyn Monroe". Documentary. Reelz Channel, 2012,

*Sharon Tate: Murdered Innocence.* Documentary. A&E Productions, 2002.

# Photography & Graphics

All images included in this book, except for those listed below, are from the author's personal collection, in the public domain, or from the New York Public Library Billy Rose Collection. Every effort has been made to credit the appropriate people for these works, and if any errors have occurred, contact the author at the address provided on the Copyright page so that any necessary corrections can be made to the next edition.

Page viii photo from Film Star Vantage (https://www.flickr.com/photos/classicvintage/) used under (CC BY 2.0) unmodified from https://www.flickr.com/photos/classicvintage/9194759559/in/photostream/ .

Page 17 photo by A.J. Marik

Page 27 photo by Taph Madison used under (CC BY-SA 4.0) unmodified from https://commons.wikimedia.org/wiki/File:Wallace_Reid_Urn.JPG.

Page 37 painting by Alberto Vargas is Public Domain from http://commons.wikimedia.org/wiki/File:Oliveartistic.jpg.

Page 53 photo is Public Domain from http://commons.wikimedia.org/wiki/File:Natalie_Wood_Still1.jpg.

Page 64 photo by Howie Berlin used under (CC BY-SA 2.0) unmodified from http://commons.wikimedia.org/wiki/File:Heath_Ledger.jpg.

Page 65 photo from Francisca(https://www.flickr.com/photos/_aldu/2235506870) used under (CC BY-ND 2.0) unmodified.

Page 66 photo from Tea Drinker(https://www.flickr.com/photos/14945397@N00/sets/72157603782777031/) used under (CC BY-ND 2.0) unmodified.

Page 67 image by Ben Foster(http://grudg3.deviantart.com/art/The-Dark-Knight-The-Joker-3-77260974) used under (CC BY-SA 3.0) unmodified.

Page 77 image by Wilfredor is Public Domain from http://commons.wikimedia.org/wiki/File:Vivien_Leigh_Gone_Wind_Restored.jpg.

Page 89 promo card scan courtesy of Shane Peters of Salem, MO.

Page 94 image is Public Domain from http://commons.wikimedia.org/wiki/File:Blackbeard_the_Pirate_(1952)_1.jpg.

Page 105 photo by Jeffery Scott Holland(http://visualslushpile.blogspot.com/2011/06/dw-griffiths-grave.html) used per his terms.

Page 107 photo is Public Domain from http://commons.wikimedia.org/wiki/File:Chaplin,_Charlie_(His_New_Job)_03.jpg.

Page 108 top is Public Domain from http://commons.wikimedia.org/wiki/File%3ACharlie_chaplin_karno_portrait.jpg.

Page 110 photo by First National Studios is Public Domain from http://commons.wikimedia.org/wiki/File:Chaplin_A_Dogs_Life.jpg.

Page 112 photo is Public Domain from http://commons.wikimedia.org/wiki/File:Chaplin_-_Modern_Times.jpg.

Page 114 photo is Public Domain from http://commons.wikimedia.org/wiki/File:Chaplin_family_1961.jpg.

Page 117 photo by Giramondo1(https://www.flickr.com/photos/8974833@N07/3762833996) used unmodified under (CC BY-ND 2.0).

Page 120 photo by Kate Gabrielle(https://www.flickr.com/photos/slightlyterrific/5190939248/) used unmodified under (CC BY 2.0).

Page 126 photo is Public Domain from http://commons.wikimedia.org/wiki/File:Ann_Savage_and_Tom_Neal_in_Detour.jpg.

Page 132 photo by Film Star Vintage(https://www.flickr.com/photos/classicvintage/) used unmodified under (CC BY 2.0) from https://www.flickr.com/photos/classicvintage/9363564374/.

Page 134 photo Film Star Vintage(https://www.flickr.com/photos/classicvintage/) used unmodified under (CC BY 2.0) from https://www.flickr.com/photos/classicvintage/9079557352/in/photostream/.

Page 149 photo by Frank H. Brueckner is Public Domain from http://commons.wikimedia.org/wiki/File:James_Dean_Park_Cemetery_Fairmont.jpg.

Page 150 used unmodified under (CC BY 2.5) from http://commons.wikimedia.org/wiki/File:James_dean3.jpg.

Page 152 photo by Enrico(https://www.flickr.com/photos/onefromrome/2497625272/) used unmodified under (CC BY 2.0).

Page 155 photo by Alan Light used unmodified under (CC BY 2.0) from http://commons.wikimedia.org/wiki/File:River_Phoenix_-_hi_res_scan_(cropped).jpg.

Page 160 photo is Public Domain from http://commons.wikimedia.org/wiki/File:Errol_Flynn1.jpg.

Page 164 photo by Los Angeles Times photographic archive - Digital collections –

UCLA Library(http://unitproj.library.ucla.edu/dlib/lat/display.cfm?ms=uclalat_1429_b295_102416&searchType=subject&subjectID=213914) used under (CC BY 4.0), from http://digital2.library.ucla.edu/viewItem.do?ark=21198/zz0002rswk.

Page 167 photo by Los Angeles Times photographic archive - Digital collections – UCLA Library(http://unitproj.library.ucla.edu/dlib/lat/display.cfm?ms=uclalat_1429_b295_102416&searchType=subject&subjectID=213914) used under (CC BY 4.0), from http://digital2.library.ucla.edu/viewItem.do?ark=21198/zz0002tv21.

Page 168 image by Dylan John Mazziotti(https://www.flickr.com/photos/mullingitover/441567382) used under (CC BY-NC-ND 3.0) unmodified.

Page 169 photo by Dylan John Mazziotti(https://www.flickr.com/photos/mullingitover/441567382) used unmodified under (CC BY 2.0).

Page 173 photo by Jde2399 is Public Domain from http://commons.wikimedia.org/wiki/File:Farleygrave.jpg.

Page 179 photo by Russell Ball is Public Domain by copyright non-renewal (Photoplay).

Page 187 photo is Public Domain from http://commons.wikimedia.org/wiki/File:Freddie_Prinze_Jack_Albertson_Chico_and_the_Man_1974.JPG.

Page 191 photo by Alan Light used unmodified under (CC BY 2.0) from https://www.flickr.com/photos/alan-light/4749086165/.

Page 199 photo is Public Domain from http://commons.wikimedia.org/wiki/File:Marie_McDonald_re-enacts_scene_from_her_story_of_kidnaping_at_home_in_Encino,_1957.jpg

Page 201 photo by Allison Marchant(https://www.flickr.com/photos/carbonated/2183888642/in/photostream/) used unmodified under (CC BY-NC-SA 2.0).

Page 203 photo by David H. Kennedy is used unmodified under (CC BY-SA 2.0).

Page 205 photo by Gianluigi Bertin(https://www.flickr.com/photos/drammatico/5039954257) used unmodified under (CC BY-NC-SA 2.0).

Page 208 image from ADiamondFellFromTheSky(https://www.flickr.com/photos/37775831@N02/3685577764) used unmodified under (CC BY-NC 2.0).

Page 209 photo by RKO Radio Pictures is Public Domain from http://commons.wikimedia.org/wiki/File:Jimmy_Durante_Lupe_Velez_Mills_Brothers_Strictly_Dynamite_1934.jpg.

Page 221 photo by Mu used unmodified under (CC BY-SA 3.0) from http://commons.wikimedia.org/wiki/File:Tombe_Jean_Seberg,_Cimeti%C3%A8re_du_Montparnasse_(2).jpg.

Page 255 photo by IllaZilla used unmodified under (CC BY-SA 3.0) from http://commons.wikimedia.org/wiki/File:Tate_family_grave.JPG.

Page 257 image by Laura Loveday(https://www.flickr.com/photos/likeabalalaika/3607485811) used unmodified under (CC BY-NC-SA 2.0).

Page 261 photo by Allison Marchant(https://www.flickr.com/photos/carbonated/255867469/in/album-72157594152370795/) used unmodified under (CC BY-NC-SA 2.0).

Page 273 photo by Lisa Burks(http://lisaburks.typepad.com/photos/uncategorized/2007/06/07/ourbaby.jpg).

Page 294 image by Mikel Agirregabiria(https://www.flickr.com/photos/agirregabiria/3654393584) used under (CC BY-NC-SA 2.0), with minor cropping and scaling.

Page 298 photo by Richard Avedon is used under (CC BY 2.0), from https://www.flickr.com/photos/aamaianos/4359635676.

Page 299 photo by Allison Marchant(https://www.flickr.com/photos/carbonated/2183888642/in/photostream/), used under (CC BY-NC-SA 2.0), with minor cropping purely for layout-related reasons.

Page 300 photo used unmodified under (CC BY 2.0) from http://commons.wikimedia.org/wiki/File%3AMarilyn_Monroe%2C_Korea%2C_1954.jpg.

Page 301 photo is Public Domain from http://commons.wikimedia.org/wiki/File:Marilyn_Monroe_Niagara.png.

Page 302 photo by Elliot Erwitt used unmodified under (CC BY 2.0), from https://www.flickr.com/photos/orionpozo/6895133616/.

Page 307 glorious image via Choo Yut Shing(https://flic.kr/p/azr6QE) used unmodified under (CC BY-NC-SA 2.0). If you're reading this on paper, this image alone is worth typing that URL, or buying a color ebook edition. It's that awesome.

Page 309 image is Public Domain from http://commons.wikimedia.org/wiki/File:Marilyn_Monroe,_The_Prince_and_the_Showgirl,_1.jpg

Page 310 photo from Ana Carolina Braga(https://www.flickr.com/photos/aclbraga/2299679135) used unmodified under (CC BY-NC 2.0).

Page 315 photo by Cecil W. Stoughton is Public Domain from http://commons.wikimedia.org/wiki/File%3AJFK_and_Marilyn_Monroe_1962_larger.jpg.

Page 316 photo by George Barris is Public Domain from http://commons.wikimedia.org/wiki/File:Barris_Marilyn_Monroe.jpg.

Page 326 image from James Vaughan, licensed unmodified under (CC BY-NC-SA 2.0), from https://flic.kr/p/8zX2gU.

Page 348 photo from George/Encato_Sunland(https://www.flickr.com/people/georgie56/) used unmodified under (CC BY-NC 2.0) from https://www.flickr.com/photos/georgie56/8202986268/.

Attributions including Creative Commons references require that the link to the license itself be provided. For legibility, links to those license definitions are summarized below:

    (CC BY 2.0)        https://creativecommons.org/licenses/by/2.0/
    (CC BY 2.5)        https://creativecommons.org/licenses/by/2.5/

(CC BY 4.0)　　　　　https://creativecommons.org/licenses/by/4.0/
(CC BY-NC 2.0)　　　https://creativecommons.org/licenses/by-nc/2.0/
(CC BY-ND 2.0)　　　https://creativecommons.org/licenses/by-nd/2.0/
(CC BY-SA 2.0)　　　https://creativecommons.org/licenses/by-sa/2.0/
(CC BY-SA 3.0)　　　https://creativecommons.org/licenses/by-sa/3.0/
(CC BY-SA 4.0)　　　https://creativecommons.org/licenses/by-sa/4.0/
(CC BY-NC-ND 3.0)　https://creativecommons.org/licenses/by-nc-nd/3.0/
(CC BY-NC-SA 2.0)　https://creativecommons.org/licenses/by-nc-sa/2.0/

# Conjuration & Summoning

General construction, otherwise unexplained strange phenomena, and that strange feeling of being watched by David Hayden.

By the way, Jessica Rabbit is property of Walt Disney Productions/Touchstone Pictures.

Here is a recent photo taken by the author of the Roosevelt hotel where Marilyn spent a lot of time:

# Index

**A**
*A Countess from Hong Kong* 115
*A Guide for the Married Man* 242
*A King of New York* 115
*A Sainted Devil* 12-13
*A Streetcar Named Desire* 78-79, 135
*A Woman of Paris* 110
*A&E Biography* 279
Abbey of the Psalms 346
Acker, Jean 11-13
Adams, Stanley 289
*Airport* 218
*All About Eve* 299
*Aladdin and His Lamp* 72
Anger, Kenneth 3, 13, 31, 212, 233
Arbuckle, Roscoe 346
Arthur, Jean 261
Astor, Mary 267

**B**
Bacall, Lauren 303
Baker, Gladys 296
Baker, Norma Jeane 296, 316
Ball, Lucille 71, 335, 337
Ball, Suzan 70-73
*Barabbas* 248
Barris, George 315, 358
Barrymore, John 21-22, 165, 267
Barrymore, Lionel 267
Bathing Beauties 29
*Bell, Book and Candle* 238
Bello, Marino 258-259, 263, 267-268
Bergen, Candice 251
Bern, Paul 180-181, 249, 261-266, 320-322
Berry, Wallace 267
Beymer, Richard 248
Bickford, Hughlina 30
Biograph Pictures 17-18, 100
*Birth of a Nation* 25, 45, 100-103
*Blood and Sand* 13, 95
Blue Book Modeling Agency 297
Bogdanovich, Peter 155, 281-284
Bolender, Albert & Ida 296
*Bombshell* 267
*Bombshell: The Life and Death of Jean Harlow* 321, 354
Bow, Clara 80-85, 261
*Breathless* 217
Bridges, Lloyd 287

Bridges, Todd 224-225
Brody, Sam 241-244
*Buck Rogers* 279
Bugliosi, Vincent 348
Bugs Bunny 3
Burke, Billy 36, 267
Burton, Richard 249
*Bus Stop* 241, 307
Buss, Jerry 333

## C
Cagney Productions 288
*Camille* 13
Cannes 242
Capote, Truman 306
*Captain Blood* 162
*Carmen Jones* 121
Carmichael, John & Winifred 264
Carpenter, Mont Clair 257
Carpenter, Harlean Harlow 257-262
Cassity, Tyler 345
*Cat on a Hot Tin Roof* 54
*CBS News* 56
Chaney, Lon 338-339
Chaplin, Charlie 40-41, 47, 104-116, 135, 210
Chapman, Winifred 253
Chateau Elysee 42-43
*Chicago Tribune* 13
*Chief Crazy Horse* 72
*China Seas* 266
*Chinatown* 255
Chippendale Dancers 170, 280
Cielo Drive 249-254, 322, 348-349
Cimber, Matt 241-242
*City Beneath the Sea* 72
Clift, Montgomery 130-139, 312
Cohn, Harry 298, 345
Coleman, Gary 224
Collins, Joan 240
Columbia Pictures 235, 298
Conover, David 296
Conover, Harry 60
Cooper, Gary 210-212, 288
Cotton, Joseph 300
Crawford, Joan 30-31, 288, 304
Curtis, Jeanne 95-96
Curtis, Tony 311

## D
*Dallas* 288
Dandridge, Dorothy 118-122
Darnell, Linda 92-97

Davenport, Dorothy  25
de Saulles, Blanca & John  11
Dean, James  54, 62, 135-136, 142-151
*Death of a Salesman*  306
DeMille, Cecil B.  209, 345
Desmond, Norma  vii, 352
*Diff'rent Strokes*  223-226
*Different Strokes: The Story of Jack and Jill...and Jill*  226
DiMaggio, Joe  302-305, 314
*Dinner at Eight*  267
Disneyland  2
*Doctor Jekyll and Mr. Hyde*  21-22
Dominguez, Beatrice  11
*Double Speed*  25
Dougherty, Jack  180
Dougherty, Jimmy  296
Dressler, Marie  267
*Drums in the Deep South*  289

**E**
*East of Eden*  136, 144-146
*East of Sumatra*  72
Easter Bunny  2
Eastwood, Clint  218
Entwistle, Peg  192-195, 342
*Excuse My Dust*  25
*Eye of the Devil*  249

**F**
Fairbanks, Douglas  45, 104, 179, 210, 333
Falcon's Lair  13, 249
Famous Players-Lasky  25-26
*Fantasy Island*  279
Farley, Chris  168-172
Farrow, Mia  250
Feldman, Phil  287
*Female Jungle*  234
Fleming, Victor  77, 346
Flint, Larry  240
Flynn, Errol  160-167, 197, 336-337
Folger, Abigail  253, 348
Ford, Harrison  154
Forest Lawn Glendale  270, 345
*From Here to Eternity*  54, 135
Frykowski, Wojciech  253, 348

**G**
Gable, Clark  138, 210, 262, 267, 270, 296, 312-313
Gardner, Hyde  238
Gary, Romain  217-219
Gaynor, Mitzi  305
Gefsky, Hal  248

*Gentlemen Prefer Blondes* 241, 302-303
Gerke, Sonny 29
Gifford, Frances 125
Gifford, Charles Stanley 296
Gilbert, John & Leatrice Joy 9, 180, 210, 262
*Gilligan's Island* 241
Goddard, Paulette 112-113
Goodman, Daniel 40-42
*Gone with the Wind* 2-3, 40, 75-78, 101
Grable, Betty 299, 303
Grabowski, Marilyn 281
Grauman's Egyptian Theatre x, 146
Grauman's Chinese Theater 260, 303
Greene, Amy & Milton 306
Greenson, Ralph 313
Griffith, D.W. 17, 98-105
Guild, Leo 293

**H**
Hargitay, Mary 238
Hargitay, Mickey 235-238, 341
Harlan, Kenneth 29-30
Harlow, Jean 180, 231, 249, 256-273, 296, 321
Harrison, Ron 243-244
Hawks, Howard 133, 303
Hayes, Allison 89
Hayes, Bernadine 270
Hefner, Hugh 162, 206, 240, 278-284, 298
*Hell on Frisco Bay* 235
*Hell's Angels* 260-261
*Helter Skelter* 348
Hemingway, Ernest 139, 178, 203, 284-285
Hemingway, Margaux 202-207
*Hemingway's Adventures of a Young Man* 248
Hoffa, Jimmy 241
*Hold your Man* 266
*Hollywood Babylon* 3, 13, 31, 212, 233
Hollywood Forever 14, 17-19, 31, 344-347
Hollywood Memorial Park 14, 31, 345
Hollywood Roosevelt Hotel 328
Hollywood Sign 194-195, 342-343, 347
Hollywood Theater 6
Holy Cross Cemetery 254-255
Hope, Bob 288
*House at the End of the Drive* 349
*How to Marry a Millionaire* 303
Hughes, Howard 30, 260-262
*Human Wreckage* 26
Humperdinck, Engelbert 341
Huston, John 138-139, 312-313
Hyde, Johnny 298-299

## I
*Illegal* 235
Ince, Thomas 38-43,
Inceville 39-40
Independent Motion Picture Company of America 18
*Intolerance* 45, 103-104
*Island in the Sun* 122

## J
Jane, Leone 261

## K
Karger, Fred 299
Kelley, Gene 197
Kelley, Tom 298
Kennedy, Arthur 144
Kennedy, Bobby 314-315
Kennedy, Jackie 314
Kennedy, John 314-315
Kennedy-Lawford, Pat 314
*Keystone Cops* 346
Keystone Studios 29, 96, 108-110, 116
Kinski, Nastassja 255
*Kiss Tomorrow Goodbye* 288, 292
Kleiner, Dick 322

## L
La Marr, Barbara 174-183, 261, 353
LaBianca, Leno & Rosemary 254
*Ladies of the Chorus* 298
Laemmle, Carl 18, 39
Lambert, Lenny 225-227
Lange, Hope 306
Lawrence, Florence 16-19
Lawrence, Max 178
Ledger, Heath 64-69, 330-331
Leigh, Vivien 2, 74-79
Lemmon, Jack 115, 238
Lemmon, Lenore 325
*Let No Man Write My Epitaph* 217
*Lets Make Love* 312-314
LeVey, Anton 242
*Lilith* 217
*Lipstick* 205-206
*Limelight* 114
*Los Angeles Times* 41, 194, 218
Lyon, Ben 297
Lytell, Beth 177
Lytell, Wilfred 21
Lytess, Natasha 298-302

## M

*Macho Callahan* 219
Madison, Guy 289
Mannix, Toni 325
Mansfield, Jayne 3, 60, 200, 232-245, 340-341
Mansfield, Mariska 243
Mansfield, Martha 20-23
Mansfield, Miklos 243
Mansfield, Paul 233-234
Mansfield, Zoltan 241-243
Manson, Charles 251, 254, 322
Martin, Dean 314-315
Mathis, June 11-14
Mathis, Samantha 155-157
Maxie 30
Mayer, Louis B. 264-266
McDonald, Marie 196-201
McDowall, Roddy 19
McGrew, Chuck 258-259, 262
Melcher, Terry 251-252
Merman, Ethel 305
MGM 121, 125, 180, 197-198, 261-270, 321
Miller, Arthur 138, 306-313
Millette, Dorothy 264-265, 321
*Moment to Moment* 217
Monroe, Marilyn 138, 235, 237, 240-241, 278, 284, 294-317, 325, 328-329
*Monsieur Beaucaire* 13
*Monsieur Verdoux* 114
Montand, Yves 312
Moore, Colleen 82, 259
Mortensen, Martin 296
Mount Lee 194, 342-343
*Mousy* 219
*Mr. Annual* 235
*My Week with Marilyn* 295
*My Wicked, Wicked Ways* 165-166, 337

## N

National Film Preservation Board 19
Nazimova, Alla iii
Neal, Tom 124-129, 289-291
Negri, Pola 13-14
Nelson, Ozzie 334
*New York Herald Tribune* 216, 311
Newman, Paul 238
*Newsweek* 218-219
*Niagara* 300-301
*Night Trap* 226
Novarro, Ramon 13

365

## O

O'Conner, Donald 305
O' Neill, Oona 113-116
Olivier, Lawrence 76-79, 308-309
Oman, David 349
*Only the Valiant* 288
Oswald, Lee Harvey 242
*Ozzie and Harriet* 90, 334

## P

*Paint Your Wagon* 217
Palmer, Herbert & Vera Jayne 233
Paramount Pictures 25, 83, 197, 217, 251, 296, 345
*Paranormal Witness* 343, 349
*Paris Match* 307
Paris Opera House 338-339
*Pawn's Destiny* 18
Payton, Barbara 125-128, 286-293
Payton, John 287
Peck, Gregory 289
*Pendulum* 217
*Personal Property* 268
*Pete Kelly's Blues* 235
*Petticoat Junction* 248
*Phantom of the Opera* 338-339
Phoenix, River 152-159
*Photoplay* 303
Pickfair 332-333
Pickford, Mary 33-35, 104, 333
Pierce Brothers Memorial Park 328
Pink Palace 340-341
Plato, Dana 222-229
Plato, Kay 222-229
*Playboy* 89-90, 206, 225-226, 238-240, 275-284, 298
Polanski, Paul Richard 254
Polanski, Roman 247, 249-255
*Porgy and Bess* 122
Powell, William 267-270
Preminger, Otto 121-122, 215-217, 305
Presley, Elvis 54, 59-63
*Pretty Baby* 224
Prevost, Marie 4, 28-31
Prinze, Freddie 186-191
*Promises, Promises* 200, 240

## R

Rabbit, Jessica 236
*Rally Round The Flag, Boys!* 238
Rambova, Natacha 13
Rappe, Virginia 346-347
*Rebel Without a Cause* 52, 145
*Reckless* 266

*Red Dust* 266-267
Reeves, George 324-327
Reid, Wallace 24-27
*Return To Boggy Creek* 224
Reynolds, Debbie 234
Riklis, Meshulam 333
*River of No Return* 304
Roach, Hal 210, 259
*Robin Hood* 162
Rogers, Charles 333
*Rolling Stone* 66, 68
Roosevelt, Eleanor 268
*Rosemary's Baby* 250-251
Rubens, Alma 44-47
Ruby, Jack 242
Russell, Jane 234, 302-304

**S**
*Saint Joan* 215-216, 220
San Francisco Film Festival 242
Sanders, Alexander and Maxine 249
*Saratoga* 268-269
Schenck, Joe 298
Scherbatoff, Mara 307
Seberg, Diego 217-220
Seberg, Jean 214-221
Sebring, Jay 249-253, 320-322, 349
Selznick, David O. 75-77, 264
Sennett, Mack 29
*Shades of Grey* 250
*Shadow of a Doubt* 51
Shahrokh, Hatami 252
Shearer, Norma 264
Shepherd, Cybill 281
Signoret, Simone 312
Skolsky, Sidney 304
Slade, Ira & Paul 307
Smith, Anna Nicole 328
Snider, Paul 275-284
Solter, Henry 17-19
*Some Like It Hot* 310-311
*Something's Gotta Give* 314-315
*Splendor in the Grass* 52, 55, 249
St. Francis Hotel 346
Starr, Ringo 341
*Stars and Stripes* 247
Stern, Howard 223, 226-227
Stewart, James 238, 335
Strasberg, Lee & Susan 308
Stratten, Dorothy 274-285
Stratten, Louise 283-284
Strickling, Howard 264

## T

Tashlin, Frank 237
Tate, Sharon 246-255, 320-323, 348-349
Taylor, Elizabeth 33, 52, 133-139, 144-149, 179, 199, 249
*Tess of the d'Urbervilles* 252, 255
Thalberg, Irving 264
*The Adventures of Ozzie and Harriet* 90, 334
*The Asphalt Jungle* 235, 299
*The Beast of the City* 262
*The Beautiful and the Damned* 29-30
*The Beverly Hillbillies* 249
*The Broken Oath* 18
*The Brothers Karamazov* 306
*The Burglar* 235
*The Daily Mirror* 29
*The Dark Knight* 67-68
*The Eagle* 13
*The Exorcist* 224
*The Fearless Vampire Killers* 249
*The Four Horsemen of the Apocalypse* 11
*The Girl Can't Help It* 235
*The Girl from Missouri* 268
*The Girl in Pink Tights* 305
*The Gold Rush* 110-111
*The Gong Show* 224
*The Great Jesse James Raid* 291
*The Hollywood Reporter* 288
*The Kid* 110-111
*The Killing of the Unicorn* 283
*The Last Picture Show* 281
The Legion of Decency 268
*The Mark of Zorro* 95
*The Marriage Circle* 29
*The Misfits* 138-139, 312-314
The Motion Picture & Television Country House and Hospital 31
*The Mouse That Roared* 217
*The New York Daily News* 270
*The New York Times* 172, 216, 250, 300
*The Postman Always Rings Twice* 126, 291
*The Prince and the Showgirl* 308-309
*The Racket* 30
*The Roaring Road* 25
*The Sandpiper* 249
*The Saturday Night Kid* 261
*The Seven Year Itch* 305, 310
*The Sheik* 13
*The Sheriff of Fractured Jaw* 238
*The Son of the Sheik* 13-14
*The Valley of the Giants* 26
*The Warrens of Virginia* 21
*The Wayward Bus* 237

*They All Laughed* 281-283
*Thirteen Chairs* 252
*Thirty Days* 26
Thomas, Olive 32-37
Thomas, Terry 243
Tone, Franchot 125-126, 288-290
*Trapped* 287
Twentieth Century Fox 65, 93-95, 179, 237-240, 259-260, 297-306, 315
*Twilight Zone* 3
Tyler, Judy 58-63

**U**
*Underwater* 234
United Artists 13, 104, 114, 197
Universal Studios 18, 71, 139, 197, 217, 287, 338

**V**
Valentino, Rudolph 10-15, 249, 345, 351
*Valley of the Dolls* 247, 250
Van Praagh, James 331
Velez, Lupe 208-213
Vickers, Yvette 88-91
Victor Film Company 18

**W**
*War Arrow* 72
Warhol, Andy 204, 306
Warner, Jack 29
Warner Brothers 29-31, 211, 234, 288-289
Weinstein, Henry 314
West, Mae 235
*West Side Story* 52
Westwood Memorial Park 284, 328
*Wife vs. Secretary* 266
Wilder, Aubrey & Billy 310-311
*Will Success Spoil Rock Hunter?* 235-236
Williams, Michelle 67-68, 331
Williams, Tennessee 78, 137, 306
Wood, Natalie 50-57, 145-146
Woodward, Joanne 240

**Y**
Young, Gig 289

**Z**
Zaca 163-164, 337
Zadora, Pia 333
*Ziegfeld Girl* 197
Ziegfeld Follies 21, 33-34, 60, 196-197
Ziegfeld, Florenz 33-34, 36